. . .

INTELLIGENCE ANALYSIS
AND POLICY MAKING

. . .

INTELLIGENCE ANALYSIS AND POLICY MAKING

The Canadian Experience

THOMAS JUNEAU and

STEPHANIE CARVIN

STANFORD UNIVERSITY PRESS
Stanford, California

STANFORD UNIVERSITY PRESS
Stanford, California

Printed in the United States of America on acid-free, archival-quality paper

Library of Congress Cataloging-in-Publication Data
Names: Juneau, Thomas, author. | Carvin, Stephanie, author.
Title: Intelligence analysis and policy making : the Canadian experience / Thomas Juneau and Stephanie Carvin.
Description: Stanford, California : Stanford University Press, 2021. | Includes bibliographical references and index.
Identifiers: LCCN 2021023213 (print) | LCCN 2021023214 (ebook) | ISBN 9781503613508 (cloth) | ISBN 9781503632783 (paperback) | ISBN 9781503629714 (epub)
Subjects: LCSH: Intelligence service—Canada. | National security—Canada. | Canada—Foreign relations. | Canada—Military policy.
Classification: LCC JL86.I58 J86 2021 (print) | LCC JL86.I58 (ebook) | DDC 327.1271—dc23
LC record available at https://lccn.loc.gov/2021023213
LC ebook record available at https://lccn.loc.gov/2021023214

Cover design: Rob Ehle

Cover photo: *Veins*, David Linscheid

Typeset by Kevin Barrett Kane in 10/14 Minion Pro

CONTENTS

ACKNOWLEDGMENTS

Given our experiences working in the area of intelligence, defense, and national security, we were motivated to write an article on the Canadian intelligence policy nexus. With the initial encouragement of Stéfanie von Hlatky, we recognized that there was a bigger story to tell. We then applied for and were successful in obtaining funding from the Social Sciences and Humanities Research Council of Canada's Insight Development Grant program to make this project a reality.

We are extremely grateful to the sixty-eight individuals who agreed to a formal interview with us for this project. It would simply not have been possible to write this book without their trust and our frank discussions with them about the state of intelligence policy relations in Canada. As little fieldwork in this area has been done, it should be acknowledged that there is a risk in trusting two academics with information that highlights certain weaknesses in the performance of departments and agencies—many of which are not familiar with being in the spotlight. While our interviewees may not agree with everything in this book, we hope they feel the final product contributes to an ongoing conversation about improving how intelligence is used in Canadian policy making. We are deeply thankful for the time they gave us, and for their trust. In addition to these interviews, we are also grateful to the many informal conversations we have had over the years with serving and retired members of the national security and intelligence community; these debates have significantly shaped and informed our views.

In addition, throughout this project we have received feedback from academics and practitioners. While many of these individuals have requested anonymity, we wish to thank Philippe Lagassé, who provided comments on the powers and structure of the Canadian government throughout the project that are integrated especially in the appendix. We would also like to thank Steve Saideman, Craig

Forcese, and two anonymous reviewers. We also have presented various portions of this book at multiple conferences and workshops over the years, including at the International Studies Association, with the Canadian Association for Security and Intelligence Studies, and in the context of various events held with the government of Canada. We are grateful for the feedback we received at these events.

In addition, we thank the Social Sciences and Humanities Research Council (SSHRC), one of Canada's federal granting agencies, for its support at multiple stages of this project. This allowed us to hire research assistants, participate in conferences to articulate and test our ideas, and support the publication of this book.

We also wish to thank the research assistants who provided us with invaluable support at various stages of this project: Ariane Calvert, Mark Farfan De Los Godos, Arathy Handakumar, Jaskaran Lamba, and Natasha Lopes.

We would also like to thank Caroline McKusick, Jessica Ling, Athena Lakri, and Alan Harvey at Stanford University Press for helping to navigate this book through the review process.

Finally, we would like to thank our families for their love and support throughout this process. Thomas Juneau would like to thank Marie-Hélène, Rémi, and Philou. Stephanie Carvin would like to thank Darcy, Tom, and Chris Carvin, and Malaika Babb.

ABBREVIATIONS

ACDI	assistant chief of defence intelligence
CAF	Canadian Armed Forces
CBSA	Canada Border Services Agency
CDI	chief of defence intelligence
CFINTCOM	Canadian Forces Intelligence Command
CRO	client relations officer
CSE	Communications Security Establishment
CSIS	Canadian Security Intelligence Service
DFIB	*Daily Foreign Intelligence Brief*
DGInt	Director General Intelligence (used for both the position and the organization)
DIR	*Defence Intelligence Review*
DM	deputy minister
DMIC	Deputy Minister Intelligence Committee
DMNS	Deputy Minister National Security committee
DMOC	Deputy Minister Operations Committee
DND	Department of National Defence
FBI	Federal Bureau of Investigation
FDP	Foreign and Defence Policy (a PCO secretariat)
FINTRAC	Financial Transactions and Reports Analysis Centre of Canada

GAC	Global Affairs Canada
GSRP	Global Security Reporting Program (of GAC)
IAB	Intelligence Assessment Branch (of CSIS)
IALP	Intelligence Analyst Learning Program
IAS	Intelligence Assessment Secretariat (a PCO secretariat)
ICA	Investment Canada Act
INR	Bureau of Intelligence and Research
ISROP	International Security Research and Outreach Program
ITAC	Integrated Terrorism Assessment Centre
NGO	nongovernmental organization
NIA	National Intelligence Assessment
NSA	national security adviser to the prime minister
NSIA	national security and intelligence adviser to the prime minister
NSICOP	National Security and Intelligence Committee of Parliamentarians
NSIRA	National Security and Intelligence Review Agency
OSINT	open-source intelligence
PCO	Privy Council Office
PMO	Prime Minister's Office
PSC	Public Safety Canada
RCMP	Royal Canadian Mounted Police
S&I	Security and Intelligence (a PCO secretariat)
SAT	structured analytic techniques
SIGINT	signals intelligence
SIPP	Security and Intelligence Policy Program

. . .

INTELLIGENCE ANALYSIS
AND POLICY MAKING

. . .

INTRODUCTION

INTELLIGENCE ANALYSIS is essential to the development and implementation of optimal foreign, defense, and national security policy (Jervis 2010; Fingar 2011). Yet its performance—the quality of the analysis and its ability to inform and shape policy making—outside the US context has been neglected by scholars. In Canada, several federal government departments have intelligence analysis units, but how their products are used by policy makers is poorly understood—often even by the analysts themselves. In this context, our book addresses these important questions: *How well does intelligence analysis support policy making in Canada, and how can it be improved? What lessons does the Canadian experience hold for other intelligence communities?*

This research will be of interest in and beyond Canada. In Canada, there is no book available for the thousands of members of the intelligence and national security community or for scholars and students interested in the role of intelligence analysis in federal policy making. Moreover, Canada is a close intelligence partner for the US, and a member of the most important intelligence-sharing partnership in the world, the Five Eyes (Australia, Canada, New Zealand, the UK, and the US). This book, as such, represents the first comprehensive empirical study on this topic and an important case study for the field of intelligence studies by proposing an analysis based on the Canadian case but relevant to other national contexts.

Scope of the Book: Intelligence Analysis and Policy

It is important, first, to delineate the scope of this book. Our research focuses on how intelligence analysis supports high-level foreign, national security, and defense policy making in Canada. Our parameters exclude important areas such as intelligence support to law enforcement or to military operations.[1] We also do not study the multiple operational aspects of the intelligence machinery, especially not the collection of various types of intelligence.

This makes our purpose quite specific: analysis represents a small portion of the intelligence enterprise, as far more human and financial resources are devoted to collection and operations. Yet much of the interactions of senior policy makers with the intelligence world, in the bureaucracy and in the political realm, focus on analytical products. Analysis is thus far more important in terms of high-level policy making than its limited budget suggests.

This raises a first, essential question: What is intelligence analysis? There are, of course, multiple definitions, most of which are US-centric. Jack Davis, a former Central Intelligence Agency analyst who wrote considerably on the topic, defines it as such: "The mission of intelligence analysts is to apply in-depth substantive expertise, all-source information, and tough-minded tradecraft to produce assessments that provide distinctive value-added to policy clients' efforts to protect and advance US security interests" (2015, 124). According to another definition by Adda Bozeman, intelligence analysis should "facilitate the steady pursuit of long-range policy objectives even as it also provides guidance in the choice of tactically adroit ad hoc responses to particular occurrences in foreign affairs" (1992, 2).

Narrowing the scope of these broad definitions, Loch Johnson and James Wirtz explain that intelligence analysis, at the strategic level, "contributes to the processes, products and organizations used by senior officials to create and implement national foreign and defense policies. Strategic intelligence thus provides warning of immediate threats to vital national security interests and assesses long-term trends of interest to senior government officials. Strategic intelligence is of political importance because it can shape the course and conduct of US policy" (Johnson and Wirtz 2004, 2).

In this book, we define intelligence analysis as the process whereby analysts gather and synthesize data obtained through a wide range of sources, both unclassified (open source) and classified, and present their findings in a range of products, written and oral, disseminated across government and with international partners. The core value-added of the work of intelligence analysts is to extract insights from the available data. These insights aim to be not merely interesting for the consumers of their written and oral products but also useful to their work in developing and implementing foreign, defense, and national security policy (see George and Bruce 2008; Marrin 2011; and Lowenthal 2017 for comparable definitions).

The second element in framing the scope of our research, after defining intelligence analysis, is to emphasize that the focus here is not on tradecraft (i.e., the methodology of intelligence analysis) or subject matter expertise (the need for analysts to acquire a body of empirical knowledge on the area of their work), the two dimensions typically receiving the most attention in intelligence studies. Instead, we focus on a third dimension: the relevance of the work of analysts, or how it is integrated into broader policymaking processes. Indeed, as the conclusion to what is probably the most important textbook on US intelligence analysis clearly states, "Analysts are of no use to their official customers by being merely the smartest and best-informed experts on a topic. They must address the policy needs of whoever now sits in the White House, executive departments, and congressional offices" (George and James 2008, 304). This cannot be emphasized enough and is the central pillar upon which this book is based. As the chapter on intelligence analysis of the 2005 report by the Silbermann-Robb Commission (often known as the WMD Commission) argues, "The best intelligence in the world is worthless unless it is effectively and accurately communicated to those who need it" (Silberman and Robb 2005, 26).

The third element, and arguably the most difficult, is to define success as it pertains to the impact of intelligence analysis on clients. There is no consensus among scholars or practitioners on how to define, let alone measure, success (Marrin 2012a). At the most general level, analytical units perform optimally when they generate insights that help clients develop and implement better policy. Successful analysis educates and enlightens policy makers and allows them to better do their work (Ghez and Treverton 2017). Kovacs eschews such ambitious goals and suggests more modestly that analysis is "useful" when it "makes a difference—either by bringing about a change in policy or decisions, or by supporting an existing policy which was about to be changed" (1997, 148). Similarly, Betts argues that the "most useful analysis . . . is that which helps to make policy something other than it would have been in the absence of the analysis" (1988, 187). This is a useful starting point, but it remains general and can carry different implications.

Some analytical products focus on a narrow topic, aimed at only one or a few clients, for a specific purpose (a yes or no decision). Others are produced for a more general audience, with a broader (and difficult to measure) objective, such as educating this readership on the topic in question, without necessarily directly supporting a particular decision process. Therefore, to succeed, an analytical product can aim to achieve a range of outcomes, including description, explanation, prediction, and achievement of policy leverage. For example, if there is a crisis in Venezuela, what do policy makers expect in terms of analytical support? Depending on their mandate and the circumstances, they might require a product, written or oral, that describes or explains the crisis (what are its drivers and consequences), makes predictions (where is it heading), or supports the development of policy leverage (what can Canada do, what are the consequences of adopting certain courses of action).

As many interviewees highlighted during the course of our research, it is difficult to measure how intelligence analysis supports policy making, in Canada or elsewhere. Senior policy makers are rarely willing to provide the detailed feedback to analytical units that would be necessary to rigorously determine whether their requirements are fulfilled. In the words of one interviewee, "You know when you fail, but you don't know when you succeed."[2]

In the Canadian context, moreover, senior policy makers rarely perceive that they have a strong need for intelligence, in the sense of having a clear, well-defined intelligence question to which they require a precise answer, which they will then knowingly and actively incorporate into their decision-making process. More often than not, as we discuss throughout the book, intelligence tends to fall more into the "nice-to-know" or "interesting" category of inputs into their work, and less frequently into the "need-to-know" or "need-to-have" category.[3] In the words of one interviewee, "Many requests for briefings we get are from senior policy makers who are interested in an issue and want context, but they rarely have a direct, precise need. . . . We are often told, 'I learned a lot,' but rarely are we told, 'I needed that.'"

In this context, it is challenging for intelligence analysis units to produce timely, well-informed, rigorous, and most importantly relevant analysis. That is, analysis answering the appropriate policy questions, in the right format, at the right time, and for the right people. These insights should be accurate, timely, forward-looking, and help avoid unwanted surprise (Betts and Mahnken 2003). To achieve this, analytical organizations must foster the development of subject matter expertise and rigorous tradecraft skills, which they often do, but they must also develop a deep understanding of the policy process—which they often fail to do (Juneau 2017). Indeed, as will be discussed in this book, this third element is easier said than done; it is at this level that the intelligence community in Canada faces some of its most important challenges.

Finally, the book covers a period starting with the attacks of September 11, 2001 until 2019. We chose this starting point because there is a clear "before and after": intelligence's role suddenly increased as it assumed a more prominent place in Canadian national security policy deliberations. Client expectations increased, in the realm of counterterrorism and in foreign policy making more generally. We conducted our research in 2018 and 2019, and we wrote the book in 2019 and 2020. The COVID-19 pandemic that started in 2020 serves as a useful cutoff point. It has undeniably affected how the intelligence community, at the levels of both analysis and operations, functions. We suspect, in particular, that some of the trends we describe in this book, such as the growth of senior policy makers' needs for intelligence and enhanced ties between the intelligence community and nontraditional partners, will intensify. We intend to explore this in future projects; without the benefit of more hindsight, it would be difficult to study this systematically.

Methodology

Our research relied on multiple data-gathering methods. First, we conducted sixty-eight interviews with serving and retired national security practitioners, mostly from Canada but approximately 15 percent from allied countries. Within Canada, interviewees were individuals with experience on the analytical (as analysts or managers) and the consumer side (policy makers using intelligence analysis). Interviewees ranged from desk officers and analysts all the way to deputy ministers (equivalent to deputy secretaries in the US) and heads of agencies. We also interviewed senior political advisers to current and past ministers and prime ministers. Finally, we also interviewed serving and retired practitioners in the US, which allowed us to better understand the Canada-US intelligence relationship, on which Canada is so dependent, and to draw some limited comparisons between the Canadian and US experiences. Our interviewees thus represent a broad sample, both in the nature of their work and their level in the hierarchy.

While interviews represent the main source of primary and original data, we also rely on other sources: mining of official government documents (e.g., the annual *Report on Plans and Priorities*, parliamentary testimonies, and reports by review and oversight bodies), media reports, conferences and conversations held under the Chatham House rule, and (limited) academic literature on the topic in the Canadian context. Moreover, senior officials in the Canadian intelligence community provided us with declassified internal reports on intelligence policy relations.

Our own experience—we worked in the national security community for a combined total of fourteen years prior to joining academia—also guided our research. One of the two authors (Juneau) has also been actively involved with the Canadian intelligence community since he left government, notably to provide training on strategic intelligence support to policy making. This experience allows him to continuously explore, through what amounts to participant observation, intelligence policy dynamics in Canada.

Throughout the book, we highlight similarities and differences between the roles, missions, and procedures of Canada's intelligence analysis community and that of its main counterparts. Comparisons with the US are possible, but differences in size and structure imply that the analytical function in Canada must position itself differently to optimally support clients. Comparisons with other countries are thus useful: the Australian and British intelligence communities (and those of other democracies to a lesser extent) are closer to the Canadian one in size and structure. In this context, our study of the Canadian case positions us to offer lessons that are generalizable to other national contexts.

Finally, we wish to highlight the limitations of the book. Researching the work of any country's intelligence community is inherently challenging, since there is little publicly available information. If conducting such research is a challenge in the US, it is an even greater problem in Canada, where there is less publicly available information about the national security and intelligence community. That said, we believe we have been able to mitigate these challenges. Our book focuses on the process and machinery of intelligence analysis and its interaction with the policy world, not on the substance of the analysis. Some specific aspects of the machinery of the intelligence policy interface must remain classified, but as many of our interviewees emphasized, much can be said without revealing information that should remain away from the public eye. Certainly, more can be said about structure and machinery than about the content of the analysis, much of which is classified. We also do not study other aspects of intelligence that need to remain highly inaccessible, especially on the operational side. Even though we recognize that our research can simply not reveal the complete picture, we are confident that we uncovered sufficient information, especially through interviews, to provide an overview of the evolution of the relationship between intelligence analysis and policy making in Canada since 2001.

Interviews: Approach and Context

We based the recruitment of participants on our preexisting contacts and on "snowball sampling," where existing study subjects assist in the recruitment of further interviewees. We targeted individuals who had experience producing, consuming, and/or managing intelligence analysis; many had experience in two or all three of these areas. Upon accepting an invitation, we sent interviewees a list of questions in advance that formed the roadmap for a semistructured interview. We conducted interviews between October 2018 and May 2019 in Ottawa, in a range of locations, including government offices, our offices at the University of Ottawa and Carleton University, public spaces (such as restaurants), and over the phone. We also conducted sixteen interviews with Canadians and Americans in Washington, DC, in May 2019. Most interviews lasted between sixty and ninety minutes, although some went longer.

Ultimately, we were pleasantly surprised with the access we achieved. Our requests were seldom turned down, and individuals often proved very helpful in providing further contact information, if needed. The atmosphere of most interviews was relaxed, with several interviewees stating that it had been a rare opportunity for them to think of "big picture" questions. Others expressed that they felt the interview was a kind of "therapy" to try to work out some of the issues they had been mulling over the course of their career.

Unsurprisingly given the subject matter, interviewees agreed to speak on the basis of strict anonymity. As such, we never identify interviewees, either by name or place of work. Even where interviewees (mostly retired individuals) agreed to go on record, we have chosen to keep their comments anonymous, for the sake of consistency and also on the grounds that the Canadian intelligence and national security community is so small that the identification of one person might accidentally lead to the identification of another, if only by process of elimination.

A note on context is also necessary, to understand the environment in which interviews took place and the scope of what our interviewees could speak to. We conducted our interviews during one of the greatest periods of change in the Canadian national security and intelligence community in terms of its legislative framework, the evolving threat environment, and expectations of transparency.

In June 2017, the government of Canada introduced sweeping legislative changes now known as the 2017 National Security Act.[4] This legislation overhauled national security and intelligence oversight and review mechanisms with a view to enhancing accountability and, to a certain extent, transparency. Notably, departments with national security responsibilities that had never been subject to comparable external scrutiny before (Global Affairs Canada and the Department of National Defence / Canadian Armed Forces in particular) are now subject to review and oversight by a range of bodies. When we conducted our interviews, however, these changes were still in their infancy and their full impact was not yet known.

The new legislation granted the Communications Security Establishment new powers to engage in "active" (offensive) and "defensive" cyber activities and the Canadian Security Intelligence Service (CSIS) the ability to legally obtain, store, and use datasets. Even though core mandates and functions within the intelligence community largely remain unchanged, it was clear that many interviewees were unsure about what enhanced review and oversight would mean for their organization, including for analytical units.

Moreover, these legislative changes came at a time when the threat environment was fluid. This period continued to see concern over threats to democratic institutions and electoral meddling from malicious state actors, especially heading toward a Canadian federal election in October 2019. In addition, there were rising concerns about foreign state and state-championed investment in sensitive economic sectors. The growing salience of these issues came in the aftermath of the emergence of the threat from extremist travelers / foreign fighters and returnees following the rise and decline of the Islamic State in Iraq and Syria (Canadian Security Intelligence Service 2018).

While these threats had existed in some fashion for decades, their new manifestations required the readjustment of tools and mindsets as well as growing cooperation with nontraditional partners such as Elections Canada, Passport Canada, and, increasingly, Innovation, Science, and Economic Development Canada (formerly Industry Canada). This was yet another series of novel steps the intelligence and national security community had been taking only relatively recently, as we conducted our interviews.

Finally, these changes were taking place at a time when Canadian citizens and the media were demanding greater transparency and accountability of the intelligence community. Since the massive leak of information about the US intelligence community and its allies (including Canada) by Edward Snowden in 2013, concerns over the activities and oversight of intelligence services in Western countries have increasingly turned into demands for more transparency about what these agencies and departments are doing in the name of national security. Canada has been no exception. There has been pressure exerted by the Trudeau government, coordinated through Public Safety Canada, to improve how the intelligence community engages and informs Canadians about what it does. This includes the establishment of the National Security Transparency Advisory Group in 2019, cochaired by one of the authors (Juneau)—although this occurred immediately after we completed our interviews (Public Safety Canada 2019).

In this sense it is important to appreciate that our interviews took place during a period of reform, transition, and uncertainty for the intelligence community. While we believe our data to be broadly accurate, our findings must also be understood as providing an overview of key trends affecting the intelligence/policymaking nexus up to 2019. Indeed, the community continues to evolve as this book goes to press, out of a need to respond to legislative reforms, evolving threats, and, of course, its own desire to improve.

Key Findings

Overall, our research identified three broad conclusions on the performance of intelligence analysis in Canada since 2001.

Scope for improvement. Interviewees differed on the details, but a clear overall consensus emerged. The performance of the Canadian intelligence analysis community in supporting policy making has improved since 2001 but remains far from optimal; it has gone, roughly, from poor to satisfactory. In the 2000s, the world of intelligence analysis in Canada was largely disconnected from strategic-level policy making. Analysts and their managers had few connections with their clients, while the latter rarely asked for it or perceived a benefit from using it. By the end of the 2010s, the situation had evolved in a generally positive direction: though there remains much scope for further improvement, analytical units have become better connected to the wider policymaking process. Yet these improvements are uneven, with interviewees describing pockets of excellence, pockets of mediocrity, and everything in between. As many interviewees noted, the community has "consistently underperformed," too often contenting itself with "muddling through."

Structural barriers to improvement. Because Canada is a relatively safe country, policy makers often believe that they have a limited need for intelligence, especially because of Canada's geographic location and proximity to the US. Moreover, Canada has traditionally been able to neglect security and intelligence issues because the costs of missteps are usually low. As a result, Canada's national security culture is immature and unsophisticated in comparison to its allies. This implies, in particular, that even though there remains scope for much improvement, further improving the community's performance will be difficult.

Electroshocks. Much of the improvement of recent years appears to be the result of what we call *electroshocks* to the system. These result from the sudden emergence of a new threat that the national security and intelligence community is initially poorly set up to address, forcing it to adapt. Importantly, these shocks are different from intelligence failures and strategic surprises (typically the source of major reform in other national contexts). They did not lead to sudden, important negative consequences like the 9/11 attacks in the US. In the Canadian experience, we identified four such post-9/11 shocks: war in Afghanistan (2005–2011), foreign investment by adversarial states (2012), emergence of foreign fighters (2013), and rise of online threats to democratic institutions (2016). Such events steadily increased the incentive for consumers to take intelligence analysis more seriously, a reflex that most senior members of the Canadian national security policy and diplomatic communities have not traditionally strongly had. These events also drive the analytical community to "get its act together," in the words of one interviewee. We also fully expect that with hindsight, we will eventually view the COVID-19 pandemic—which falls outside the scope of this book, since it is still ongoing as we finish writing it—as another such shock.

Overview of the Book

The book proceeds on the assumption that four elements are required for a successful intelligence policy dynamic: overall governance and structure of the community; management of individual analytical organizations; management of the interface between intelligence analysis and policy; and approaches to analysis. Using this framework, the following four chapters assess the performance of intelligence analysis in Canada. They identify its main strengths and flaws and propose explanations. They also each conclude with a case study.

Chapter 1 provides an overview of the Canadian intelligence and national security community. It highlights some of the characteristics that drive the nature of the community's internal dynamics. Weak central leadership, in particular, implies that personalities are especially important in the Canadian system relative to our allies. Next, the chapter looks at some of the structural factors that impact the performance of the analytical community: poorly defined niches and mandates, a lack of a foreign human intelligence service, and uncertainty regarding the impact of changes related to enhanced oversight and review. The chapter concludes with a case study of the Privy Council Office's Intelligence Assessment Secretariat.

Chapter 2 examines in detail how the intelligence community manages its analytical units. It highlights the importance of everyday bureaucratic practices to a successful intelligence policy dynamic, including hiring, training, offering exchanges and secondments, and defining career paths. Our findings build on the assessments of chapter 1: given the decentralized nature of the intelligence and national security community and the importance of personalities, we find that the management practices of analytical units lack standards in terms of hiring, training, and defining career paths. We then offer a case study of the Intelligence Assessment Branch of CSIS at the end of the chapter.

Chapter 3 focuses on the cultural factors that impact the management of intelligence policy dynamics. This includes the relatively low intelligence and policy literacy that pervades the policy and intelligence communities respectively, challenges with the intelligence priorities process, different approaches to client relations, and continued problems with silos between the various intelligence analysis bodies. We also explain here why there is no hard politicization of intelligence analysis in Canada—contrary to the experience in the US. The chapter ends with a case study of the relationship between Global Affairs Canada and intelligence matters.

Chapter 4 presents the findings of our research on what makes an intelligence product useful, including format and responding to government priorities, and what kinds of analysis are desirable. The chapter also examines the tendency to overclassify in the Canadian system, which has a serious impact on the ability to share and use intelligence in policy making. The Canadian Forces Intelligence Command within the Department of National Defence / Canadian Armed Forces is the concluding case study.

Chapter 5 provides recommendations to address the problems and challenges identified throughout the book. We examine what can be done to remedy or mitigate certain weaknesses and propose measures that the intelligence community can take to improve its performance. Moreover, we examine how this can be accomplished in an era requiring enhanced transparency amid a series of fluid national security challenges.

Finally, the conclusion offers a synthesis of the book's key themes. It begins with a discussion of whether we can truly say there is a Canadian intelligence and national security community, and what the experience of this "community" says about the role of expert communities more broadly in government. It also reflects on what the findings of the book suggest for how international structure shapes outcomes within a government context. And, the conclusion examines challenges ahead for the Canadian intelligence and national security community and its analytical bodies: What happens if Trumpism continues to deteriorate the foundations upon which Canada's national security has rested upon for decades? How should the community focus its evolution? Can Canada draw upon the experiences of its allies? And, can the intelligence community manage relations with nontraditional partners when addressing unconventional threats when it struggles to maintain relationships within itself?

We also offer, in a short appendix at the end of the book, an overview of the main organizations that form the Canadian national security and intelligence community. Readers unaccustomed to its structure and the mandates of its key players may wish to read it before moving on to chapter 1.

1 GOVERNANCE AND STRUCTURE

WE BEGIN BY FOCUSING on the governance and structure of the analytical function in the Canadian intelligence community. Overall, five key factors create the context in which analytical units function: institutions, personalities, mandates, capabilities, and accountability.

First, our research shows that the institutions of Canada's intelligence and national security community are relatively decentralized, especially compared to those of its allies, while the national security and intelligence adviser to the prime minister has limited authority over the rest of the community and a constrained ability to play a coordinating role. Second, the analytical community is heavily affected by individual personalities: whether senior leaders have an appetite for analysis or not tends to have a disproportionate impact on the salience of intelligence. Third, niches and mandates are not always clearly defined, leading to some confusion over responsibilities, which can foster competition rather than collaboration, even in a small community like Canada's. Fourth, the lack of a foreign human intelligence agency means that Canada is dependent on its allies. This reduces Canada's potential for deeper allied engagement and raises concerns over whether current arrangements rely too much on intelligence that does not necessarily have Canadian interests or perspectives at their core. Finally, we examine the emergence of new and evolving oversight and review bodies, and how they can impact the intelligence and national security community's relationship with policy makers. We find that there is potential for enhanced transparency to generate greater social license and improve Canada's weak intelligence culture. However, a failure to build trust may result in the opposite: retrenching bureaucrats who might aim to slow or even shut down the process of greater transparency if they believe the new system is unfair or may be abused. The chapter concludes with a case study discussing the evolution of the Intelligence Assessment Secretariat in the Privy Council Office (PCO).

Centralization

The intelligence community in Canada is relatively weakly centralized: its central department, PCO, exercises limited authority over its parts; coordinating mechanisms are relatively underdeveloped; and there is only a limited sense of community. That said, our interviews demonstrated that the situation has improved in recent years thanks to the creation of new positions and structures as well as the slow but steady development of a stronger national security culture and of more solid norms of cooperation.

A RELATIVELY WEAK CENTER

PCO is the prime minister's department. Its mandate is to coordinate public service support to the prime minister as the head of government and to act as the secretariat to the cabinet (Brodie 2018; Savoie 1999). PCO coordinates all sectors of government activity, including security and intelligence, and organizes itself by small thematic secretariats. The national security and intelligence adviser to the prime minister is the senior PCO official responsible for coordinating the security and intelligence community and to support the prime minister and cabinet as they carry out their responsibilities in this area. The position was formally created in 2004, when what had been known since 1985 as the security and intelligence coordinator became the national security adviser (NSA). In 2012, the NSA also became responsible for foreign and defense policy, based on the idea that combining this responsibility with security and intelligence would lead to a fusion of the advice to the prime minister on national security more broadly. The name was changed to the national security and intelligence adviser (NSIA) in 2017 to reflect the growing role of intelligence in the position. The NSIA holds the rank of a deputy head (deputy secretary equivalent in the US). Many holders of the position have been senior deputies, but this has been variable. In theory he or she reports to the clerk of the Privy Council, the highest-ranking public servant and deputy minister (DM) for PCO, though in practice some NSIAs in recent years have had a direct line to the prime minister.

The NSIA was, from 2012 to early 2020, responsible for three secretariats: Foreign and Defence Policy, which supports the prime minister and cabinet on foreign and defense policy matters; Security and Intelligence (S&I), which supports the prime minister and cabinet on security and intelligence and is responsible for the overall coordination of the community on policy and operational issues; and the Intelligence Assessment Secretariat (IAS), the intelligence community's central, all-source analytical unit (see the case study at the end of this chapter).

In contrast to its Five Eyes counterparts, PCO lacks clout in its relations with policy and operationally focused line departments throughout the security and intelligence community. Its role is not to direct their work but to bring people together and try to coax them into coordinating policies and operations. Its main asset is its proximity to the prime minister, but it lacks the size and authority to play a more forceful coordinating role. In 2018, the NSIA branch was fairly small, as it included about ninety individuals, with a budget of CA$11 million.[1] The three secretariats thus have limited bandwidth relative to the larger line departments with which they work. PCO's mandate is also similar in some ways to those of Public Safety Canada (PSC) and Global Affairs Canada (GAC), which are tasked with coordinating, respectively, domestic and international security and intelligence issues. (PSC's portfolio includes the Canadian Security Intelligence Service, the Royal Canadian Mounted Police, Correctional Services Canada, and the Canada Border Services Agency.)[2] This can lead—to some extent depending on the personalities involved—to some friction.

On the analytical side, in particular, the IAS has limited authority to play a leadership and coordination role. It can, in theory, write papers formally representing the consensus view of the community as a whole, but it rarely does, largely because it is a time-consuming and frustrating process that offers limited reward. The IAS has also slowly broadened its mandate in recent years, for example writing on climate change.

Views diverged among interviewees on the need for a stronger center. A minority argued that the situation is not perfect, but that it is more or less the best that can be hoped for and that more centralization would not be the answer to improve the analytical community's overall performance. The NSIA, in this view, already brings different perspectives together in a sufficiently flexible way in its support for senior policy makers. Decentralization, in this view, can act as an antidote against groupthink. It can also foster a degree of healthy competition among analytical units as well as the production of more tailored products for clients and the development of specialized knowledge. These are valid concerns;

more centralization would certainly come with a certain cost. These arguments would have more weight, however, if the Canadian intelligence community were already centralized. That is not the case; its center is weak both in terms of its authority and size. A moderately stronger NSIA—the office itself and the secretariats underneath, especially the IAS—would therefore allow the analytical function to better position itself and enhance its ability to shape policy.

A relatively weak NSIA—that is, a center with limited ability to coordinate the work of the intelligence community as a whole and with a small staff and limited capacity to coerce or cajole counterparts to work together—does have negative implications. It is constrained, in particular, in its ability to define intelligence analysis priorities and to mobilize the community in their pursuit and enforce follow-up (see chapter 4 for more on the priorities process). Weak central leadership also makes it more difficult to optimize resources and the work of individual departmental budgets in a more coherent manner.

Limited centralization and coordination in Ottawa also prevents the community from maximizing its opportunities in terms of its intelligence relationships in Washington, DC, and other capitals. Because Canada is a net importer of intelligence from its allies and partners, especially the US, these relationships are vital. However, as one interviewee argued, "we underplay ourselves" by missing opportunities to better leverage these relationships through a more coordinated approach. The CSIS station in Washington,[3] for example, talks to the Federal Bureau of Investigation (FBI) and the Central Intelligence Agency (CIA) (and to eleven of the seventeen US intelligence agencies), but mostly about operational issues; analytical issues tend to fall under the remit of GAC's Intelligence Liaison Office, while the embassy's political section talks to the National Security Council and to Congress. There is informal coordination between these different Washington- and Ottawa-based actors but, according to most interviewees, far from enough.

IMMATURE COORDINATING STRUCTURES

To illustrate the relative immaturity of community-wide coordinating institutions and their limited ability to connect intelligence analysis with policy development, one interviewee provided the example of a cabinet committee meeting to discuss Canada's Middle East strategy, early in the Trudeau government's first Parliament (2015–19). According to this individual, the intelligence community did not shape cabinet discussions in this instance; it did not speak with one voice by providing a holistic assessment of the situation, which could have served as a foundation for discussions. Instead, the community's work was siloed (see chapter 3 for more on this). There was, in particular, not enough of a process to identify key intelligence gaps. There was also, as will be discussed throughout this book, limited ability and willingness to connect intelligence assessments with the process of developing and implementing policy. In addition, interviewees highlighted that there was not enough coordination between the international and domestic angles of the issue. Multiple interviewees—here, and on many other topics—emphasized how the Joint Intelligence Committee and the Office of National Intelligence, roughly the IAS's equivalents in the UK and Australia, perform such functions, and typically do it quite well.

The pillar of these coordinating mechanisms in Canada is a structure of three DM committees:[4] one on national security (DMNS, responsible for policy), one on operations (DMOC, responsible for operations; it meets weekly but can be convened rapidly and frequently, as necessary), and one on intelligence (DMIC, with deputies responsible for reviewing IAS products and approving them for circulation to the prime minister; this committee was named the Deputy Minister Intelligence Assessment Committee until 2020).[5]

The UK example was key in informing processes and roles as Canada refined PCO's functions in the intelligence domain. For example, the Deputy Minister Intelligence Committee (DMIC) is the central high-level body for intelligence analysis. It was established by NSA Marie-Lucie Morin in the late 2000s, at the recommendation of IAS executive director Vincent Rigby (who subsequently became the NSIA in 2020), with the UK's Joint Intelligence Committee in mind.[6] It meets once a month, usually to discuss IAS papers known as National Intelligence Assessments (NIAs), which offer analysis of important topics, with a box of key judgements upfront. NIAs may be highly general, dealing with regional or thematic topics, or more specific (such as focusing on a particular crisis or conflict).

NIAs are not meant to formally reflect the consensus view of the community to the same extent that National Intelligence Estimates in the US do. The IAS consults others, but ultimately it holds the pen.[7] DMIC is not a decision-making or policymaking body. Its members discuss NIAs and then approve their distribution to the prime minister and cabinet. More broadly, the committee's role is also to inform the community of deputies on key issues, whether to shape specific discussions on the policy implications of specific assessments or to help build their knowledge base.

The significance of DMIC's role remains a matter of debate; it is still an evolving and somewhat immature process. Some deputies believe that discussions on the assessment itself are of limited value; they argue that at this level, deputies' focus should shift relatively rapidly to the implications for policy. Proponents of this view thus typically supported the decision to shift the committee's work in 2020 more toward the "so what" of assessments and less on the "what." Others, however, believe that holding intelligence-focused discussions is useful in itself. The point of the committee, according to this second view, is to agree on an assessment regarding an important issue, which educates deputies and allows them to reach a consensus to pass on to the prime minister and cabinet. The discussion on policy can then occur at the Deputy Minister National Security (DMNS) committee. That said, in practice, many interviewees noted that this distinction cannot, and should not, be rigidly enforced. It is inevitable that deputies will at some point shift the debate toward policy, but the fiction of the separation allows them to wall off some time for discussion of the analysis.

There was a consensus among interviewees that the quality of NIAs and of discussions around them have steadily improved over the years, though all recognized there is still significant scope for improvement. Five years ago, in the words of one interviewee, "it was kind of show and tell," with papers poorly linked to policy priorities and deputies often unprepared to engage in substantive discussions. More recently, deputies have been taking the committee more seriously. They ask their staff to provide them with better support and attend more regularly; as a result, discussions are better informed. The result is the slow institutionalization and routinization of a culture of working with this more sophisticated process. This improvement is, according to some, in part the result of more serious attempts by the IAS to reach out to the policy community to figure out what topics would be useful to the committee, as opposed to its past method of more or less self-generating papers on topics that it thought would be interesting.

Despite these improvements, DMIC still faces challenges. The committee represents, in theory, the top of the pyramid for intelligence analysis, but not every deputy sees the linkage to their policy concerns. The NSIA from 2018 until 2020, Greta Bossenmeier, was herself, according to interviewees, skeptical of the value of the process. Many interviewees were indeed still critical of committee discussions. They often agreed that most IAS products (though not all) are "intellectually consistent, very well crafted, and thoughtful" but are still too long, and often far too long, and often too narrow and detached from the high-level priorities of deputies. One interviewee gave the example of a paper on Russian policy in Africa, which did not seem relevant to core Canadian interests: it was "well done and interesting, but not important."

More broadly, the relatively immature national security culture in the federal government acts as a powerful constraint on the optimization of DMIC's work. As one interviewee reported, assessments are regularly pushed up the committee structure too quickly as decisions are delegated upward.[8] As a result, DM-level committees regularly end up spending a portion of their scarce time on minute details, sometimes even editing documents. Other interviewees noted that there is still far too much resistance on the part of intelligence agencies to share information with policy counterparts and to take interdepartmental coordination seriously. In their view, too many deputies (and other senior officials) are still too parochial in their approach to DMIC's work. "They care more about ensuring their department's paragraph is in the final document" as opposed to making the best document possible.

THE IMPORTANCE OF PERSONALITIES

Weak centralization and the relative immaturity of institutions implies that personalities have a disproportionate impact on the successes and failures of intelligence analysis. When leaders at the top have an appetite for intelligence, there is a strong trickle-down effect, incentivizing consumers below the leader to read and use it and producers to write better analysis. The higher up the official and the stronger his or her appetite, the more powerful this trickle-down effect is. Conversely, high-ranking officials—the highest being the prime minister—with little appetite for intelligence analysis have the opposite effect, disincentivizing those below, throughout the system, to consume analysis and producers to take their work more seriously.

A direct implication is that when there is a change in senior leadership, the status of analytical units can also change, more than in a system in which the role of analysis is better institutionalized. To some extent, this is normal in any bureaucracy; the personalities of top leaders always have an impact on how the system operates. But as institutions are relatively underdeveloped in Canada's intelligence community, changes in leadership have a greater impact than in other contexts in which institutions are more mature. The transition with the most impact, of course, occurs when a new prime minister takes office; the lower the position, the lesser the impact of a change of personalities.[9]

The evolution of the status of the intelligence analysis community under prime ministers Jean Chrétien (1993–2003), Stephen Harper (2006–2015), and

Justin Trudeau (2015–) confirms this impact of personalities. Chrétien was well known to be generally uninterested in intelligence analysis, incentivizing the system to take it less seriously. In the words of one interviewee, a view repeated by others, Chrétien generally thought intelligence analysis was "pointless." He understood the role of intelligence in the broader system but had little personal appetite for it—with the exception of counterintelligence, which he viewed as crucial. Because he did not read much intelligence, the various levels below him perceived little incentive to invest much time in reading it themselves. Predecessors to DMIC, as a result, were poorly attended, and senior officials often did not take them very seriously.[10]

The situation changed under Prime Minister Harper. As confirmed by multiple interviews, political staffers, ministers, and senior public servants realized that he became an avid consumer of intelligence analysis. He showed little interest upon taking office in 2006, but this steadily changed. In the words of one official, Harper became "very interested; he read, commented, had questions," while another emphasized that Harper "read intelligence, appreciated it, and engaged with it a lot."[11]

There was a clear trend throughout the early Harper years of a growing role for intelligence analysis. During the Harper government's first Parliament (2006–08), spontaneous generation of analysis was "close to zero," in the sense that the machinery rarely sent up products that had not been requested; this was a legacy of the limited interest of the past. This is a reliable indicator of progress: by the end of the Harper government's third Parliament (2011–15) and then under Trudeau, the relationship between the IAS and the Prime Minister's Office (PMO) was on firmer ground, with the latter requesting regular oral briefings and written products and the IAS spontaneously generating more written products.

Stephen Rigby, who was the NSA under Harper (2010–14), worked hard to steer the bureaucracy to better support this new prime ministerial requirement for regular analysis. He started personally briefing the prime minister on security and intelligence issues on a weekly basis and set up regular intelligence briefings by the IAS for PMO staff, two innovations. Rigby also supported the creation of short daily written products, tailored to the prime minister's interests (see chapter 4). These focused on extracting salient points and implications for Canada, as opposed to the longer, more abstract products the IAS had traditionally produced. Perhaps most importantly, Prime Minister Harper had significant trust in his NSA, and the two of them rapidly built a strong personal relationship, as confirmed by multiple interviews.

This had an important trickle-down effect on the policy side; it incentivized officials to stay aware of, and even contribute to, the process of preparing those products (attending meetings, tasking staff with preparing supporting material, and providing feedback) and to actually read the products that reached them. This cascade of incentives trickled down the various lines of authority. According to an interviewee, "Harper was interested, with a memory like a computer"; he "wanted a lot of intelligence," and this greatly shaped the consumption pattern of senior officials around him. This informal trickle-down effect slowly became more institutionalized.

Because Harper read intelligence, appreciated it, and engaged with it, this "pushed the machinery to take it more seriously." As a result, the head of the IAS in the years roughly corresponding to the second Harper Parliament (2008–11), Vincent Rigby, started holding weekly meetings with the foreign and defense policy adviser in PMO, Ross O'Connor. Gordon Venner, then the assistant secretary for foreign and defense policy in PCO, usually also attended, and even Ray Novak (principal secretary to the prime minister, then chief of staff) sometimes did. PMO officials also started contacting the IAS increasingly frequently when they had questions. As the intelligence community steadily realized, however, there was a price to this newfound success. Notably, because the bureaucracy knew that Harper would read many of them, its written products became increasingly tangled in consultation processes and vetted by senior officials on their way up the chain. It began to take longer to approve products, reducing nimbleness.

When Justin Trudeau came to power in 2015, the IAS had by then an imperfect but established tradition of providing oral and written analytical support to the prime minister and his staff. But every PMO is different in terms of its organizational structure, the influence of different personalities, its interest in intelligence, and its consumption patterns. Under Trudeau, PMO has been, in general, more informal than the Harper one. Interviewees agreed that even though Trudeau is not the voracious reader of intelligence that Harper was, he is nevertheless an interested consumer, and his PMO is very much interested in receiving analysis. Once the dust settled after the election, the IAS was thus able to provide it with regular oral briefings and written products. Reflecting the new prime minister's style, the ratio has skewed toward more oral briefings including regular, usually weekly briefings to Katie Telford, the chief of staff, and Gerry Butts, the principal secretary (until his resignation in 2019). These usually consist of a one-hour briefing, covering two topics. Some topics are requested by PMO, while others are suggested by the IAS. As interviewees pointed out, that

Telford and Butts, with their busy schedules, agreed to attend these briefings on a regular basis testifies to the IAS's success in delivering—unlike in the past—relevant and useful products.

The success of the IAS in positioning itself to satisfy PMO's intelligence needs illustrates, once again, the importance of personalities and how building relationships based on trust is a necessary condition for success. Many interviewees highlighted the role of Martin Green, the assistant secretary for intelligence assessment since 2015, along with his senior staff, in building relations with key officials and his ability to read individuals and understand their needs and to engage in proactive marketing of IAS products (see the case study at the end of the chapter).

Interviews in Washington, DC, with officials with policy and intelligence experience described partially similar dynamics. According to one interviewee, President Barack Obama was a good consumer of intelligence; he read a lot and was thoughtful about it. He read, in particular, the *Presidential Daily Brief* and asked many questions. This sent a strong signal throughout the system and had an important spillover and trickle-down effect. It strongly incentivized officials, in the White House and the National Security Council as well as in line departments, to also consume intelligence to make sure that they would be up to date. Obama's two secretaries of state, Hillary Clinton and John Kerry, and one of his secretaries of defense, Robert Gates, notably, were major consumers because it corresponded to their management styles but also because they feared a scenario whereby the president would have read a specific piece of analysis before them and would ask them about it in a meeting. This trickled down below the secretary level, down the hierarchy. Even though his management style was different, a similar trickle-down effect occurred under President George W. Bush. After the attacks of September 11, 2001, Bush became very interested in tactical responses to terrorism threats. As a result, the Terrorism Threat Integration Center (later renamed the National Counterterrorism Center), started generating a threat matrix. This created significant pressure and incentives for government departments to also become interested; secretaries and heads of agencies wanted this matrix and asked their staff about it, generating a trickle-down effect throughout line departments and agencies.

But there is a fundamental difference between the US and Canadian contexts in terms of how these trickle-down and spillover effects function. In the US, as interviews in Washington showed, changes in presidential administrations are typically less consequential than changes in personality at the top in Canada.

Structure imposes different sets of incentives for both: the US is a global super-power with global interests, while Canada is a midsize power and fundamentally a safe country with far fewer global interests. The US, as a result, has built over the decades much more mature institutions.

When President Trump came to office, it was immediately clear that he was less interested in intelligence analysis. He asked for less, read far less, and followed up less. But below him, many other officials, in the National Security Council and in line departments, were not very different, if at all, than in other administrations in terms of their patterns of consumption. In that sense, cabinet secretaries and their senior advisers, senior National Security Council officials, senior military officers, elected members of Congress, and their staff still wanted intelligence analysis. The reality that President Trump himself consumed far less intelligence analysis had a dampening effect on their appetite but did not completely eliminate it. There was a negative trickle-down effect, in other words, but it was less important than in Canada. If, hypothetically, a prime minister openly uninterested in intelligence had succeeded Stephen Harper, this negative trickle-down effect would likely have been much stronger. That is, personality matters everywhere, but it matters more in shaping intelligence policy dynamics in Canada than in the US because structural incentives are weaker and more diffuse.

Mandates and Niches

In addition to weak centralization and the important role of personalities, the third factor that shapes the functioning of the intelligence and national security community are the mandates and niches of each department and agency. For the purpose of this book, *mandates* refers to areas of responsibility defined in policy or law, and *niches* refers to informally defined responsibilities based on the common understanding of what an agency is best fitted to do. For example, CSIS is formally mandated through legislation to collect and analyze security intelligence on threats to the security of Canada. PCO's Intelligence Assessment Secretariat (PCO/IAS) has no formal mandate, but its niche, as discussed, is foreign political intelligence. Here, we ask whether niches and mandates provide sufficient guidance to define the roles and responsibilities of the various institutions within the community and to allow them to coordinate their work when it comes to analysis. As one interviewee noted, niches are important "because otherwise you are, as a cohesive unit, condemned to irrelevance" and "the first one to the chopping block" if you cannot prove your use. Moreover, in the absence of a defined line of products, or deliverables, it is harder to make a case for more resources. In this sense, niches and mandates are not just about dividing the work; they are also about who is heard on certain issues and who gets resources.

As it stands formally, many agencies and departments, such as GAC, the Integrated Terrorism Assessment Centre (ITAC), and PCO/IAS, do not rely on statutory authority to perform their security and intelligence analysis functions. While it is true that most countries' analytical methods and best practices are not stipulated in law but are promulgated in agency regulations and informally among analysts and analytical units (i.e., niches), it is worth examining these arrangements .

The Department of National Defence (DND) is unique in that its mission to collect, assess, and produce defense intelligence is relatively clear. The authorities for engaging in intelligence operations are also well established, falling under the authorities provided by the National Defence Act and under the "Crown prerogative" (powers of the Crown recognized by common law).[12] The use of and limitations on these Crown powers are typically given in ministerial directives, some of which have been made public. The governance framework for defense intelligence is outlined in the Ministerial Directive on Defence Intelligence, which is issued under the defense minister's authority under the National Defence Act.[13] While this one is unclassified, other directives, such as the Ministerial Directive on Defence Intelligence Priorities, are classified.

More granularity with regard to the Department of National Defence / Canadian Armed Forces (DND/CAF) intelligence function is provided in defence administrative orders and directives (DAODs, issued through the DM and the chief of the defence staff), especially DAOD 8008–0, Defence Intelligence (Department of National Defence 2017a) and DAOD 8002–2, Canadian Forces National Counter-Intelligence Unit (Department of National Defence 2017b). DAOD 8008–0 describes the purpose of defense intelligence activities in Canada and broadly outlines limitations on intelligence capabilities. When it comes to analysis, DAOD 8008–0 notes that defense intelligence is "a critical component of the ability of [the government of Canada] to make informed policy, partnership and program decisions in matters concerning national defence, national security and foreign affairs." It states that defence intelligence "may also assist senior [DND/CAF] and [government of Canada] decision-makers in achieving ongoing situational awareness of defence intelligence priority issues and in having strategic warning of impending crises in support of policy development regarding national defence, national security and foreign affairs objectives."

A second agency with relatively defined analytical responsibilities is the Financial Transactions and Reports Analysis Centre (FINTRAC), created in 2000 through the Proceeds of Crime (Money Laundering) and Terrorist Financing Act. This legislation details the analytical obligations of the center, more than is the case for most other units. It establishes an agency that collects, analyzes, assesses, and discloses information to assist in the detection, prevention, and deterrence of money laundering and of the financing of terrorist activities, and to assist the minister of finance in carrying out the minister's powers and duties.[14] The legislation also details which reports FINTRAC is responsible for and to which agencies it may disclose information.[15]

Yet even a strong legal mandate regulating security and intelligence activities does not guarantee clear guidance on analytical roles. Although they may provide strict guidance on the use of their powers, the statutes of intelligence organizations are usually mostly focused on operations or unique intelligence specializations and capabilities. References to "analysis" or "advice" are generally vague, providing little in the way of specifics on either roles or responsibilities. For example, *analysis* appears only briefly in the Canadian Security Intelligence Service Act (CSIS Act), often in relation to the processing of electronic datasets for the protection of privacy. While the act stipulates that CSIS is to "advise" the government on threats to the security of Canada, it does not provide guidance on how this should take place.[16] Similarly, the Communications Security Establishment Act only mentions analysis in the context of protecting the privacy of Canadians. It does, however, provide a bit more specifics in that the Communications Security Establishment (CSE) is to provide "advice" on its foreign intelligence collection and cybersecurity and information assurance mandate, as well as advice to the minister of public safety and emergency preparedness on matters relating to the Investment Canada Act and, specifically, on the impact of the integrity of supply chains and trustworthiness of telecommunications equipment from potential foreign investment.[17]

Finally, as previously noted, several departments and agencies have no specific statute or available guidelines. PCO, as the prime minister's department and the secretariat to the cabinet, does not have any statutory authority that defines its role. In addition, there is no mention of intelligence analysis in the Department of Foreign Affairs, Trade and Development Act. It is likely that some of the activities for GAC's Global Security Reporting Program (GSRP) fall under the act, which allows the minister of foreign affairs to "carry out any other duties and functions that are by law assigned to him or her" (Department of Foreign

Affairs, Trade and Development Act, s. 10 2.c). However, for the most part, the authorities for intelligence activities of both GAC and PCO/IAS are sourced in the Crown prerogative, as is the case with defense. But unlike the latter, neither organization has made any of its processes and procedures in this area public.[18]

In this sense, with the exception of FINTRAC and DND, there is little in the way of laws or statutes that institutionalizes and describes the analytical roles and responsibilities of the security and intelligence community in Canada. As such, the mandates and niches of individual units within the community appear to reflect collection activities (where present) but also heavily depend on established understandings built over time.[19]

Interviewees pointed to a lack of formal coordination mechanisms and, as a result, uncertainty over roles. As one argued, the community needs to "map [its] capabilities better" for the purpose of improving how each organization leverages the work of others. This was echoed by another who recalled that "we were tripping over each other, and we were doing a lot of the same coverage, and I used to say in a community this small, (a) we should be able to get along and work well together; but (b) we should be able to really do a better job at figuring out who is doing what." An end result of this state of affairs is that some individuals within the community, or policy makers, do not always understand who has the responsibility for what function or who is best placed to answer a question.

A second issue inhibiting cooperation is competition because of rivalry and territoriality. This should not come as a surprise; anyone familiar with bureaucracy will appreciate that the Canadian national security and intelligence community is hardly alone in suffering from such problems. The premise of the well-established "bureaucratic politics model" explains that government policies "can be understood largely as a result of bargaining among players positioned hierarchically in the government" (Allison and Halperin 1972, 43). In other words, competition and rivalry in bureaucracies are unavoidable.

Moreover, rivalry in other intelligence communities, particularly in the US, is well documented. In the last two decades, tension can partly be attributed to the blurring of foreign and domestic threats, resulting in overlapping agendas. Moreover, rather than cooperating, US agencies have often preferred to develop their own capabilities, causing more overlap (Lowenthal 2017, 61–63). In the eyes of one critic, "the [US national security establishment] is less efficient and effective than it should be because of institutional rivalries, overlapping authorities, and a host of other deficiencies constrained by the shortcomings in its constituent elements and shaped by structural and serendipitous imbalances in the relative clout of individual agencies and the leaders who head them" (Fingar 2017, 186).

This state of affairs prompted the George W. Bush and Barack Obama administrations to undertake efforts to improve community-wide coordination (including through the creation of the Office of the Director of National Intelligence), but improvements have remained elusive. Today the US intelligence community is known for "praising the virtue of interagency collaboration in principle but resist ceding their autonomy in practice" (Rosenwasser and Warner 2017, 29).

In this sense, rivalry in the Canadian context is neither surprising nor exceptional. This was apparent in our interviews, where views about agencies' willingness to cooperate was often less than complimentary; the Intelligence Assessment Branch of CSIS (CSIS/IAB) was described as "not a team player," CSE as "a little on its own," PCO/IAS as "a little bit nose up in the air" and "an ivory tower," the Canadian Forces Intelligence Command (CFINTCOM) as "too tactical," and "poor ITAC." While interviewees described all analytical units as territorial, the most frequent example of rivalry was between CSIS/IAB and ITAC. There was a general consensus that there is still confusion over their roles. In the words of one interviewee, "part of the problem was that nobody knew what ITAC's role was. So how were they distinct from IAB?" And in the view of others, mandates have been "exceptionally fuzzy over the course of those two organizations' existences"; as a result, "ITAC duplicates the work of IAB."

It is possible to trace the origins of this situation with internal problems in both agencies. On the one hand, given that for most of its history CSIS/IAB has been managed by intelligence officers, it has not always had a consistent client in mind for its products—alternating between focusing on operations, its own executive, and the rest of government. This prompted one interviewee to ponder if "IAB analysts know who their client is." This inconsistency has ultimately hurt CSIS/IAB's ability to establish its own niche. Yet while CSIS's problems vis-à-vis ITAC may stem from its inability to define a role for itself, ITAC has itself suffered from an inconsistent mandate from its very beginnings. Established as an "all threats" and "all source" assessment unit that would provide products to virtually the entire government as well as frontline responders, it had gradually morphed by 2011 into a unit focused solely on terrorism, with its main clients as "senior decision-makers" in the government.

The fact that ITAC is physically housed within the CSIS building and that its management committee includes the CSIS director adds to the confusion. These are two intelligence analysis units, both with an exclusive or major focus on terrorism, generally using the same sources to produce analysis for the same or similar clients.[20] While one interviewee argued that ITAC had driven CSIS/IAB into an "identity crisis," others noted that ITAC has yet to "truly find its groove" and as such is underused. While the rivalry between CSIS/IAB and ITAC is a unique case, it is emblematic of the larger problems related to a failure to better define roles and coordinate across the intelligence and national security community generally.

A third issue is that the mandates analytical units adopt sometimes depend as much or more on the capacity and capability of analysts than on a strategic plan. As one interviewee noted, the issues ITAC covers depend more on its ability to attract certain kinds of expertise: "It was just a matter of who was in which organization at the time and who was taking up that space. It wasn't necessarily directed by management." In other words, the ability of an analytical unit to write products on certain issues, such as terrorist financing or cybersecurity, is sometimes shaped by the capabilities of individual analysts as well as by strategic design. This is one major difference between Canada and the US. Whereas the latter often has several intelligence analysts within the same organization working on the same or similar files, Canadian analysts are often responsible for a larger number of functional or geographic areas. When there is staff turnover, it may take months, sometimes years, to bring someone new up to the same level. In this sense, similar to how personalities play an outsized role in the broader functioning of the intelligence community, the capabilities of individual analysts can impact what topic or areas some units cover.

This discussion begs these questions: Is cooperation overrated? Is competition good for the security and intelligence community? And could it even lead to better results? Here the views of interviewees were split. Some were adamant that in a small community, overlap is bad: "We need to get rid of any remnants of competition between the different agencies." Another observed that within the Canadian community, "there was a lot of competition and it wasn't particularly healthy competition. . . . Do we need three or four assessments on a specific subject? In a community this small, could we not really pool our resources and produce joint products?"

On the other hand, others felt that a certain degree of competition is beneficial. One provided the example of CFINTCOM, which has gradually expanded its coverage on a wider range of topics that do not always have an immediate DND/CAF nexus. In the view of this individual, if an agency has the expertise and receives questions from policy makers on a topic, it should write on it: "They should not say 'this is not my mandate.' You should offer the client what the client wants." PCO/IAS, for example, can write on topics that touch on military issues if asked by PMO, and CFINTCOM can write on terrorism when asked by its leadership. In this view, rather than causing friction, overlap "leads to, actually, more coordination." Analysts are forced to check in with analysts in other units, promoting communication and cooperation. It also has the benefit of helping to avoid gaps and cracks between niches and mandates (even where poorly defined).

Ultimately, in our view, intelligence analysis units cannot entirely avoid overlap between them. This is due to the poorly defined mandates of some departments and agencies, but also because a minimum of overlap is impossible to avoid in bureaucracies generally. Moreover, our interviews suggest that two factors contribute to a sustained, but limited, overlap. First, major steps to better define the community's niches and mandates are unlikely. Second, the largely decentralized reality discussed previously and the lack of an established interagency process for most intelligence products mean that individual units, and possibly analysts themselves, will remain responsible for doing outreach to ensure this overlap does not grow too large. Otherwise, there could be a wasting of scarce resources when the capacity of the system is already low. The bottom line is that limited overlap with appropriate coordination between analytical units is positive; it provides policy makers with a diversity of views on key issues important to Canadian defense and national security.[21]

Foreign Intelligence

Canada's relatively limited capabilities represent the fourth factor shaping the intelligence policy nexus. Canada is one of the few Western countries and the only G7 country to not have a foreign human intelligence service. Here, we understand *foreign intelligence* to be information or intelligence relating to the capabilities, intentions, or activities of any foreign state or group of foreign states, or any person other than a Canadian citizen or permanent resident or Canadian corporation [Canadian Security Intelligence Service Act 1985, s. 16 (1)]. Instead, Canadian human intelligence is focused almost exclusively on domestic *security intelligence*, that is "intelligence on the identity, capabilities and intentions of hostile intelligence services, organizations or individuals, who are or may be engaged in espionage, sabotage, subversion, terrorist activities, organized crime or other criminal activities" (Department of National Defence 2017a).[22]

There is no obvious explanation for this, though there are several hypotheses. Reg Whitaker, Gregory S. Kealey, and Andrew Parnaby argue that it can be explained by Canada's colonial legacy. While the UK took steps to protect and preserve the British Empire abroad, Canadian leaders saw their job as preventing subversion from within, including from Fenians and South Asian radicals. As the role of Canada's protector shifted from the UK to the US, Canada's focus on internal security remained (2012, 3–60). Kurt F. Jensen argues that a combination of factors prevented Canada from maintaining its World War II foreign intelligence activities, even as the Cold War was ramping up. Jensen highlights the fact that Canada's political leaders had been largely distant from the creation of foreign intelligence activities and collection and were not invested in their continuation. In his view, this led to the "absence of a foreign intelligence culture" (2009, 173–79).

Canada is a net recipient of foreign intelligence: it receives a large amount from its allies, particularly the Five Eyes intelligence-sharing partnership (Australia, Canada, New Zealand, the UK, and the US). Yet the lack of a foreign human intelligence agency does not mean that Canada is devoid of foreign intelligence. Canadian foreign intelligence collection is conducted by agencies that are constrained by statute. There are currently four organizations with some element of foreign intelligence collection in their mandate. CSE and DND have the most obvious mandates, although CSE is limited to signals intelligence and DND to activities tied to its mandate (the collection of intelligence essential to the preparation and execution of military policies, plans, and operations). CSIS has the ability to collect foreign intelligence *within Canada* upon the request of the minister of foreign affairs or minister of national defence. Essentially, CSIS may collect information about certain foreign topics, but any collection must take place on Canadian soil. CSIS may also operate abroad so long as its operations are directly tied to a threat to the security of Canada. Finally, the Global Security Reporting Program (GSRP), discussed in chapter 4, provides diplomatic reporting from abroad.[23]

Over the years there has been a low-key debate in the margins of Canadian foreign and defense policy studies over whether Canada should consider establishing a foreign human intelligence collection program, either by providing CSIS with an enhanced mandate or by establishing a new organization (Collins 2002; Farson and Teeple 2015; Livermore 2009; St. John 2017; Tierney 2015). While interesting, this question falls outside the scope of this book. Instead, we ask if the absence of a Canadian foreign intelligence service has an impact on the ability of analytical units to draft useful products for policy consumers.

As with many other topics discussed in this book, there was no consensus among our interviewees on whether a foreign human intelligence service would improve intelligence analysis in Canada. While no one downplayed the importance of foreign intelligence for policy making generally, there was a great deal of skepticism among many interviewees about whether Canada would truly benefit from such a capability. Some referred to the often cited "traditional" arguments against a foreign human intelligence service: there is no obvious department that could house such an agency, it could be a distracting resource drain, the cost would be too great, and Canada does not have the culture to support such an institution. Some interviewees also argued that foreign human intelligence would add little, as policy makers would not necessarily know what to do with it.

Others, however, felt that a foreign human intelligence service would provide more information and would improve policy making. One interviewee described the lack of a foreign human intelligence service as "a huge gap" that has a negative impact on policy making. "How are you supposed to make a foreign policy? GSRP is a great opportunity, but it is also a sign there is more that we are missing." This was supported by another interviewee who indicated that the lack of foreign intelligence meant that "often we cannot answer questions we get." (Of note, no other interviewee made such a claim.) One interviewee suggested that most of the material they read, over 50 percent, was not from Canadian sources.

The most cited reason in favor of having a foreign intelligence service had less to do with directly supporting policy makers and more with relations with allies, especially the US. In particular, some interviewees stressed the need to be seen as "carrying our weight." In Washington interviews, both Canadians and Americans emphasized that US allies are better off when they bring something meaningful to the table. As one interviewee observed, "In the US, security is a currency. What you provide gets you access. You have to buy yourself in." In other words, Canadians need to remember that to get something, they also need to give.

Despite the lack of a Canadian foreign intelligence service, allies generally hold Canada in good standing and view it as reliable; at worst, some interviewees suggested that Canada simply did not come up that often in high-level meetings. At the same time, Canada's allies would like it to contribute more to the overall Five Eyes intelligence effort.

One of the most common ways that the Canadian and US intelligence communities interact is through analytical exchanges. An interviewee noted that exchanges between Canadian and US analysts are frequent, with some agencies meeting with their US counterparts every two weeks. They noted that these meetings serve as a kind of "vetting" of draft intelligence products, helping to make the analysis of both countries stronger. Similarly, another interviewee noted that workshops and conferences organized by Canadian intelligence agencies help to build relationships with allied counterparts: "We get a lot of products from the US, but this helps us give back." Specifically, the interviewee noted that these events help to identify Canadian interests to the US and build relationships for other opportunities down the road.

Numerous interviewees noted that while the analysis Canada brings to the table is usually good, it is often strategic (discussing general trends), while US counterparts also often focus on more tactical products (such as detailed information about the specific capabilities of a terrorist group or adversarial state); Canada has more limited resources and cannot always dive that deep. As such, for one US interviewee, analytical exchanges are more about relationship building than a genuine sharing of information; they are a form of intelligence community diplomacy. This is an issue, as "the US system puts emphasis on tactical granularity." One interviewee suggested that Canada's limited ability to provide this kind of information means that the US often brings its "B-Team" (as opposed to its top analysts) to analytical exchanges with Canadians. In this sense, we find that Canada would be able to benefit more if it showed up with more proprietary information and analysis. At the same time, Canadian analysts' ability to look at the bigger picture—which their far larger and more specialized US counterparts sometimes lose track of—can be much appreciated in Washington.

Additionally, when it comes to the Five Eyes, Canada lags behind others, especially the UK and, on some matters, Australia. Both invest substantial efforts to maintain a robust presence within the US intelligence and national security community, including by placing a higher number of liaison officers in their embassies and embedded within US defense and national security agencies. Interviewees also described them as better at leveraging tactical and strategic analysis in creative ways. Some interviewees noted that Canadian intelligence and national security officials were sometimes reluctant to visit Washington, DC, as often as they could, despite the ability to do it as a daytrip from Ottawa.

Does this matter for intelligence analysis? Our findings suggest that it does; while Canada's relationships with its allies and partners are strong, almost all interviewees felt they are suboptimal and could be improved if Canada contributed more. Moreover, by failing to engage as actively as it could with US counterparts or to bring more resources to the table, its own intelligence analysis occasionally suffers. "We get the information, but how much are we helping to shape the information?"

CANADIANIZATION

In the absence of its own foreign human intelligence service, are Canada's analysts and analytical units successful in presenting views that reflect Canadian interests to policy makers? Some of our interviewees are skeptical about if this is being done as well as it could be. One interviewee stressed the need for analysts to do better to "Canadianize" intelligence analysis. This argument for "Canadianization" stresses that in the absence of a foreign human intelligence service, and given Canada's heavy reliance on the Five Eyes, it is important for analytical units within the Canadian intelligence community to develop their "own parochial lens" through which they develop understandings of issues and make sure assessments reflect Canada's interests. As an interviewee described it, Canadianization is "how you understand your job and the perspective you are supposed to bring to the problems and your work and your product. What's my job? Who am I working for? What am I supposed to be doing here? What is our angle on this?"

The problem is that Canada's heavy reliance on raw and finished US intelligence means that its own interests and perspectives become lost. It is hard to quantify exactly how much intelligence Canada receives from the US, but it is a great deal more than it collects itself. This means that the bulk of the intelligence Canada consumes largely reflects the world through a US prism. Moreover, given that the US determines which information Canada receives, this prism is shaped by US interests. As one interviewee argued, it is a legitimate question for Canada to ask whether "we are developing our own resources enough or are we relying too much on essentially second-hand information that we learn from others?"

A few interviewees also mentioned that in some instances, senior Canadian officials can give more credibility to US intelligence and intelligence assessments. A few thus identified a halo-effect problem, suggesting that some—though by no means all—senior Canadian officials are in awe of US capabilities and assessments. This can give rise, on occasion, to pressure by senior policy makers to take the information given to Canada at face value. Alan Barnes, for example has argued that during the Iraq War in 2003, mid-level managers and some analysts within the Canadian intelligence community pressured analysts in PCO/IAS to bring their assessments of the threat of weapons of mass destruction more in line with US (and British) assessments (2020, 939–40).[24] One interviewee suggested such pressure toward groupthink was "our natural Canadian inferiority complex. We think, well our view can't be right because there are five hundred guys down there in Washington that think differently." Another suggested that some Canadians can be too timid to disagree: "If we [come to a different assessment than] the CIA, there is pressure to agree. If we do not agree with the CIA, senior policy folks want to know why we do not agree."

Beyond the halo-effect, a further issue is that Canadian officials do not always scrutinize US intelligence for implicit bias, even though—according to some interviewees—America's greater intelligence capabilities influence its analysis. For example, because the US can leverage its geopolitical, geoeconomic, and military power to encourage or pressure countries to act in certain ways, it sometimes produces assessments that reflect these capabilities, or perhaps that reflect a misplaced faith in those capabilities. Canadians, assessing the same information but lacking the same ability to leverage other states, might therefore come to different conclusions about what is actually possible or likely. As one interviewee stated, "I think the Americans think differently about things and we have to always watch out for this." Another argued that Canadian policy makers are making decisions "based on someone else's read. Information may not reflect relevance to our needs."

What would Canadianization look like in practice? One interviewee suggested that it would require stronger analytical training and a better definition of what Canadian priorities are. It would also require analysts to be bolder in presenting a different view to senior policy makers and allies. An interviewee noted that while analytical units in the Australian intelligence community make their bottom-line assessments known, Canadian organizations like CSIS still sometimes "speak in hushed tones." The argument for resisting the "pack mentality" is that, ironically, Canada "would be more respected" by its partners for making its own view clearer. Moreover, it would suit Canada to help shape the debate on issues of critical importance, such as the security implications of foreign investment by Chinese state-owned enterprises, the intentions of states sponsoring terrorist groups, or the risks posed by disinformation campaigns in Western elections (Carvin 2021b).

Oversight, Review, and Scrutiny

Traditionally, the oversight and review of the Canadian intelligence and national security community has focused almost exclusively on assessing operations and legal compliance rather than the functioning of analytical units. The issue of oversight and review may therefore not seem to have direct relevance to the overall question of the performance of intelligence analysis. This view is too narrow, however. First, recent legislation introducing efficacy review, beyond mere compliance, means that the performance of intelligence analysis will be evaluated for the first time. Second, oversight and review enhance transparency and, ideally, generate confidence in the system. This boosts the social license of intelligence and national security agencies. Third, if done well, review and oversight could contribute to the establishment of a more sophisticated intelligence culture which may drive further demand for intelligence products and improve the conversation about national security issues generally. All of this has an impact on how intelligence supports policy makers.

Before beginning, a number of clarifications are necessary. First, while it is common to hear *oversight* and *review* used interchangeably, both terms have specific definitions in the Canadian context. "*Review* refers to the ability of independent bodies retrospectively to evaluate security activities. A reviewer does not have operational responsibility for what is being reviewed. . . . *Oversight* refers to a command and control process—the power to issue directions, influencing conduct before it occurs. Review bodies do not have the power to oversee [national security] activities, though they can make findings about failings and can make recommendations on improvements" (Forcese and Roach 2015, 362–63).[25]

In Canada, most institutions tasked with ensuring accountability are review bodies, whereas *oversight* rests with ministers (usually of national defence, foreign affairs, or public safety), the courts (through warrants), and/or independent bodies led by retired judges, such as the intelligence commissioner (discussed below).

A third concept, *scrutiny*, is important here—although it has traditionally played a less important role in the Canadian context. Scrutiny in Westminster parliamentary systems ensures political accountability. Elected members of a legislative body ask questions or scrutinize the government, often but not exclusively in the legislative chamber. As noted, in the Canadian system, ministers are accountable to Parliament for the performance of the departments and agencies under their control. In the context of intelligence and national security, ministers are often asked to approve certain operations and missions that are high risk and dangerous, and in this way they provide a kind of oversight—albeit one that does not often see the light of day, unless a mission goes wrong and is brought to the public's attention.

Parliamentarians have the opportunity to scrutinize the performance of a government department or agency through parliamentary committees in the House of Commons and the Senate. Ministers and senior bureaucrats can be called to answer questions and provide details about an operation or issue (Friedland

1997). In recent decades, these committees have tended to be hyperpartisan rather than a venue for sober inquiry. Moreover, as Canadian members of Parliament and senators are not provided with security clearances and these meetings are held in the open, they cannot discuss classified information. As such, the ability for committees to engage in robust scrutiny is limited.

Nevertheless, scrutiny is an important aspect of Westminster systems. It differs from review and oversight in that parliamentary scrutiny offers political accountability, rather than administrative or operational accountability. Scrutiny therefore has the ability to bring important issues to the public's attention through questioning the government or senior civil servants from the intelligence and national security community.

A second clarification is the time period in which we conducted our research. The framework upon which oversight and review in Canada takes place was rapidly evolving when we conducted interviews in 2018–19. Prior to this period, Canada had one of the weakest oversight and review frameworks of any of its peers. Review was conducted by stovepiped bodies that looked only at CSIS (the Security Intelligence Review Committee) or CSE (the Office of the Communications Security Establishment Commissioner), neither of which were permitted to look at the actions of other government departments or agencies to see how they used the products or information provided to them by the intelligence services. Interviewees described both as having been underfunded and struggling to keep up with the volume of work.

Two federal institutions also play important but limited roles that apply to all federal government departments and agencies: the Office of the Auditor General, which conducts periodic independent audits of federal government operations, including government departments, and the Office of the Privacy Commissioner, which enforces federal privacy laws that set out the rules for how federal government institutions must handle personal information. Most information collected as a result of intelligence activities constitutes personal information under Canadian law (Privacy Act, [R.S.C., 1985, c.P-21, s. 3]).[26] These bodies are limited in their size, however, and do not always have the expertise to delve into the complicated world of intelligence operations and national security (Forcese and Roach 2015, 401).

Finally, all government departments have their own internal compliance units, such as the Internal Audit at CSIS, GAC's Inspector General, and DND's Assistant Deputy Minister of Review Services.[27]

RESTRUCTURING OF OVERSIGHT AND REVIEW

In 2015, the Justin Trudeau government was elected on a platform that included reform of intelligence and national security, leading to a complete overhaul of the oversight and review architecture. This was primarily done through the creation of three new institutions: the National Security and Intelligence Committee of Parliamentarians (NSICOP), Canada's first executive review body for the national security and intelligence community composed of parliamentarians; the National Security and Intelligence Review Agency (NSIRA), an independent body with the authority to review the use of intelligence in any government agency; and the Intelligence Commissioner, a quasi-judicial role with an office that has both oversight and review powers concerning the collection, assessment, storage, and use of certain datasets, as well as certain cyber operations to ensure that the privacy of Canadians is protected (West 2021).

This brief background is important for two reasons. First, all major departments and agencies are now subject to external review for the first time, including the Canada Border Services Agency, DND/CAF, and GAC. While these reviews are limited to intelligence and national security issues, they constitute a major change in how these departments do business, causing a certain amount of concern. Second, even for departments and agencies used to external review, such as CSIS and CSE, the new arrangements have been enhanced to a degree where they will be answering to not just a more robust agency but also politicians for the first time. This too has given rise to some concern.

Given such a major shift in how the intelligence and national security community operates, it is important to assess the degree to which this will have an impact on departments and agencies that produce analysis. Overall, no interviewee indicated that enhanced review and oversight, *in principle*, is a bad idea. Some discussed the factors needed to establish an effective relationship that will improve accountability. Overall, three broad factors emerged for both the new agencies and the units they are tasked with reviewing: the appropriate resources, time to get everything up and running (probably a few years), and trust (the review bodies need to show good will, and the community needs to buy in). In the view of several interviewees, good will can be demonstrated where the review bodies are transparent about their intentions. Without this goodwill, it is clear that the process will not work optimally. Answers provided by agencies "will be scripted to say nothing" to the oversight and review bodies. In this scenario, feeling threatened, the natural inclination of the intelligence and national security community will be to shut down. While there is, for now, a certain amount of goodwill, our interviews suggest that there remains "a lot of discomfort in the intelligence community." Another interviewee stated that the intelligence and national security community generally is still uncertain as to how review will actually work: "I don't think people are grumpy. . . . We are nervous." Other concerns included the risk of politicization, particularly through NSICOP, and the potential for political abuse through the leaking of sensitive information by its members for political ends.

Two advantages of enhanced review and oversight frequently came up. First, it will provide *social license*. More oversight and review is part of the process of developing trust with Canadians, many of whom are concerned about government surveillance. Reflecting on this, one interviewee observed, "When there isn't clarity and some level of transparency, then people will assume the worst." Indeed, some interviewees raised the idea that transparency can help credibly explain issues to a skeptical public when controversy arises: "It becomes easier to also talk about threats, and people don't ignore it or they don't think we are overreacting." That said, one interviewee questioned if this really will be the case, suggesting that the idea that review enhances the community's social license still "is a hypothesis that needs to be tested." A second set of benefits might be described as *practical* advantages that may come out of enhanced oversight and review. The new structures could bring new voices and perspectives into a closed world. "We are just always talking amongst ourselves. It is a small community. . . . So we need to have a different viewpoint." Others also suggested that even if departments and agencies were not being specifically targeted for review, it would encourage them to look at their governance and intelligence practices with a view to reforming them for the better. For example, one interviewee noted that they hoped that the potential for review would "make them look at their internal governance, their policies, how they brief the minister, whether there are reporting obligations to the minister . . . whether those reports are as complete as they should be." For the most part, interviewees were more concerned about the impact of enhanced review on their resources than on their analytical work, given how labor-intensive the new process can be.

There appears to be a cautious optimism among many (though not all) interviewees that more transparency through strengthened oversight and review will help achieve a better functioning intelligence and national security community, more confidence in the system, and even a more sophisticated intelligence culture. For analytical units, this could eventually mean an improvement in the environment in which their products are received. Yet there is a clear risk that if the new process is not able to operate on the basis of trust, it will be hampered by officials who drag their feet or do the bare minimum rather than actively participate. This would have the opposite effect on intelligence culture, making the situation worse. Although we did not hear truly negative perspectives on enhanced review in our interviews, both authors have been present during multiple informal conversations where individuals with experience in the national security and intelligence community have expressed deep skepticism over whether the new review bodies will be free from politicization (in the case of NSICOP) and suggested the new bodies were likely to be too hard on certain departments (such as DND and GAC) without truly appreciating their functions.

To recap, we find that to establish an effective relationship between the new review bodies and the intelligence and national security community, three broad factors are essential: resources, time, and trust. Interviewees agreed that the new arrangements are going to be resource intensive for departments and agencies that have never been reviewed before. It is important to note that no new resources were allocated to support the new review obligations—resources had to be found from within existing budgets. One interviewee noted that it can take many hours to prepare to meet with one of the review bodies. A review can require a department to produce years of paperwork, to have their employees taken away from their jobs to prepare for interviews or meetings, and to spend time preparing and answering pointed written or oral questions.

Of these three factors, the most important is the need to build trust. The new oversight and review bodies as well as the departments and agencies themselves need to work together to ensure that this new arrangement functions well. The former need to show good will and the latter need to buy in. Interviewees emphasize transparency, with many stating that it is important for review bodies to state not only what they are reviewing but also why. Tone also matters. If the process becomes overly adversarial, it will not work well. Finally, interviewees suggested that it would help if the new oversight and review agencies could better explain the benefits of review. "Market your value added, explain why it is much better to sit down in a room to answer tough questions for two hours and try to convince people that going through that process will help them and save them time five years down the road." In this way, wary or skeptical departments and agencies might be able to better understand the advantage of investing in the process.

Conclusion

This chapter argues that the Canadian intelligence and national security community is small, with weak centralization and coordination mechanisms, and that it lacks many of the tools (notably a foreign human intelligence service) that most of its main allies and partners possess. Americans often refer to the "interagency process" when it comes to decision-making, but the equivalent in Canada is weaker and poorly institutionalized.

The implication, confirmed by our interviews, is that the influence of personalities becomes dominant in the functioning of the intelligence and national security community. Leaders who are able to successfully network with senior policy makers (particularly in central agencies) are more successful in having their products read. Similarly, the ability for the community to coordinate and work together depends on the ability of senior executives, mid-level managers, and analysts to establish and maintain relationships.

Nevertheless, this situation is slowly changing. The establishment and strengthening of DM committees where intelligence issues and products are discussed has improved coordination, exchanges, and collaboration. The establishment of enhanced review means that the efficacy of the community will come under greater scrutiny, improving incentives to work more efficiently together.

Case Study: The Intelligence Assessment Secretariat

Intelligence was not a priority in PCO in the 1990s: Prime Minister Chrétien was not interested in intelligence while Canada, like its allies, was focused more on benefiting from the post–Cold War peace dividend. The assistant secretary for security and intelligence chaired an assistant deputy minister (ADM) level committee that reported to a ministerial committee (the Ministers' Meeting on Security and Intelligence) once a year to submit a memorandum to cabinet seeking authority on intelligence priorities (in addition to a few small agenda items). In the words of one interviewee, "neither S&I nor the IAS were mainstream players in PCO at the time; they did not contribute much, except for specific episodes, like the 24 Sussex break-in, where they had a role to play."[28]

The IAS was created in 1993, after budget cuts led to the elimination of the analytical function in the foreign ministry (see the case study at the end of chapter 3). Initially, the IAS rotated one team in the foreign ministry headquarters, while Foreign Affairs (as GAC was then known) seconded roughly a half-dozen analysts and the deputy executive director to PCO; the goal of this burden-sharing was to maintain the appearance of a close relation between the two. The quality of these secondees was unequal; a good number were "deadwood, dumped from Foreign Affairs" as a convenient way to get rid of them. This arrangement ended with 9/11, after which the IAS got an infusion of cash. This reorganization suited both sides. Foreign Affairs wanted the office space vacated and needed the personnel it had been seconding to the IAS, while the arrangement had in practice become unwieldy and troublesome for PCO.

The IAS in the 1990s was small. Margaret Purdy, who was deputy secretary for S&I in 1998–2001 (the predecessor position to the national security adviser), believed in the value of the IAS; she asked the clerk of the Privy Council at the time, Mel Cappe, for more resources, but he turned her request down. The IAS was also not very dynamic. According to one official, "Nobody was asking the IAS for products. It had very few direct requests, so it had to set its own deadlines and priorities. . . . It was writing blind and rarely got feedback."

The IAS was, on paper, modeled after the Joint Intelligence Committee in the UK, but with far less impact; in fact, according to one interviewee, in a view supported by others, "it failed miserably" in its early years at producing analysis relevant for policy clients.[29] Senior officials simply did not take it seriously. This came from the very top. Prime Minister Chrétien did not have an appetite for intelligence analysis, as discussed, providing little incentive for senior officials to be interested.[30] This was reflected in the work of the predecessor to DMIC at the time, which was poorly attended and was "basically not much more than an editing committee." Meanwhile, on the operational side, the equivalent committee was working better.

By 2001, and still for a few years afterward, IAS products rarely had impact. The organization focused on writing long pieces largely disconnected from the policy context. To the extent its work was focused on clients, they were at Foreign Affairs, not PCO. The IAS executive director at the time, Greg Fyffe (2000–2008), barely ever met with his assistant secretary counterparts in PCO (for security and intelligence, and for foreign and defense policy), for example. Until 2006, the IAS was "isolated, out of the mainstream." It had virtually no contact with PMO and the political world.

The situation started evolving after September 11, 2001. The IAS received an infusion of money as part of government-wide efforts to improve counterterrorism capabilities, allowing it to grow. To connect itself to policy, it started producing a daily brief, at Foreign Affairs' request, a two-pager with short paragraphs and links to longer papers. The IAS also started producing shorter papers and aimed to make its products more visually appealing (e.g., with two columns per page, to make them easier to scan quickly). Another initiative was to adopt a format whereby it put key judgments at the beginning of papers. Despite these efforts, the IAS was starting from a low point. Its impact on policy making in the early 2000s remained limited. The policy literacy of its analysts, in particular, remained excessively low; most were content with writing long papers with little care for the questions of who their readership was, and what it needed.

Major events or crises tend to have an important impact on the role of intelligence; senior policy makers become keener to obtain up-to-date, relevant information and likelier to set clear requirements and to demand more frequent and higher quality products. The attacks of 9/11 represented such a shock to the system, and so did the Iraq war in 2003. There are two major questions concerning the Chrétien government's decision not to support the US-led intervention in Iraq: What was the view of the Canadian intelligence community? And what was the impact of its analysis on the decision? The intelligence community got the assessment right, but this had at most a limited impact on the decision. It did, however, boost its credibility.[31]

The IAS's assessment was that it could "see no evidence that there were weapons of mass destruction in Iraq." This was not the same as assessing that there were none; the IAS simply judged that it was not in a position to say so definitively. Underlying this assessment was the view that "a lot of inconclusive evidence does not make it confirmed." In addition, according to one official, "the Al Qaeda in Iraq angle was so ludicrous we barely spent any time on it," referring to the George W. Bush administration's claim that Saddam Hussein's government had ties to the terrorist movement. An IAS analyst similarly discredited the US claim that Iraqi oil would pay for the invasion. The US government also argued that Iraq had a smallpox program, leading it to inoculate its deployed personnel. The Canadian government, seeing no evidence to support this, decided not to do so. The IAS produced about twenty-seven papers in total in the run-up to the invasion in March 2003. All were CEO (for "Canadian Eyes Only," meaning not for distribution to allies or partners), which is unusual; normally, a far greater proportion of papers are shared, especially with the Five Eyes.[32]

The IAS got the assessment right, but did it shape Canada's decision not to join the war? According to the majority of our interviewees, intelligence did not actually play an important role in shaping Chrétien's decision but rather reinforced his political instinct to stay out. This validation mattered, as "the last thing we wanted was for Canada to say no and then for [weapons of mass destruction] to be found in Iraq." Importantly, a point to which we return in chapter 4 in our discussion of politicization, all interviewees agreed that there was no political pressure on the IAS to come to any specific conclusion. But even if the IAS analysis had a limited impact in driving the decision, the fact that it got it right made a positive difference for its reputation; senior policy makers, who had mostly neglected it until then, became more responsive to its analysis afterward. The events allowed the IAS to build credibility and increase aware-ness of its products—both credibility and awareness had been low until then.

The other key element to the evolution of the IAS—after the shocks of 9/11 and the Iraq war, and then the evolution of Stephen Harper as prime minister, as discussed previously—was the nomination of two experienced policy officials as executive directors to succeed Greg Fyffe, first Vincent Rigby in 2008 (who, until then, was ADM for policy at the Department of National Defence) and then Rob McRae in 2010 (who was a career diplomat and former ambassador to NATO). Both Rigby and McRae worked hard to push the IAS to be better connected to client needs, and to make its papers shorter and less academic. While the IAS in the past had mostly hired PhD graduates with high levels of specialization, it started hiring more generalists. It also sought to hire mid-level managers with policy backgrounds instead of to solely promote analysts.

Progress was real, and the IAS became, during those years, increasingly re-sponsive to the needs of clients. But its position remained fragile, with many senior officials still skeptical of its value. This was best illustrated when Stephen Rigby, who became national security adviser in 2010, seriously considered elimi-nating the IAS to allow PCO to achieve its budget-cutting targets at the time of the Deficit Reduction Action Plan in the early 2010s under the Harper govern-ment. For Rigby in particular, the IAS's meager contribution and its large size relative to the other two secretariats under him (responsible for security and intelligence, and for foreign and defense policy) made little sense.

The transformation of the IAS toward greater relevance continued under Martin Green, who succeeded Rob McRae as assistant secretary in 2015 (after Stephen Burt, the director of operations and number two official, had held the position on an acting basis for about one year). In the words of one interviewee, expressing a position supported by others, Green and key members of his team have done a "fabulous job" in continuing to modernize the IAS and improve its ability to serve clients. This official argued that "the IAS is getting to" the level of the Office of National Intelligence, its Australian equivalent, which has a strong reputation in the Five Eyes community ("the best products, high quality, relevant, succinct"). IAS products, in particular, have become "sharper, shorter, and more responsive." According to one interviewee, clients "are [now] not shy to ask specific questions" to the IAS and to request oral and written products, a different reality from only a few years before.

The quality of IAS products has undeniably improved over the years, but does it actually shape decisions on a regular basis? Here, interviewees presented a more mixed picture. One consumer could think of one instance in which an IAS product made a noticeable difference on a decision; "It had a real value-added in shaping how we responded." But on a day-to-day basis, the IAS rarely impacts decisions in a measurable way. Rather, for many interviewees, its strength mostly lies in its ability to explain the context, to frame the issue, notably on "relationship questions: who talks to whom, who is connected to whom, who influences whom."

There is, as such, still room for improvement for the IAS; for all its progress of recent years, its work remains "mixed in quality and relevance." There remains, in particular, a culture in the IAS of producing analysis that is still often viewed by many in policy as too long and too academic, detached from their concerns, interesting but not useful enough—despite important improvements in the past ten years or so. In the words of one interviewee, there is still in the IAS a tendency to "write long papers, then they throw them up over the wall, nobody reads them, and they go back to their coffee breaks."

2 MANAGING ANALYTICAL UNITS

ALTHOUGH THERE HAVE BEEN thousands of books and articles written about intelligence agencies around the world, telling their stories of success and failure, few focus on the issues of how the spies got there in the first place: human resources and management practices. While not exactly the stuff of a James Bond novel, the everyday bureaucratic management of intelligence agencies is vitally important to how they operate. Agencies with processes that do not hire people with the right skills or fail to provide adequate training will result in suboptimal performance. Worse, they may be doomed to a cycle of repeating bad practices if they fail to invest in the policies and procedures that create the backbone upon which the intelligence and national security enterprise runs.

In what little literature exists, there is consensus that managers are crucial for the success of analytical units.[1] This includes forging relations with policy, human resources (especially hiring), training, and career management. But how managers should carry out these tasks and the challenges they face in doing so is underexplored.

This chapter seeks to add to the literature on the management of intelligence analysis units, albeit within the Canadian context. Our findings build on the assessments of the last chapter. Given the decentralized nature of the Canadian intelligence community and the importance of personalities, we find that the management practices of analytical units lack standards in terms of what is required of managers, hiring, training, and defining career paths. Canadian practices also fall behind those in the US. Of course, some of this divergence can be attributed to the difference in size between the two communities. The US can afford to hire more analysts and managers, so it is able to create arrangements and opportunities with more flexibility. However, deficiencies on the Canadian side can also be attributed to a lack of attention by upper management to the human resources issues crucial to the operation of intelligence analysis units. As with many other aspects of the Canadian intelligence community in recent years, there are signs of improvement. An increase in resources dedicated to training and the development of a small but important community-wide secondment program, for example, are first steps toward a more professionalized workforce.

The chapter proceeds as follows. We first provide a brief overview of the literature on managing intelligence analysis units and what is known about the Canadian context. Next, we examine human resources practices, especially hiring, diversity, and targeted recruitment programs. We then discuss how the Canadian intelligence community trains its analysts and what further training is needed. We follow with a discussion of exchanges and secondments and of why there are still such few opportunities. We also offer competing views over the need for better defined career paths for analysts.

The chapter concludes with a case study discussing the evolution of CSIS/IAB.

Management of Intelligence Analysis Units: A Gap in the Literature

Anyone who has worked in a bureaucracy knows that management has a significant impact on how well a particular unit performs. The world of intelligence and national security is no different. Although the community is unique in some of its responsibilities and capabilities, it is comprised of government departments and agencies that are required to coach their employees, conduct performance evaluations, arrange for training, allocate budgets, and respond to requests.

Yet despite the central importance of management to the operation of intelligence units, there is very little written on the topic. John A. Gentry describes the lack of scholarly analysis of intelligence management practices as "a glaring hole." He argues that this may lead to bias in assessing the performance of intelligence analysis; when problems with intelligence arise, few scholars consider the context in which analytical units operate and turn to the analysts themselves. "Rather than analyzing managers of analysts, intelligence agencies and scholars focus on cognitive causes of analytic errors and possibilities for real but limited improvements in analysis in areas such as 'tradecraft' training, use of 'structured analytic techniques' (SATs) that are standard methods for helping analysts avoid errors, and information technologies" (Gentry 2016, 154; see also Gentry 1995).

In other words, discussions about improving analysis are often about the analyst—but not changing or reforming the environment in which they find themselves. As John C. Gannon argues, "the bottom line is that immediate supervisors have the greatest impact on the morale and motivation of analysts, who complain most about the managers closest to them" (2008, 213–14).

It is not obvious why this is the case—perhaps because it is easier or perceived as more interesting to write about the craft of intelligence analysis. Gentry's more cynical view suggests that focusing on analysts provides opportunities to develop courses and training materials that can then be sold back to the intelligence community (2016, 165). There simply may also be a bias toward looking at the product and how clients read and receive it rather than at the conditions under which analysts produce it—something that is less tangible and harder to capture in a scholarly format. Alternatively, there may be an assumption that the traditional literature on bureaucratic management may not apply to the intelligence community. Whatever the reason, the lack of studies on management practices is a significant gap.

A further complication in the Canadian context is that virtually all of the limited literature in this area has been written from a US perspective. While some of the general insights about the importance of management likely carry across borders, there are important differences between the US and Canada that limit the applicability of this literature to the latter. First, the US literature generally assumes that managers were analysts—something that is not always true in the Canadian experience (Gannon 2008; Gentry 1995). Many managers at CSIS, DND, and GAC, for example, have had other backgrounds, including as intelligence officers, foreign service officers, and active military personnel. For most of its history, analysts in CSIS/IAB were barred from entering the management cadre, even within their own unit, although this has recently changed.

The only research on the management of intelligence analysis in Canada comes from a series of studies conducted by the Thinking, Risk, and Intelligence Group within Defence Research and Development Canada between 2010 and 2012 (Derbentseva, McLellan, and Mandel 2010; Adams et al. 2012).[2] The group, which we discuss later, describes its mandate as "to support Canada's defence and security community through applied behavioral science aimed at promoting human effectiveness in risk management and intelligence production" (Mandel 2009).[3] In addition, much of the focus of these reports remains on the analysts and their needs rather than on the practices of management. The 2010 study interviewed seven managers from what is now CFINTCOM and PCO/IAS, and the 2012 study interviewed twenty-three individuals within the intelligence and national security community, including analysts, managers, and trainers. While these studies had different objectives in mind, they do represent a starting point to compare the results of our survey.

Management

In the 2010 study, managers identified their role as "shaping the environment in which intelligence production occurs." This includes generating a production outlook for their unit or group, maintaining an interface with clients, managing community products, ensuring rigor and timely delivery, mentoring and furthering development, evaluating performance, fielding human resources issues, training, and shielding analysts from pressures (Derbentseva, McLellan, and Mandel 2010, 59). Some of the challenges managers indicated they face include evaluating performance, dealing with underperformers, constructively challenging analytic assessments, and distributing budget resources (especially for training) (Derbentseva, McLellan, and Mandel 2010, 60–62). For the most part, these findings are consistent with our interviews. Nevertheless, we were able to go into further detail with regard to how individuals in the community view the most important tasks and challenges facing managers of analytical units.

BUILDING BRIDGES BETWEEN INTELLIGENCE AND POLICY

Overwhelmingly, the most important role of managers identified by our interviewees is the ability to build bridges to the policy world, marketing products to consumers, and conveying the needs of policy makers back to analysts. Managers play a key role in "the whole information flow between senior management and the analysts to understand where that need is." Traditionally, achieving this goal has been a challenge given that many managers in the intelligence and national security community, particularly in collection agencies, have often not had policy experience. As a result, they are unfamiliar with the needs of the consumers of their products, making it more difficult to guide analysts in producing policy-relevant work.

More recently, some departments and agencies (particularly PCO/IAS and CFINTCOM) have addressed this by bringing in managers, in some cases from outside the intelligence community, with stronger policy backgrounds. At the same time, this comes with a cost, in that these managers often have little-to-no prior intelligence experience. We found that there is little support or training for them as they take on these new positions and that they have to learn about the nature of intelligence (sourcing, collection, etc.) by themselves. Some managers therefore struggle to support and direct their analysts. In our view, we believe this is an acceptable trade-off for the purpose of trying to improve the policy relevance of intelligence products. Ideally, it should be manageable as individuals from the policy world tend to be generalists, able to adapt quickly.[4]

Other departments and agencies have been slower to change their management profile. For example, CSIS/IAB put intelligence officers as managers, traditionally to serve as a kind of security check on intelligence analysis given concerns that sensitive intelligence might leak outside the organization through intelligence products. While outsiders with policy experience have been brought in at the levels of assistant director, director general, and middle management since 2005, these have tended to be the exception rather than the rule. That said, as discussed in the case study at the end of this chapter, CSIS now also allows analysts to apply for managerial roles.[5]

HIERARCHY

Another issue identified by our interviewees is that the management of the intelligence community is hierarchical, with many bureaucratic levels, which means response times can be slow. Hierarchy is, of course, important. It ensures accountability and that the appropriate managers are aware of who is speaking with whom, especially when those clients are senior. At the same time, getting the appropriate approvals for a briefing requested by high-level officials can take hours, and often days—meaning that intelligence organizations sometimes fail to inform senior policy makers in a timely manner.

In this sense, rather than facilitating the delivery of intelligence analysis, management practices often slow the process. Within our cohort of interviewees, some senior consumers indicated that "the analyst is often the person I want to talk to" but speaking with them has been a challenge (that said, as we discuss in chapter 4, this has improved in recent years, with the growing frequency of oral briefings provided by analysts). These senior consumers were aware that reaching out to the analyst directly might be seen as going outside the correct channels or a kind of interference. However, going through the correct layers of management meant that information would not be available when needed.

"When I need information, I need it in the next twenty-four hours, and lining up all of the approvals to get the analyst to be allowed to talk to me usually takes more than twenty-four hours." Interestingly, one interviewee indicated that they had come up with novel ways to get around the problem of working through layers of management: "I will call a meeting with everybody, including the super junior people to explain exactly what I want. . . . Some of the management are thinking I am stepping on their toes, and I am stepping on their toes. I am also trying to teach people how to do their work."

EDUCATION AND QUALITIES OF GOOD MANAGERS

A further consideration is that there are few resources available to help managers of intelligence analysts learn and prepare for their role and no set expectations for what skills a good manager should have. While some intelligence agencies have leadership development programs to coach the next generation of executive managers, there is little to guide new managers on how to perform their duties. Learning must be done on the job with few resources other than institutional culture and patterns of behavior from their peers.[6]

Moreover, while there are many resources dedicated to the characteristics of a good analyst, there is not much in the way of guidance for what makes a good manager of analysts. Arthur S. Hulnick argues that the model for managers suggested by the policy or intelligence cycle does not match reality. Policy makers and intelligence consumers do not provide guidance to intelligence managers. Instead, they "assume that the intelligence system will alert them to problems, or provide judgements about the future" (Hulnick 2015, 81). As such, Hulnick argues (consistent with our findings) that managers must be able to know what policy makers are up to and will have to make good judgements about the subjects that ought to be covered.

Our findings suggest at least four key skills. The first is, simply, the ability to manage people: "If you are going to be a manager, you need to be able to manage people and issues, and not just be the smartest guy in the room. It's not enough to be a great intelligence analyst then become a director general or an assistant deputy minister if you don't have these other skills." A second skill is the ability to cooperate and work across silos with other organizations: "You don't want people who are particularly turf-ish. You want people who have a reputation for working cooperatively, who promote that kind of work." Third is entrepreneurship—someone who excels at reaching out to consumers with products, scheduling "deep dives" and roundtables on key issues. Finally, consistent with the sparse literature on managing analytical units, interviewees noted the importance of building a culture that promotes the integrity of analysis.

Not everything can be taught, of course. As shown in the previous chapter, much depends on the personalities and personal initiatives of managers. But the lack of training for managers of intelligence analysts to ensure they have a better understanding of the clients they support is an important gap, which contributes to and perpetuates suboptimal performances.

Human Resources: Hiring

Human resources issues are central to most scholarly writings on managing intelligence analysis units (Gannon 2008, 219; Gentry 1995, 176). Writing about the US intelligence community, Gentry notes that managers of intelligence organizations are "first and foremost, stewards of their agencies and their careers" (2016, 156). Several interviewees emphasized the importance of hiring and recruitment for the Canadian intelligence community, with one indicating that it was their "number one corporate risk."

Hiring practices in the intelligence community are uneven; all the major departments and agencies have their own specialized recruitment, with a great deal of control over the process. CSIS and CSE have their own human resources entirely, separate from the rest of the public service. Although less frequently than in the past, GAC runs its own competitions for foreign service officers, the source of most GSRP officers. PCO/IAS and CFINTCOM run their own recruitment processes for analysts as well. Other departments and agencies on the fringes of the community, such as Transport Canada, also either have their own programs or go through broader public service recruitment processes.

Overall, while noting there are many talented individuals in the intelligence community, interviewees were often severe in their criticism of current hiring practices. According to one, for example, "public service human resources is a major impediment to everything we do in government." Another described hiring in the public service as "a mystery," adding that "we have our own archaic process which seems to change every time." The fact that the process often seems inconsistent was echoed by other interviewees, with one noting that "it seems we start from scratch every time." Beyond being opaque and confusing, one interviewee described the hiring processes as often run by "mediocre people." "They don't know what to look for. They hire people like them. To have competent, driven, smart people, you need to put competent, smart people in charge of recruitment, and it's a mistake that all organizations are making. . . . And the problem with that is instead of having very strong hiring and a new batch of very strong analysts, you will hire a batch of okay, but not more than okay, analysts."

While several interviewees indicated a desire to improve, standardize, or systematize hiring practices, it is clear that for a long time the hiring process has been "all over the place." There has also often been a lack of a baseline from which to judge qualifications. One interviewee argued that hiring in parts of the intelligence community seems to be "done on a little bit of a wink and handshake for a while, with mixed results as you would expect." In this sense, there is a need to develop a more regularized model, at least within intelligence analysis units, if not across the community as a whole.

Part of the problem is that analytical units are small, misunderstood, and traditionally undervalued by departments that approve the funds for hiring, especially the Treasury Board of Canada Secretariat.[7] In the view of one interviewee, "if CSE asked for a billion dollars for some new computer equipment, they would get it. If you asked for ten million for assessment staff, the answer was no."

Finally, a major and consistent complaint about the current system is that it is slow, while the need for employees to obtain high-level security clearances adds an additional layer to the process. Every unit discussed here requires its analysts to have at least a top-secret security clearance. Obtaining such a clearance, however, is a difficult and expensive process that can take up to eighteen months, and sometimes longer. Even if an individual holds a top-secret clearance in one organization, it does not automatically transfer over to another organization such as CSE, CSIS, and ITAC, which maintain strict control over their own clearance processes. This means that even current government employees face lengthy delays in trying to transfer to another department. While Canada is not alone in having hiring and recruitment processes take time (it can take up to two years to get into the CIA), the small size of its intelligence community does not mean that the process is faster. Aware that this is a problem, as strong candidates may find alternative employment while waiting for a security clearance to come through, some organizations, such as CSE, have tried to speed up the process, getting the wait down to two or three months in some cases, although this is far from a community-wide timeline. Other analytical units such as CFINTCOM have tried to find other solutions during the lengthy wait, such as having new analysts work in nonsecure environments or as open-source analysts while they wait for their high-level clearance.

WHAT MAKES A GOOD ANALYST?

As noted, human resources issues are a fixture in the limited literature on managing intelligence analysis units. There is, however, a wider range of resources on what qualities good analysts should possess, which dovetails with the hiring process.[8] Our interviewees identified several traits that they look for in good analysts. This includes having outside experience and interests "because you need outside perspective," analytic skills, the ability to work in a team, the ability to communicate well, and the ability to deliver high quality work quickly. Interviewees were most likely to highlight the need for analysts to be flexible and adaptable to changing circumstances. This is sometimes referred to in the literature on intelligence management as "analyst fungibility" or "analyst agility" (Lowenthal 2017, 173).

Relatedly, academic or research specialization is not necessarily seen as an advantage. Many interviewees were more likely to recommend hiring generalists rather than specialists. Here, generalists can be understood as "those who have significant knowledge on many different issues, but are not deep on any particular one," whereas specialists or experts are individuals possessing "significant or deep knowledge" on one particular issue or area (Marrin 2011, 67). Roi and Dickson note that this move toward hiring more generalists rather than specialists in the intelligence and national security community "paralleled the shift that was taking place across the broader public service with the introduction of new thinking in public management" (2017, 237).

While there is a debate in the US-dominated literature on the merits of hiring generalists or specialists, there are a number of reasons why hiring more generalists and fewer specialists seems to be preferred in the Canadian context. Some interviewees linked generalists to the need for flexibility. This is understandable in a context in which most analytical units are small and analysts often have to switch or take on new files as demand changes. A second reason reflects the desire for strong communications skills. One interviewee felt there is a risk that experts may not be good at speaking to nonexperts: "The subject matter, they can learn. The ability, the skill to actually take a lot of information, make sense of it, and write in a coherent fashion quickly, that is harder to develop. . . . We have hired people that had a good knowledge base but didn't have that bit, and they are laggards." Another noted that while expertise is important, the trade-off is that specialists are often too detail-oriented for briefing senior clients who require information and insight at a more strategic level. Several interviewees bemoaned that the intelligence community had "recruited too many academically oriented people without the skills in timeliness and policy relevance that are required." Interviewees were aware that there are trade-offs in choosing generalists over specialists. One noted that key countries, such as China and Russia, and important technical matters, such as missile and nuclear proliferation, do require some level of specialization. However, in a relatively small intelligence community like Canada's, too much specialization is suboptimal; that is why, in recent years, the community has moved toward shifting the balance to more generalists.

DIVERSITY

Increasingly, discussions about hiring in the intelligence community are about not only what skills are important but also who is hired and the experiences they bring. Diversity has been touted as being important to ensuring a variety of "identities, abilities, backgrounds, cultures, skills, perspectives and experiences" that are representative of the population (Treasury Board of Canada Secretariat 2017b). Diversity also supports better organizational outcomes and performance. These findings are consistent with a 2010 study by CSIS that found that greater diversity and inclusion would enhance its ability to attract talent and establish relations with communities across Canada (National Security and Intelligence Committee of Parliamentarians 2020a, 5). The importance of diversity for organizational performance is also highlighted in reports by Canada's intelligence allies, including the US and UK (Central Intelligence Agency 2015; Intelligence and Security Committee of Parliament 2018). These findings were also confirmed by one interviewee in Washington, DC, who emphasized that "diversity is one of the strengths of the US intelligence community. . . . It provides better opportunities to avoid groupthink."

In 2019, NSICOP completed a study on diversity for its *Annual Report 2019*. It found that "challenges to increasing diversity and inclusion . . . persist in the security and intelligence community despite decades of legislation, multiple reports and repeated calls for change" (National Security and Intelligence Committee of Parliamentarians 2020a, 2). Additionally, "organizations in the security and intelligence community have put in place measures and programs to support employment equity, diversity, and inclusion. However, the degrees to which those organizations are diverse differs significantly" (2020a, 53). Although the report found that overall diversity is lower than in the rest of the Canadian public service, there were positive trends in that "organizations across the security and intelligence community show steady or slightly increasing representation of members of designated groups over the past three years" (2020a, 28). The representation of women and Indigenous peoples is higher than their estimated workforce availability in the majority of Canadian organizations under review, but the representation of visible minorities and people with disabilities is lower than their estimated workforce availability. This, however, did not hold true at the executive level where representation of women and visible minorities is lower than their estimated availability. There was not enough information available on Indigenous peoples to make an assessment. People with disabilities were represented at a higher level than their estimated availability (2020a, 28).

Generally, interviewees stressed the importance of diversity in two respects. The first was a need to bring in individuals with different experiences. "We tend to promote from within, which is a bad idea," said one interviewee. Another noted the problem that recruitment tended to be from the same "gene pool" and that "we weren't bringing in people from the outside." As such, interviewees observed that analytical units are now increasingly trying to recruit from a range of educational backgrounds. Otherwise, "if we stacked up on intelligence officers who are nothing but criminologists, we would be in deep trouble."

The second aspect of diversity relates to representation. Some interviewees noted that the situation has improved over time. For example, one observed that there has been some progress, "Our demographics as far as women, minorities—is it perfect? No, but it is a lot better than it was." Interestingly, many interviewees who discussed diversity were more interested in diversity of experience rather than representation. Our findings suggest that the main concern is avoiding monoculture within analytical units to avoid echo chambers. The extent to which this carries over to representation is unclear. As we did not ask interviewees directly about representative diversity, it would be inappropriate to draw strong conclusions on this issue, other than to highlight this issue as important for future research on the Canadian intelligence community. Of note, NSICOP's study indicates that while organizations it reviewed have diversity "champions," there are still problems in this area, including ensuring leadership accountability and a lack of established goals and performance measures (2020a, 32–35).

TARGETED RECRUITMENT

Interviewees highlighted three recruitment strategies for hiring analysts. First, there is targeted university recruitment where representatives attend job fairs to encourage students to apply. Some organizations like CSE and PSC run competitions on campuses such as "hackathons" to introduce themselves to students, but these mainly target those in science, technology, engineering, and mathematics (STEM) programs rather than serving as a gateway for analysts. In addition, co-op programs are a major source of recruitment for the intelligence community. In these programs, students from across Canada receive security clearances and often a pathway to join the organization while they finish their degree.

An additional form of recruitment are boutique, targeted programs that seek to hire exceptional graduate students. There are several programs to which students may apply, although they normally take in small numbers each year (from as little as one or two, to a few dozen). This includes policy-oriented programs such as the Advanced Policy Analyst Program, DND's Policy Officer Recruitment Programme, and the Recruitment of Policy Leaders Program (Government of Canada 2019).[9] While these programs are policy-oriented, they can include the opportunity to rotate through an intelligence policy or analysis unit.

A new addition to these development programs specifically geared to intelligence is CFINTCOM's Defence Intelligence Officer Recruitment Program. This is a unique program within the federal government that targets graduate students specifically for defense intelligence analyst positions. While waiting for their security clearance, some hirees can spend their first year working in a policy position in DND's policy group, the equivalent to the undersecretary of defence for policy organization in the US, learning about the jobs and needs of future clients. Next, recruits move on to different positions within CFINTCOM, both on the analytical and intelligence policy teams, where they receive training courses as well as on-the-job experience. The idea is not only to recruit top graduate students but also to ensure that future intelligence analysts have exposure to policy. Recruits are also given English or French language training if required. A potential downside of the program is that some of the recruits find that they prefer policy work, leading some to try to stay with the policy side. Nevertheless, while the program is only a few years old, interviewees who spoke about it described it as a success that has helped foster a more dynamic workforce in defense intelligence. Recruits, in the opinion of one interviewee, "are actually rocking the boat for the old folks who are left, who were there to start with, because you have a bunch of these young workers now who are motivated, driven, and it is forcing the rest of the workforce to step up their game."

Training

For the purpose of this chapter, *training* (programs that provide analysts with "specific instruction to implement job-related tasks") is distinct from *education* (academic courses that normally provide individuals with knowledge and frameworks for understanding and exploiting that knowledge; Marrin 2011, 77). While training is provided (or paid for) by an employer, education typically forms the basis for the qualifications to get the analytical position in the first place (though there are programs for analysts to receive support for further education). Although analysts are typically hired partly on the basis of their education, few begin their career with specific training on how to be an analyst. In this sense, analysts require training to help them adjust to an intelligence organization's standards and expectations, and to learn about the organization itself.

In embarking on a review of this literature to compare with our findings, a caveat is warranted: like other areas of this book, the vast majority of this literature has been written in a US context, for a US audience. Much of this writing comes from the desire to improve intelligence analyst training in the US after a perceived series of intelligence failures (for which some have proposed analytical bias or other failings as possible explanations) as well as out of a sense of the need to professionalize intelligence analysis generally (Lowenthal 2017, 196–197; Marrin 2011; Pherson and Heuer 2011, 1–8).

In addition, the literature on training is based largely on certain assumptions that are only partially true in other national contexts. For example, most (but not all) intelligence and national security agencies in the US have their own analytical training schools or centers. The most famous is the CIA's Sherman Kent School, but the FBI has the College of Analytical Studies, the Office of the Director of National Intelligence created a virtual National Intelligence University, and the Defense Intelligence Agency has the Joint Military Intelligence Training Center. No other Western country has this range of schools and programs that provide training to their own agencies and act as a community resource.

A second difference is that, as noted previously, the US community operates in such a way that managers have often been analysts and have gone through some kind of analytic training. As discussed, these assumptions are not always applicable in the Canadian context. The US intelligence community also deals with consumers who are on average more familiar with intelligence. This creates a different set of needs.

Keeping these limitations in mind, we can still find insights from the literature on intelligence analyst training. First, insights emerge from the debate over the nature of intelligence analysis itself, which has implications for how organizations view training. Stephen Marrin describes this debate as between those who view intelligence analysis as an art ("depending largely on subjective, intuitive judgment") and those who view it as a science ("depending largely on structured, systematic analytic methods") (2012b, 529).[10] Those who favor the former are more likely to place emphasis on cultivating innate qualities and on training analysts in specific types of expertise. The latter, for their part, emphasize training in scientific methodologies using modeling and forecasting, known as structured analytic techniques (SATs) (Marrin 2012b, 539). While most believe that intelligence analysis must combine the strengths of both art and science, how much emphasis individual units place on one or the other has a significant impact on their training regimes.

Interestingly, there is some literature discussing the Canadian context here, albeit in a one-sided way. For the most part, scholarly papers and research on improving intelligence analysis in Canada have been dominated by the idea that intelligence analysis is (or should be) more science than art. This view has been promoted by what might be described as a Canadian behavioralist school of intelligence analysis. Based out of the Thinking, Risk, and Intelligence Group (previously mentioned) in Defence Research and Development Canada, these individuals—especially David R. Mandel and Alan Barnes (a now-retired, long-serving director for the Middle East and Africa team in PCO/IAS)—published studies between 2009 and 2018 promoting scientific methods (especially quantitative methods and behavioralism) and the use of numeric probabilities and geopolitical forecasting in intelligence analysis (Barnes 2016; Mandel 2009; Mandel, Barnes, Richards 2014; Mandel 2015; Mandel and Barnes 2018).

There is no consensus in the literature on the value of SATs and scientific approaches. While Randolph H. Pherson and Richards J. Heuer, as well as the Canadian behavioralists, argue that formal training in SATs and behavioralist methods provides rigor, discipline, and clarity, others such as Mark Lowenthal argue that there is a disconnect between those designing and promoting these approaches and the reality of analysts: "Too many programs have been developed without regard to how analysts think and work" (2017, 197–98).[11] Similarly, though he does not object to SATs being taught, as he sees them as one part of analysts' formal training, Marrin cautions that "mandating the use of structured methods is problematic given the general intuitive approach that analysts use and the relative paucity of data showing that structured techniques would improve accuracy" (2007; 2011, 78–80).

Instead, Marrin argues there are three distinct types of expertise required to produce quality analysis: substantive expertise (subject matter expertise about a country, region, or thematic area required to describe, explain, evaluate, and forecast effectively); disciplinary or functional expertise (theoretical perspectives used to interpret substantive information such as economics for economic analysts, military sciences for military analysts, or psychology for leadership analysis), and process-oriented analytic tradecraft ("mechanisms and methodologies used to produce intelligence analysis")—essentially the SATs discussed previously (2011, 77).

TRAINING PROGRAMS IN THE CANADIAN INTELLIGENCE COMMUNITY

The Canadian intelligence community does not have an analyst training infrastructure remotely comparable to what exists in the US. Instead, there are a number of department and agency-specific programs, as well as one community-wide program managed out of PCO/IAS, the Intelligence Analyst Learning Program.

Each specific training program is different. For most of its history, CSIS offered limited training opportunities for its analysts, which included courses on SATs offered internally. Since 2019, new analysts have been attending the intelligence officer training program to become better acclimatized to CSIS's mission and culture. This is similar to the way CIA analysts sit on the same course as officers at the outset of their training. ITAC has created a "training journey" composed of mandatory and recommended courses that analysts need to complete within their first six months. However, it depends on the course offerings of other organizations to provide the training, including CSIS, CFINTCOM, and PCO. Similarly, FINTRAC devotes considerable resources to training but depends on the community for courses to be available for its employees. CSE has its own Analyst Learning and Development Program.[12]

CFINTCOM has developed one of the most comprehensive programs. CAF personnel working in intelligence attend Canada's only government school dedicated to intelligence, the Canadian Forces School of Military Intelligence, based in Kingston, Ontario (with satellite locations across Canada). According to its website, the school offers thirty basic and advanced intelligence courses each year (Department of National Defence 2019a). Many are not for analysts, however, notably those on interrogation and source handling. Others are on analysis, but with a more tactical focus, such as the imagery analyst course. The school also offers courses in basic intelligence analysis. For a time, civilian intelligence analysts with CFINTCOM were sent on a forty-day residential course. But as it has hired more civilian analysts, this became (in the words of one interviewee) "not economically feasible," and stressful for individuals who were separated from their families for long periods. Therefore, since 2015, civilian analysts in CFINTCOM have followed the Strategic Defence Intelligence Analyst Course, composed of nine modules with topics including the intelligence community, writing, researching, analytical thinking, oral briefing, requirements of policy clients, and ethics.

Finally, there are intelligence courses offered by the Canadian Police College, particularly for the Royal Canadian Mounted Police (RCMP). The emphasis at the college is on tactical analysis, focusing on the skills analysts need when working as part of a criminal investigation. Skills taught include link analysis and looking at associations between individuals, properties, locations, and the like. Essentially, these courses teach how to develop a sense of a network, who is involved, and more. Individuals at the college are taught about the importance of timeliness, written reports, and geomapping, and they are given information about the history of criminal intelligence analysis. The college offers a strategic analysis course, but it focuses on how to present strategic criminal intelligence at the municipal, provincial, and national levels. (While localized gang violence is not a national issue, at the municipal level it needs to be understood strategically.) In addition, much of the training on these courses emphasizes SATs, exercises, and major projects. New analysts in the RCMP are also paired with a mentor who helps ensure they are prepared to work either at headquarters in Ottawa or in a smaller detachment.

The Intelligence Analyst Learning Program

There is only one community-wide resource for analysts, the Intelligence Analyst Learning Program (IALP). It is not a formal school but a program with "a large suite of courses" (a 2016–2017 PCO report suggests there are up to ninety courses available; Government of Canada 2020b) attended by analysts from "core agencies as well as the more peripheral agencies in the community."

The IALP started as one entry-level course focused on SATs shortly after 9/11. Its existence since then has sometimes been precarious. Despite a widespread understanding that there was a need for community-wide analytical training, the program long lacked a stable home or funding. The original idea for the IALP was that at the beginning of each year, members of the intelligence and national security community would each decide whether they would want to participate and contribute to the IALP. The result was that individuals running the program could never be certain how much funding they would have or how much demand there would be for courses, making long-term planning difficult. Moreover, the program's costing model was a source of frustration, particularly as PCO/IAS was not set up to work on a cost-recovery basis. As one interviewee noted, it is difficult to deliver a program across the community in these conditions. They went on to observe that programs like CFINTCOM's Strategic Defence Intelligence Analyst Course was set up in part because they could not count on the IALP offering the courses that were needed on a regular and predictable basis.

Part of the problem is that the IAS did not consider the IALP to be part of its "line of business." One interviewee noted that even IAS analysts were often not interested in taking IALP courses. Instead, many analysts and managers viewed the IALP as "not very professional" and of limited use. In this context, it is unsurprising that as government departments were targeted by budget cuts in the early 2010s, PCO/IAS was eyeing the IALP as a target. The program survived and, in 2014–15, new staff within the IAS saw the problem differently. There was a realization that although IAS analysts saw limited interest in the program's courses, analysts from smaller analytical units (such as Transport Canada) did. The IALP thus became seen as a resource, even an "instrument of influence," within the larger national security community. Although the program is still far from perfect, it is now seen as a tool that can help improve analysis throughout the community more than in the past.

In this context, the IAS put together a plan to save the IALP by putting it on a proper footing. This included steps to institutionalize the program, notably by normalizing a cost recovery model, and ensuring that material for the courses was hosted properly within government of Canada websites. The program has since become more predictable, offering a suite of regular courses. Depending on interest, a course may run up to three times per year. Interviewees who spoke favorably about the program noted that it also plays an important socialization role, as analysts from throughout the community attend and have the opportunity to network with one another. One interviewee noted that there are now high levels of participation from peripheral departments and agencies (such as the Canada Border Services Agency).

While it is clear that this new stability has helped the IALP, some interviewees continue to note problems. Some maintain that the training is still of limited value, and underutilized. One felt that the individuals giving the training do not have enough experience delivering intelligence to policy makers. Another noted that while the courses are of good quality, the IALP continues to have problems in relation to how often it offers some of them: "Where we are not satisfied is the frequency." Another interviewee noted that IALP courses are too general for some agencies and departments to meaningfully link to their core business. The interviewee noted that the program is not good enough for some departments with more of an operational focus. Importantly, however, no interviewee suggested these were unfixable flaws. Indeed, in a small intelligence community like Canada's, it is difficult to design, implement, and frequently run courses that meet all the needs of every unit. The hope among IALP advocates is that as it continues evolving, it will contribute to the professionalization of analysis within the broader intelligence and national security community by establishing clearer and higher standards.

One interviewee noted that it would be far more economical if a community resource could be developed rather than all the core agencies having their own programs, noting that "we are too small" for boutique programs. In our view, given the small size of the Canadian intelligence community as well as the specialized nature of some of the departments and agencies within it, a mix between agency-specific and community-based courses is ideal. The development of a roster of high-quality courses that apply to all or most analysts helps foster a sense of community. Moreover, from a resource perspective, it allows some departments and agencies to focus on courses that suit their specific mandate and niches.

ASSESSING INTELLIGENCE TRAINING IN CANADA

Based on our interviews, we conclude that analytical training in Canada is improving. In particular, the development of programs at CFINTCOM and ITAC as well as the stabilization of the IALP are positive steps. Nevertheless, a number of issues remain.

What Training Is Needed?

Overwhelmingly, interviewees stressed the importance of understanding consumers more than any other skill: better understanding should produce analysis that is more tailored, accessible, and useable for policy makers.[13] For some, this included educating analysts about the context they are writing in, especially the policy process. One interviewee suggested that training needs to start with explaining "the very basic intelligence infrastructure" and "what Canada does, what our adversaries do, and how [intelligence] fits into a broad government of Canada tool kit in terms of policy development." Another framed this as "knowledge transfer": "Who am I writing for? What do they need to know? What are they going to do with the answer?"

Second, interviewees put a lot of emphasis on writing and briefing skills. Several interviewees suggested that analysts need to be coached away from writing in an academic model where papers are long and only read by other analysts. Instead, building on a better understanding of clients, analysts need to improve their ability to write concisely for busy consumers. One interviewee suggested that it is not just about writing for policy but for different kinds of consumers, "because you can have three different clients asking the same question, but they are going to do three different things with the answer, which will require three different analyses." These ideas are consistent with what is often described in the literature on writing briefs as the AIMS approach, where analysts should think through "audience, issues, message, and storyline" before writing.[14]

Third, some interviewees discussed analytical tradecraft needs. This includes teaching critical thinking skills, the fundamentals of analysis, how to avoid cognitive bias, intuitive traps, and SATs. Interestingly, there was no consensus as to how useful these techniques are, although many were skeptical. This could be because some of our interviewees (especially managers and consumers) were not familiar with the techniques and were more concerned with having products that they could easily and quickly read than with how answers are formulated. While no one suggested they should not be taught, some questioned their overall usefulness relative to the emphasis currently placed on them.

Nevertheless, there are advocates for SATs. One interviewee in a management position argued that they are important for avoiding bias, ensuring predictability, and being able to reverse engineer the findings of an assessment, "because if it's completely unpredictable and just left to whatever the analyst's gut feel is that day, it doesn't work." A second interviewee agreed, noting that "you need to be able to say how you got to the answer in a reasonable way that even though your answer was wrong, based on the knowledge known at the time, this is how I arrived to that answer."

Others, mostly on the policy side, expressed deep skepticism. Several noted that there is no evidence that these techniques produce better analysis: "We have no data to tell us if it actually makes a difference. So, is it the equivalent of herbal medicine?" In addition, those who had been through SATs training did not speak highly of the experience. "I particularly find them boring and useless," said one interviewee who had been trained on them multiple times throughout their career. They also indicated that they are not amenable to the kind of products policy makers want: "It is the kind of thing that would make them flee."

As noted previously, the lack of enthusiasm from many interviewees may partly be the result of policy makers not caring about how intelligence products are made; all they seek is a clear, relevant assessment. Many proponents and critics of these techniques can probably meet in a middle position. These techniques can be a useful set of thinking tools, but only alongside training that emphasizes understanding client needs and communicating findings in an accessible manner. The difficulty is that many training programs emphasize SATs over other kinds of learning. One interviewee noted that while it is important for analysts to be able to show how they get their answers, the key is analytical "rigor" as opposed to any particular method: "It's like when I go see a doctor, I don't need him to explain to me how he comes to his conclusions. I just want to know that he has got some sort of structured way." In sum, we believe that it makes sense for analysts to learn these techniques, but the community has put too much emphasis on them relative to other areas of training that would help with other kinds of analysis and improve communications skills.

Data Exploitation Skills

One skill set that repeatedly emerged from our interviews is the ability to work with data in different ways. In an era of big data, interviewees from across the intelligence and national security community noted a pressing need to hire analysts who can develop data sensitivity and exploit open sources better. One interviewee pointed to the efforts of civilian data-journalists such as Bellingcat as an example of data exploitation skills. They called for managers to better foster the conditions where analysts can bring meaning to data, including mining data, deriving broader implications, and then "mixing the big picture with the granular data." Another interviewee noted this challenge and the ability to present data-driven findings to policy makers, "Are we seeing everything we should be seeing? Are we pulling, culling it, are we manipulating it in the right way? Can we make sense of it? How can we best reflect it? . . . How do you turn this into a chewable product for a minister? . . . Because you can't just throw thousands of whiz kids at it. You are going to need machine learning to help you cull through what we have and that is not unique to us, that is a big data issue generally . . . How do you turn that into a useable product?"

Training analysts who were hired on the basis of critical thinking and writing skills to engage in this work is difficult, however. An interviewee suggested that "as a general concept, our workforce isn't tech savvy to deal with even large quantities of data, let alone big data." While they felt that analysts need to adapt to new data-driven realities, analysts also need training to do it. This, however, is not happening enough, because training programs "forget about what is coming down the road and how you need to adapt." Rather than training analysts for future challenges, "everyone is focused on today's fire," and not enough on future priorities.

Intelligence Education for the Client

Interestingly, one of the most common suggestions for training did not involve analysts. Multiple interviewees suggested that what is also needed is intelligence education for policy makers, including politicians. It is true that when writing this book, there were no known programs for policy makers in the government of Canada to learn about intelligence—what it is, how it can be used, and its limitations. While there are some introductory courses on intelligence, these are built for and cater to entry-level intelligence analysts, not consumers. The situation, however, is slowly improving. Since 2020, the Canada School of Public Service has been providing workshops on this topic. (Initial plans were delayed due to the pandemic.) It is also planning to offer more courses and to create a flagship national security program. For now, however, junior and senior policy officials who use, or might benefit from using, intelligence have limited access to training tailored to their needs; they can mostly learn on the job.

It is thus unsurprising that many interviewees felt that to improve the performance of intelligence analysis, clients also need better training. "We spend a lot of time focusing in our organizations about how we train analysts, how we train intelligence officers, how we train various folks in the chain. We spend a lot less time as a community, I find, talking about how do we educate the clients in a way that they can maximize what it is that we are being asked to produce."

The architecture of intelligence, in particular, is not well understood among policy makers. In the words of one interviewee, "it's not understood that the machinery of intelligence is dispersed throughout the government." Another pointed out that many government executives have "no experience with intelligence, and there are no executive courses on intelligence." Or, in the words of an interviewee, "somebody shows up and hands them something, and they go 'what the hell is that?'"

Continuing Weaknesses

Overall, the quality of training for analysts has been improving. Nevertheless, challenges remain. One of the biggest challenges is that training is not a priority for many senior executives in the public service. As one interviewee noted, "there aren't training emergencies today, but you will have problems down the road if you don't take care of training and professional development."

Interviewees provided examples illustrating these issues. The first is financial: good training is expensive. While our interviews suggested that CFINTCOM, FINTRAC, and ITAC are willing to invest resources, this is not true across the board. "In the current environment of competing priorities, do you want to hire analysts, or do you want to hire trainers?" This interviewee noted that this means there is an incentive to cut training when budgets are reduced, which constantly has to be resisted. "You have to fence off resources and jealously guard them against encroachment."

Other interviewees similarly pointed to the resources that are put toward training as indicative of the reality that it remains a low priority. One also suggested that some organizations "used their training budget, from my perspective, entirely to try to address deficiencies in analysts." In the interviewee's experience, some organizations make the mistake of trying to improve weak analysts at the cost of not investing enough in stronger ones. "If you were a poorly performing analyst, you were awarded unlimited amounts of training in an effort to improve your performance, which is a maddening experience." Another interviewee agreed with this sentiment, claiming that the community generally "doesn't send its best and brightest" to training, or will often pull stronger analysts off training and bring them back to the office for urgent work, preventing them from completing a course.

On a more positive note, community cooperation is increasingly strong when it comes to training. This allows some departments and agencies to mitigate the shortage and infrequency of some courses. For example, ITAC is able to outsource virtually all of its training. Given this cooperation, an interviewee noted that it would make sense for the IALP to remain a centralized hub, while each agency has their own niche capacities to run courses, many of which can be open to the community. In this way, analyst training would be rationalized but could also serve as a vehicle for better cooperation and networking within the community. All this supports our previous recommendation that more general training should be centralized through the IALP, allowing different departments and agencies to develop their own specialized courses, which they can then also offer to others.

Exchanges and Secondments

Another way for analysts to learn about consumers is by spending time in the organizations that receive their products through exchanges and secondments. For the purposes of this section, *secondments* refer to "the assignment of a person, to another department or organization, which does not affect the person's appointment status" (Government of Canada 2020a). *Exchanges* are programs designed along the same lines where two or more individuals swap places within their home organizations.

There are few assessments of the benefits and costs of exchanges and secondments in the literature on managing intelligence analysis units. In this sense, there is not much to compare our findings to. Yet interviewees universally accepted the idea that exchanges and secondments are beneficial for both analysts and organizations, often noting that they have a strong potential to promote better understanding between consumers and producers.

Our research identifies several advantages to exchanges and secondments. One is that secondees are able to speak on behalf of or explain the needs of their home organizations, thereby educating new colleagues. This, one interviewee felt, "could help with improving the institutionalization of intelligence" across the community. Such a move is even more important now given that the intelligence community increasingly has to reach beyond its traditional partners to work with new agencies that may not have a traditional background in security or intelligence. As an example, one interviewee observed that "the community now has to work very closely with partners they had not worked with" in the past, such as Innovation, Science, and Economic Development Canada on issues related to foreign investment.

Secondments also improve mutual understanding between intelligence and policy units. As one interviewee put it, they create "more opportunities to have common conversations, to walk a mile in each other's shoes." Another suggested it is a good way for analysts to develop "a better idea of what the needs are, what the circumstances are, what the perspectives are. I am a big believer in people working in different places." Interestingly, many felt that analysts should go beyond the traditional intelligence and national security community and also work in nonintelligence jobs, notably in a central agency "where they are working in social policy or economic policy." This can help them understand the broader context of the Canadian government.

OUTSIDE OF GOVERNMENT

Multiple interviewees went so far as to argue that analysts should consider taking secondments outside government to get "a different perspective and bring that back in." Reflecting the need for analysts to write about and engage on issues in nontraditional areas such as foreign investment, one interviewee argued, "The ability to make sure that the intelligence community is going to be able to make informed assessments may mean that at some point you will want people that will be doing the assessment talking to the company that is being acquired and understanding better what is being acquired, what are the risks associated with this. That is a novelty. This is something that we would not have even contemplated, I think, five, ten, years ago."

Yet interviewees reported that attempts to institutionalize secondments to the private sector have largely failed. One recounted such an attempt at GAC, where diplomats coming back from abroad were encouraged to find an exchange or secondment in another department, provincial government, private sector company, or NGO. Employees were told that this would be given significant weight in terms of their career experience and that it would help them get a better assignment the next time they rotated on diplomatic assignment. Interest in the program was, however, low. It is possible that this was due to concerns about the permanency and strength of the program. For example, employees may have been concerned that future senior managers would not abide by the promises of current management and fail to take the external experience seriously, or even see it as a disadvantage. "And that is the kind of structural problem we have with these things. Unless you have a real concerted push with an ongoing commitment it is a hard thing to do with changes of government and changes of senior leadership, but I think it is really required."

CHALLENGES IN INSTITUTIONALIZATION

The lack of buy-in for the GAC program is not the only challenge that exchange and secondment programs face. One of the biggest problems comes down to security clearances. Although analysts across government can have access to information classified as top secret if they are appropriately cleared, their clearances are not necessarily transferrable to the core intelligence and national security agencies, especially CSE, CSIS, and ITAC. As a result, employees from other organizations must go through a renewed screening process that can take up to eighteen months. As one interviewee noted, "I only want secondees for two years. And if it's going to take me eighteen months to actually hire them, it's a very cumbersome problem." Although the community is aware of and attempting to mitigate this problem, it remains an impediment. The end result is that organizations cannot always be sure when they will be able to get a secondee, especially as that person may decide to abandon the process for another opportunity halfway through.

A second set of concerns centers around who is sent on exchange/secondment. One is the issue of *dumping*—the idea that organizations tend not to send their best analysts in an attempt to get rid of weaker ones (if only temporarily). As one interviewee noted, "some secondees can be fantastic and amazing and others not so much." Another issue is that some analysts do not want to go on exchange/secondment. One interviewee noted there is a lot of internal resistance: "Many think they were hired to write about one thing and that they will never do anything else." Some are simply not interested in policy issues and resist efforts to go on an exchange/secondment.

Given these challenges, it is not surprising that many interviewees felt that there are simply not enough exchanges within the intelligence and national security community and not enough analysts with outside experience. "How many analysts at CSIS have worked at any other position except being an analyst at CSIS?" asked one interviewee rhetorically. They also noted that the outside experience of most analysts is limited to academia, or is not relevant to policy work. Another noted, more broadly, that "the interactions, just the human movement between agencies is not as regular and deliberate as it could and should be."

Our findings suggest this is another way the Canadian community differs from its counterparts, particularly in the US. As one interviewee noted, the US intelligence community "sees joint duty assignments and exchanges as enhancing the capability" of analysts. Another observed that secondments and exchanges in the US help improve the relationship between the intelligence and policy worlds; they are more institutionalized and seen as a regular part of an analyst's career path. As noted previously, this may simply be a result of the disparity in size between the Canadian and US intelligence communities. Having more analysts and more managers means that it is easier to move individuals around and to provide them with opportunities to work in different agencies and departments. It still does not explain, however, the lower frequency of exchanges and secondment opportunities on the Canadian side.

THE SECURITY AND INTELLIGENCE POLICY PROGRAM

Interviewees did point to a bright spot, the Security and Intelligence Policy Program (SIPP), coordinated by PSC. The program, established in 2019, rotates analysts from across the community, including CSIS, CSE, ITAC, PCO, PSC, the Canadian Nuclear Safety Commission, Transport Canada, as well as Innovation, Science, and Economic Development Canada, placing intelligence analysts in a policy position and policy analysts in an intelligence analysis unit. Organizers try to avoid one-to-one swaps, preferring a distributed rotation.

The program runs for one year with the objective of allowing analysts to learn about policy or intelligence and to build their networks. In order to gel the analysts together, the SIPP requires participants to work on a horizontal project, which they present to DMs. Topics for these projects focus on issues facing the community, such as information sharing, with the aim of having analysts cooperate together to map out the issue, evaluate how it is working, determine gaps, and offer solutions. The following year, analysts stay involved with the next cohort. The SIPP also has a budget for both training and travel. Analysts have the opportunity to build their own learning plan, and a travel budget allows them to visit a Five Eyes capital to meet counterparts, bringing an international dimension to the program.

Although it is still early, interviewees familiar with the program described it as successful. There is also determination across the community to make it succeed. Some noted that the quality of participants is high and that there has been some success in fast-tracking normally lengthy clearance processes. One of the main challenges is to ensure that managers of analytical units feel the incentive to participate. As one interviewee described it, some "analysts who wanted to join were saying managers were reluctant." Given its championing by PSC, the SIPP is one of the most promising avenues to help build bridges between the policy and intelligence worlds.

Career Paths

All the previously discussed issues culminate into one question: What should a career path for an intelligence analyst in the Canadian government look like? This is another area where the literature does not have much to say. Lowenthal notes that career tracks are "a major concern" for managers, who must balance the correct times for rotations and promotions (2017, 176). However, there is an assumption in the US literature that there are rotations (something that remains precarious in the Canadian context) and opportunities to be promoted to middle management. This too is not automatic in Canada as there have traditionally been only limited promotion opportunities for intelligence analysts. When analysts wish to move up in their careers, it has often entailed departing analytical units entirely. This means that after investing time and money to provide an individual with their clearance and training, that person may leave their analyst position after five or so years if they wish to advance—just as they become, potentially, highly productive analysts.

To what extent is this an acceptable state of affairs? Do Canadian analysts need a more defined career path? Interestingly, while there was consensus about the usefulness of exchanges and secondments, we found no agreement among interviewees on this question. Views varied from supporting the development of a more standardized career path to others who did not feel this was an important issue.

Several themes did emerge. The first is whether or not there should be better standardization of analyst qualifications to assist with mobility and career development. This would mean that if individuals want to move around the intelligence and national security community, other organizations could better recognize their qualifications. When it comes to career paths, this idea was the most popular among our interviewees. "There's no baseline in terms of being accredited as an intelligence analyst, and that shows up in some places more often than not," said one interviewee. Another added, "It would make sense to come up with standards, and I will use the term *accreditation*, so that we all understand what an entry level analyst is and what a journeyman analyst is and what a senior analyst is. And to be the head of analysis, a team lead, or a director . . . or [executive level], there should actually be a path that we all agree to so that certifications/accreditation make sense."

Taking standardization to the next level could involve the development of an analyst stream within the government. Presently, civil servants in the government of Canada are classified according to occupational groups. For example, air traffic controllers are classified as the AI group and financial management as the FI group. Each occupational group has a job description, qualification standards, and evaluation standards (Government of Canada 2017a; Treasury Board of Canada Secretariat 2017a). For the most part, analysts are in the Economist and Social Science Services (EC) stream.[15]

Some thought the creation of an analyst stream would be a positive step forward in better defining standards and career paths. A few interviewees indicated that there have been discussions about developing some kind of functional speciality for intelligence analysts in government, which could be very useful. Noting that many other groups, such as financial specialists, have their own stream, an interviewee added "So why not one for intelligence specialists as well?"

Yet there are many problems with this option. A new stream could make it easier to promote analysts across the government, but it might limit who managers could hire or bring into the intelligence community in the first place. One interviewee agreed with this concern, noting that a dedicated intelligence analyst stream could make it more isolating: "Creating another classification specific to intelligence would put us in the same zone as the poor foreign service officers." Another added that the differences between the main core intelligence and national security agencies are too large for a stream to bridge and that it would be difficult to create a job stream that could blend core and specialized agencies. In any case, the tendency in recent years has been for the Treasury Board of Canada Secretariat, which is ultimately responsible for this, to reduce the number of streams in the public service, not to create new ones.

Another idea is the creation of a process similar to the CIA's Senior Analytic Service, where, rather than being promoted into management, analysts develop their specialty with a view to dedicating their career to analysis, and also to teaching, training, and helping to improve analysis within the agency (Marrin 2011, 78). Individuals who have skills better suited to analysis than management, or who have no interest in management, are then able to stay within their organizations and still have a career path where advancement is possible. This idea, however, was largely rejected by many interviewees. "We are not rich enough for that. You have to look at what you can afford." Another suggested that there are simply not enough individuals in the Canadian intelligence community for such an idea to work.

The current state of affairs is therefore likely to continue for some time. For many though not all interviewees, this is an acceptable outcome. Some noted that while analysts need to stay with a file for years to develop deep expertise, many analysts also develop cognitive bias after four or five years. Another added that the job can become "very boring in five years," noting that it is hard to have a full career as an analyst in any Canadian national security department or agency. It is thus important for analysts to move on in their careers when they feel that they are plateauing or that their motivation is diminishing. Conversely, it is essential for management to encourage and facilitate the movement of their staff, to avoid their analytical teams becoming burdened with poorly motivated analysts.

Finally, and interestingly, it is worth noting that intelligence analysts are not exceptional in not having a clearly defined career path. As one official noted, "there is no one discipline in government where you have a great career path. It's the same everywhere." A second interviewee drew a similar conclusion: "It's a problem all across government where you have people who are experts who don't want to be promoted into managerial categories or executive categories." The challenge for how to deal with experts, in other words, is a government-wide issue, not one that can be solved by the intelligence community alone.

Looking Forward

This chapter began by stressing the importance of management in the performance of intelligence and national security agencies generally, despite the lack of attention paid to this issue in intelligence studies literature. Our findings demonstrate that management practices in the Canadian context have often been haphazard, lacking standards and with few organizing principles. While each agency has unique mandates and responsibilities requiring specialized training, the community has refrained from taking a more coordinated approach (such as setting basic training requirements). It has also performed poorly in sharing best practices and lessons learned with regard to management-related issues. This is in part the result of the community's decentralized nature, with initiatives often personally driven. It is also likely because growth in the community is often driven by events (such as 9/11, the October 2014 terror attacks in Canada, and the 2016 US presidential election), when governments provide departments, agencies, and their analytical units a surge of new resources. Hiring and the concomitant need to train is therefore largely spontaneous and unplanned. Many departments and agencies suddenly find themselves with an influx of cash to hire analysts quickly, with limited thought given to how this should be done in a more organized way.

A second reason for this lack of coordination is that resources have traditionally been precarious. Funding for training and secondments is often among the first to be cut when budgets take a hit. These programs, in other words, are often seen as "nice to have" as opposed to "need to have." Moreover, there is little incentive to make changes to current management and career structures given the difficulty in obtaining resources or buy-in from senior officials.

Importantly, the story is far from entirely bleak. This chapter documents steady improvements in training and in movement toward more exchanges and secondments. It also shows that there is a willingness to improve coordination and cooperation in the community generally by better educating managers and clients who will be more informed on how intelligence products can serve them. The creation of a specific intelligence analyst recruitment program in CFINT-COM also represents a step in a positive direction.

Yet ultimately, structural factors limit how far improvements to the Canadian intelligence community can go. In particular, its small size relative to its allies means that there are always constraints on the number of community resources that can be developed. Nevertheless, there are clear paths to professionalization that can be taken, which we discuss in chapter 5.

Case Study: The Canadian Security Intelligence Service

The Canadian Security Intelligence Service (CSIS) is Canada's domestic security intelligence agency. It has a mandate to collect intelligence on threats to the security of Canada as defined in section 2 of the CSIS Act: espionage, foreign influenced activities, terrorism and extremist violence, and subversion.[16] Specifically, the act gives CSIS the ability to "collect, by investigation or otherwise, to the extent that it is strictly necessary, and analyse and retain information and intelligence respecting activities that may on reasonable grounds be suspected of constituting threats to the security of Canada and, in relation thereto, shall report to and advise the Government of Canada" (Canadian Security Intelligence Service Act, RSC s.12).

Prior to 1984, security intelligence (essentially domestic national security intelligence) was run by the RCMP. After a series of scandals and public embarrassments in the 1970s, the government formed the Commission of Inquiry Concerning Certain Activities of the Royal Canadian Mounted Police (otherwise known as the McDonald Commission), which recommended the creation of a civilian intelligence gathering service that would be separate from the evidence gathering / enforcement police force. As a result, the government of Pierre Trudeau established CSIS in 1984.[17]

The original intent of CSIS was for its activities to be purely domestic. Over time, however, successive governments loosened this restriction, allowing CSIS to conduct operations *within or outside of Canada,* so long as they directly relate to its domestic intelligence mandate. As noted in chapter 1, CSIS may only collect foreign intelligence *within Canada* and as tasked by the ministers of foreign affairs and of national defence (Canadian Security Intelligence Service Act, RSC c s.16).[18]

Intelligence analysis did not have a particularly strong start in the new organization, for a number of reasons. First, although it was intended as a civilian security intelligence service, much of CSIS's culture was inherited from the RCMP, which also did not have a strong analytical culture (Whitaker, Kealy, and Parnaby 2012, 397). A parliamentary Special Commons Committee (mandated to review CSIS after its first five years) noted in 1989 that the RCMP legacy continued to have an effect on CSIS subculture, and that its deficient human resources processes affected its ability to do operations as well as analysis. "The Committee believes the Service requires a specific type of intelligence officer and analyst: someone capable of understanding the dramatic changes now taking place in the world and their impact on the security of Canada. In particular, the Service needs recruits who can grasp the social, cultural, political, and economic contexts from which the changing threats to the security of Canada emerge" (quoted in Whitaker, Kealy, and Parnaby 2012, 398).

Analysis, however, appears to have consistently been an afterthought for the new organization. Whitaker, Kealy, and Parnaby note, "As with many intelligence agencies, the security service's capacity for collection tended to outrun its capacity for analysis and evaluation, a disparity that has persisted down to today. Even as CSIS analytical capacities have improved over the RCMP era, so too has the ever-expanding technological capacity for amassing largely unprocessed information" (2012, 528).

Second, even if there had been a strong analytical culture at CSIS, it is not clear that successive governments were particularly interested in receiving its analysis. As noted throughout this book, it is only comparatively recently, in the aftermath of the election of the Stephen Harper government in 2006, that prime ministers appear to have taken a more active interest in reading assessments provided by the intelligence community. As such, the government of the day (whether Liberal or Conservative) and CSIS largely lived in different worlds— symbolically represented by CSIS's move from several buildings in downtown Ottawa to its new building in Gloucester (a suburb approximately twenty minutes away) in 1995.

Nevertheless, based on the report of the Special Commons Committee in 1989, analysis was initially taking place in a unit identified as the Research,

Analysis and Production (RAP) branch. This unit was headed by a director general who reported to the assistant director for intelligence. According to one account, RAP underwent a reorganization in 1996–97 to improve the coordination of intelligence production with PCO/IAS, although the results of this reorganization are not clear (Rimsa 2011, 40). At the very least, it suggests an attempt at reorganization and coordination with the rest of the community just over a decade after the creation of CSIS.

There is not much that is publicly known about RAP. We do know that CSIS analysts were involved in a joint project with the RCMP on measuring China's influence in Canada in 1996. The project, however, was mired in disagreements over the quality of analysis and strength of the evidence. A watered-down assessment was completed in 1999 and was eventually leaked on the internet (Sallot and Mitrovica 2000; Whitaker, Kealy, and Parnaby 2012, 425–27). In addition, RAP published open-source analyses of national security issues for public consumption in a series called *Perspectives* in the late 1990s and 2000s.[19] These were discontinued by the early 2010s, although it is not publicly known why.

In 2007, RAP's name changed to the Intelligence Assessment Branch (IAB), although again it is also not publicly known why this decision was made.[20] It may be that, with the rise of violent extremism following 9/11, and particularly the 2006 Toronto 18 Case (Canada's first major post-9/11 terrorism investigation), there was a desire to rebrand CSIS's analytical unit. In addition, after the election of the Harper government in 2006, there was a push for higher levels of engagement with policy makers.

Despite the name change, IAB kept the same management structure but began to hire more analysts to keep up with post-9/11 demands for analysis about terrorism, foreign investment, and national security more generally. As noted previously, these analysts were managed almost exclusively by intelligence officers; while analysts could be promoted to senior analyst positions, they were ineligible to be promoted into management positions. While it is not clear if this was a formal or informal policy, the idea was likely that intelligence officers would help ensure that products were operationally relevant and that sensitive information did not leak to the rest of government.

Today, different kinds of intelligence analysts support the work of the organization. First, there are the operationally oriented tactical analysts; they are managed by CSIS's regional offices across Canada or by IAB, but they are often embedded with operational desks where they piece together collected information (typically called *selectors*). This helps investigators organize information and draw links between different elements within a case. Communications analysts help translate intercepts and work with intelligence officers to provide information and context. This book is mostly concerned with the work of strategic analysts within CSIS who are managed by IAB. There are approximately thirty strategic analysts, normally assigned a geographic region or a thematic area such as foreign investment or nuclear proliferation. Strategic analysts typically (but not always) have graduate degrees in their area of study and in some cases have work experience in a prior career, such as in academia or the private sector. They are responsible for writing the products that are consumed by policy makers and other analysts within the government (although, as discussed below, this is not their sole audience.)

Recently, there have been changes to the structure of IAB. The most important of these derives from the reorganization of CSIS as a whole in 2019, which led to the elimination of the assistant director for intelligence position and the transfer of IAB under the authority of a new position, the assistant director requirements. This position, along with its counterpart, the assistant director collection, is responsible for communicating requirements to intelligence collectors in regional offices across Canada, notably on terrorism, counterintelligence, and counterproliferation. Ironically, in trying to make IAB more policy relevant, it was put in an operational branch. There was nevertheless a certain logic to this new approach. While CSIS officials were aware of the risk that IAB would be further removed from policy, the reasoning was to put the responsibility for the intelligence cycle under one assistant director.

Additionally, strategic analysts are now allowed to apply for managerial positions within the branch (called *section heads* or *heads*). Other strategic analysts, who have traditionally been kept away from operations given their sensitive nature, are increasingly embedded in operational desks, a move that loosely mirrors steps taken by the CIA in 2014–15 to reorganize how analysis feeds into and informs operations (Shane 2015).

But perhaps the biggest change affecting IAB has been cultural: the realization by senior leadership that despite its proprietary information, CSIS's voice was not heard enough by senior policy makers across government on crucial issues such as foreign investment by state-owned and state-championed enterprises. Yet taking steps toward improving policy relevance requires CSIS to overcome a series of challenges. First, CSIS is at a disadvantage relative to other departments and agencies given that it is geographically located away from the heart of government in Ottawa's downtown core. This means it is difficult to compete for the attention of busy policy makers (or collaborate/compete with other agencies physically closer to PMO and other senior officials). This should not be overstated, however; a CSIS employee notes that CSIS has been increasingly "burning through taxi chits" to make sure they are present downtown. In addition, since the onset of the COVID-19 pandemic, most departments and agencies in the intelligence community have improved their secure video teleconferencing systems.[21]

Second, while IAB writes about important topics, many of its products are still delivered through an archaic, highly classified distribution network. Policy makers in GAC, DND, and other parts of government often need to leave their workstation and cell phone behind to enter a secure facility to access CSIS products. This cumbersome process means that timely information, when available, is not easily accessible.[22]

Third, even when its products are more accessible, IAB analyses have not always been user-friendly. For years, its Intelligence Assessments were long, written in an academic style, and disconnected from the daily priorities of senior policy makers. IAB has been attempting to fix this issue by hiring a strategic editor to help analysts develop a "bottom line up front" writing style. IAB has also been years behind other agencies in developing products that make better use of graphics and data (such as CFINTCOM's placemats; see chapter 4) and are shorter (such as PCO/IAS *Daily Foreign Intelligence Brief*), as well as in offering oral briefings. Also, CSIS has been less likely to send analysts to important meetings than higher level managers or executives, which has meant that analysts seldom met their clients.

In recent years, IAB has tried to steer its analysis along these lines. It now encourages analysts, for example, to make better use of graphics and visualizations. Intelligence assessments are now typically no longer than four or five pages, with a cover page summarizing the main findings. CSIS provides more oral briefings and has even experimented with placemats. It also aims to provide high-level officials with rapid, limited-distribution, one- to five-page products on urgent matters, each called a *National Security Special Brief*. It is also adapting to client requests, notably by producing placemats that IAB can then present through an oral briefing, increasingly given by analysts, supported by managers. In addition, IAB is taking steps toward the creation of a briefing unit that can give daily updates to senior executives as well as clients downtown. The move toward oral briefings came as CSIS realized it took too long to meet client demands in writing.

Finally, improving policy relevance requires CSIS/IAB to face a long-standing challenge: its bias toward supporting internal collection operations and investigations rather than providing advice to the rest of government. Frequently, despite bursts of personality-driven efforts to make IAB products more relevant, analysts have been encouraged to turn their attention more to supporting operations, often at the expense of products for policy makers. This situation reflects the biases of branch heads. The vast majority have traditionally been intelligence officers, who are far more familiar with intelligence gathering than the requirements of senior policy makers. As noted previously, these intelligence officers have not received training and have, at most, limited experience in supporting policy makers. It should therefore not be surprising that analysts have often been actively encouraged to write what intelligence officers know and understand (and what would likely give them higher standing among their peer group). Therefore, rather than writing for clients outside CSIS, analysts have been encouraged to write for their operational colleagues or for CSIS executives making operational decisions.

To be clear, this is a perfectly acceptable decision for an organization to make—namely that its efforts should focus on its ability to collect and investigate threats to the security of Canada. Moreover, as one interviewee noted, "security intelligence is less client driven" and more "threat driven." From their perspective, policy is better served with nonsecurity intelligence.

Yet despite CSIS's traditional inward bias, the organization has made the decision to better engage with policy discussions "downtown."[23] One interviewee noted that in the past IAB needed to focus on supporting operations when the main issue was terrorism. Today, with the rise of more strategic and geo-economic threats, there is an opportunity to provide analysis that can help inform key national security decisions, such as foreign investment by state-owned or state-championed enterprises and threats to democratic institutions. There is an added benefit in doing this for CSIS: as its operational needs and requirements change as a result of the emergence of strategic threats, helping policy makers better understand CSIS's perspective means it will be easier to obtain the resources and policy changes it seeks to support an organization still bound to legislation designed for a Cold War environment.

It is therefore not surprising that during his time as CSIS director since 2017, David Vigneault has prioritized policy relevance. Two interviewees recounted that shortly after his arrival, he unveiled a large banner in the lobby of National Headquarters that said "relevance" on it, to send the message to the organization that he was determined to make sure that CSIS's voice is better heard downtown. One interviewee did note that there remains "institutional resistance" and that "adjustment will take many years." In their view, pushing change will require senior CSIS leadership to continually challenge IAB on its practices, champion reforms, and ensure that CSIS is at the table with timely intelligence.

3 MANAGING INTELLIGENCE POLICY DYNAMICS

IN THIS CHAPTER, we outline five challenges in managing the interface between intelligence analysis and policy. We begin with a discussion of the limited, though improving, policy literacy of intelligence analysts, or their capacity to understand the policy process. We then argue that the reverse, intelligence literacy in policy circles, has followed a similar pattern: it is relatively low but also improving. We follow with a discussion of the intelligence priorities process. We then shift attention to the formal and informal client management processes, and their successes and failures. In Canada, high-level policy making mostly occurs in a whole-of-government context: the advice that DMs and equivalents provide to the government incorporates multiple priorities and perspectives. Yet the intelligence analysis they receive too often does not reflect this reality of whole-of-government policy making. Next, we explain why the hard politicization of intelligence analysis is not a problem in Canada. This is in part because of the low salience that senior policy makers attach to intelligence; there is simply limited incentive for them to politicize it. Finally, the chapter concludes with a case study discussing the relationship between GAC and intelligence matters.

Relatively Low Policy Literacy in the Intelligence Community

One of the most important conclusions of our research is that policy literacy—defined as the general understanding of and familiarity with the policy process—within the intelligence analysis community is low.[1] As with the overall performance of the community, this must be nuanced. Levels of policy literacy vary significantly, ranging from abysmal to quite advanced. It was also clear from our research that policy literacy has been on an upward trend in recent years.

Multiple interviewees, from both the policy and intelligence worlds, emphasized the centrality of this low literacy in explaining why and how intelligence analysis fails to optimally support policy. In the words of one interviewee, too many analysts write "without knowing why, who their target audience is, and what policy they support." Another similarly argued that there is "very insufficient knowledge among intelligence analysts on what policy is; it is very difficult to write analysis that can support policy if we don't understand what the policy is and how it is made." In the words of yet another interviewee, "Intelligence analysts are policy blind to the point of being detrimental . . . and they make a point of being proud of that . . . it's remarkable."

Many if not most intelligence analysts do not have a sufficient understanding of the day-to-day work of policy makers, either those at senior levels or their counterparts at the working level. They tend to hold broad oversimplifications of what policy is and of how it is developed and implemented. One interviewee, for example, argued that "most intelligence community analysts don't understand that one of the most valuable currencies in government is a time slot at Treasury Board or Cabinet" and that "most analysts don't get how busy senior policy makers are." Another interviewee, who has worked in both worlds, emphasized, "Until I went to (a policy job), I did not realize how little I knew about policy. I laugh now when my intelligence colleagues say how busy they are"; this individual viewed their secondment as "immensely eye-opening," allowing them to realize that most intelligence analysts are "not remotely connected to cabinet, parliament . . . they have no idea."

As a direct consequence of such low levels of policy literacy in the analytical community, too many analysts "write for themselves," asking questions (and providing answers) that are more of interest to them and their fellow analysts but often of little or no interest to policy clients. There is, in other words, too little ability—and incentive—to translate intelligence analysts' subject matter expertise in a way that can better inform policy.

Policy literacy is on average low, but it is also highly unequal throughout the community. It has been especially low in CSIS/IAB, where, in the words of one interviewee, there is "very little understanding and interest in downtown clients."

The organization was criticized by multiple interviewees, notably for being "too insular" and largely disconnected from the broader government context. Some of their analysts have experience working in CSIS's policy unit, but few have held policy positions elsewhere in the government. There are also limited opportunities for secondments. Instead, IAB has tended to be more operationally focused, driven by its cadre of managers dominated by intelligence officers focused on doing work to support the main business of the organization—operations— rather than supporting policy makers (see the case study at the end of chapter 2). CSIS analysis has been, as a result, not as central as it could be to high-level policy conversations.

The situation at IAB has evolved over the years. Successive directors, starting with Jim Judd (2004–2009) and followed by Dick Fadden (2009–2013), launched reforms to slowly steer IAB toward greater relevance. While ensuring that IAB would continue supporting operations, these efforts sought to shift IAB's work toward external clients, such as GAC and PCO. These efforts initially met with limited success, in part due to internal resistance and, as noted previously, a culture that prizes operations over policy relevance. The situation has continued to gradually improve under the current director, David Vigneault (in the position since 2017). More recent initiatives, for example, have seen nonintelligence officers reach mid-level management positions in IAB.

Proximity to the policy world is an important variable explaining fluctuating levels of literacy. Agencies that encourage their analysts to rotate across the policy and intelligence realms and that, by dint of the nature of their work, are better connected to the rest of the bureaucracy tend to do better. In PCO/IAS, the development of policy literacy in recent years (see the case study at the end of chapter 1) was the result of determined efforts by successive leaders, but it was also made easier by the organization's greater physical and institutional proximity to PMO and the rest of PCO. As a result, in the words of one interviewee, the IAS has emerged in recent years as "ahead" of other analytical organizations at this level. This was illustrated in our interviews with policy officials, where answers significantly differed in their appreciation of the relevance of IAS products based on the era during which they consumed them, ranging from mostly indifferent (2000s, when the organization was widely perceived as disconnected from the needs of the policy process), to mildly interested (the turn of the 2010s), to increasingly willing to put time aside for IAS analysis (throughout the 2010s).

This is different from IAB, which is institutionally and culturally separate, as well as physically distant (CSIS headquarters are in southeast Ottawa, not downtown, like the IAS). CFINTCOM's performance at this level is somewhere in between the IAS and IAB (see the case study at the end of the next chapter). It has improved significantly in recent years but still has work to do. ITAC's situation is somewhat different, since its mandate is specifically to inform decision-making more on threats and less on strategic policy making. Nevertheless, multiple interviews highlighted how, even though ITAC sometimes produces quality analysis, it continues to be viewed as marginal in high-level bureaucratic and political circles and still has much progress to do to better understand senior client requirements.

A number of reasons explain how and why the analytical community has failed to enhance the policy literacy of its analysts. Historically, the community has been insulated. Its analysts typically do not invest the time and energy necessary to understand who their consumers are, what they do, what the inputs into their work are, and how intelligence fits as one of those inputs. Analysts are told, and generally accept in an abstract sense, that their ultimate objective is to support clients. In practice, however, on a day-to-day basis the dominant trend is to view analysis as an end in itself rather than as a means to the end of supporting a client. As discussed in chapter 2, this is reinforced by a linear and insulated career structure that still often fails to encourage analysts to gain experience in the policy world. As a result, in the words of one interviewee, "certain assumptions about the other become cemented."

That said, our research has clearly shown that policy literacy has improved since 2001. As one interviewee emphasized, analysts' overall ability to serve clients is "night and day compared to where we were when I started twenty years ago," when most analytical organizations essentially "lived in autarky." Even if there remains significant room for further improvement, there is on average far more focus on serving clients and an enhanced frequency of contact with consumer organizations.

The recognition at senior levels in both the policy and intelligence realms of the need for analysis to better serve policy clients has played an important role in driving this improvement. There has also been, in parallel, a growing—and much needed—trend of filling senior positions in the analytical community with individuals coming from not only a policy background but also, in some cases, nonsecurity sectors of the public service. Martin Green, for example, who became head of the IAS in 2015, had previously served in a policy position in DND, but prior to that he had spent his career in various economic and social departments. Such individuals have helped steer their organizations toward enhanced policy literacy.

An interesting approach here is to draw parallels between Canada and other countries: Is policy literacy in the Canadian intelligence community lower, comparable, or higher than in other countries, notably Five Eyes partners? It would be beyond the scope of this book to attempt to answer this question rigorously; such an extensive comparative study has never been done, and, though it would certainly be interesting, it would also be highly complex and labor-intensive. Based on our interviews in Canada and with a dozen US and allied officials, we can say with confidence that it is certainly not higher in Canada and is most likely lower than in the US and the UK.[2] Weaker-than-ideal policy literacy is also a problem in the US intelligence community, as our interviews in Washington showed. As one official emphasized, like in Canada, a surprisingly high proportion of analysts do not have a sufficient understanding of who their clients are, what they do, and what they need in order to do their jobs. Also like in Canada, it varies. For example, in a manner somewhat similar to the IAS, analysts in the State Department's Bureau of Intelligence and Research (INR) are physically, culturally, and institutionally closer to their clients. This inherently gives them a better understanding of the policy process.[3]

The Reverse Is Also True: Low Intelligence Literacy in the Policy World

Conversely, multiple interviewees emphasized the reverse: the limited understanding among most people on the policy side of the role of intelligence. The same two caveats apply: Intelligence literacy in policy has improved in recent years, albeit from a very low to a moderate level, and it varies significantly across the foreign, defense, and national security policy worlds. Nevertheless, our research demonstrates the existence, in the words of one interviewee, of "a big education gap on the policy side on what they can ask for and what they can do with what they get" from intelligence analysis.

Low intelligence literacy in policy circles carries many implications. First, it means that many in policy have little appetite for intelligence and are not willing to spend much time, if any, to consume it; since many do not understand its potential benefits, they are less willing to incorporate it into their already busy schedules. This was emphasized by many interviewees on the policy side; in the words of a former official, for example, "I would spend five minutes per day reading intelligence." Low intelligence literacy in the policy world and the related limited appetite for intelligence also implies that important variables shaping the intelligence community's performance are outside its control. If demand and literacy are low, it is difficult for the units supplying the analysis to perform optimally, at least in the short term.

Policy makers with a limited understanding of the role of intelligence are not able to make the best use of the analytical support they receive. They also have a harder time asking precise questions to the intelligence community, making the latter's attempts at providing relevant answers all the more challenging. This risks creating a vicious cycle: poorly served, poorly educated clients further turn their backs to the intelligence community. Low intelligence literacy among policy makers, in addition, makes their efforts to reform the intelligence community more challenging, since they often have a limited understanding of its processes.

That said, like policy literacy in the intelligence community, intelligence literacy in the policy world has improved markedly since 2001. The fundamental reason, as will be discussed, is straightforward: security issues have steadily ranked higher on the political agenda. This has led to a slow but steady increase in the demand for intelligence assessments, and therefore the experience of those consuming it. Canada's contribution to the war in Afghanistan, especially its difficult combat mission in Kandahar from 2005 to 2011, left an important legacy. It "taught a generation of senior leaders how to use intelligence," boosting their understanding of what they can expect of it. In addition, analysts who worked the Afghanistan file, in Ottawa and in theater, have since steadily risen up the chain, taking with them their greater experience with intelligence matters.

Interestingly, US officials we interviewed described a similar dynamic (albeit with a far higher baseline, as prior intelligence literacy was higher than in Canada). Intelligence literacy in the US government in general is also unequal. One of the drivers of this inequality is the Afghanistan and Iraq experience. Officials who worked on these wars gained a better understanding of what intelligence can, and cannot, bring in support of policy making. Interviewees similarly highlighted the spillover effect of younger analysts who worked on these wars steadily reaching senior positions throughout the national security community.

Policy literacy in the intelligence community and intelligence literacy in the policy community are low, but it is important not to put both on the same level. Strong policy literacy is a necessary condition for intelligence analysis to be relevant. Conversely, relatively limited intelligence literacy among policy officials is mostly normal, up to a point: the job of a policy maker is to be a generalist, to integrate multiple inputs and fuse them into policy advice and then to implement it. Policy makers cannot be experts in science, engineering, law, finance, and accounting; those in relevant positions may have background in one of those fields but must use the work of experts to support them.

As a senior policy maker candidly put it, "I won't wait for intelligence. . . . Only a small proportion of what I know comes from the intelligence community, (while) the majority comes from open sources or other government sources." As a result, if "hypothetically you remove intelligence from my diet of the multiple inputs of knowledge and analysis I receive, I would not be much worse off." One interviewee went so far as to argue that the issue of intelligence literacy in the policy world is "irrelevant." The role of intelligence, in their view, is to support policy, not the other way around, and it is entirely up to the intelligence community to adapt to this dynamic or be condemned to irrelevance. This is an extreme view, shared by few, but it does illustrate the unequal balance of power between policy and intelligence, since the former has multiple inputs into its decision-making process, with intelligence being only one.

Interviewees frequently highlighted GAC as a strong example of low intelligence literacy. In the words of one, the reality is that "some seniors [at GAC] have had limited exposure" to intelligence throughout their careers, and many are "deeply skeptical" of its value. Some "don't know the difference between SIGINT and HUMINT . . . they lack even basic knowledge of intelligence." As a result, "their ability to fit intelligence within their work is not sophisticated . . . there are [GAC] executives who have literally never been in a secure boardroom." Intelligence is simply not prominent on the radar for many of the department's senior officials. Its staff receive basic indoctrination sessions when they obtain clearances but "receive no formal training, though of course we receive training on human resources and the Financial Accountability Act." As a result, senior GAC officials "often ask inappropriate questions," or simply ignore intelligence; they see raw intelligence but are not well equipped to put it in context, assess its reliability, and incorporate it into their work, as opposed to merely reading it and finding it interesting. As a result, most of the time, most of the information consumed by senior officials comes either from open sources or from internal analysis, notably embassy reporting (though, as is discussed in the case study at the end of this chapter, this is changing).

Of course, as is the case elsewhere in government, intelligence literacy in GAC is unequal. Those who have worked on international security issues—especially postings in Ottawa or abroad dealing with China, Russia, and the Middle East—typically have a stronger foundation than those who spent all or most of their career dealing with Africa, Europe, or Latin America or who come from the development and trade streams. Many working on these less security-oriented files also often do not even have top-secret clearances. There is, as a result, a minority who are expert consumers of intelligence (they know what questions to ask, and what to do with the answers), while others have "no clue," in the worst cases, or only a limited background, arguably in the case of the majority in the middle.

The Investment Canada Act (ICA) process provides another illustration of how the gap between the assumptions and perceptions of the policy and intelligence realms can lead to tension and dysfunction. The ICA, according to its section 2 (1985, c. 28), provides "for the review of significant investments in Canada by non-Canadians in a manner that encourages investment, economic growth and employment opportunities in Canada" and "for the review of investments in Canada by non-Canadians that could be injurious to national security." It is thus the government's chief mechanism for reviewing foreign investment. It led to the establishment of a complex process, led by Innovation, Science, and Economic Development Canada (formerly Industry Canada), whereby interested departments and agencies recommend to the minister or cabinet (depending on the size of the investment) whether a specific foreign investment should be accepted or rejected.[4]

The second part of this review function, which determines whether the investment would be injurious to national security, brings together a range of departments and agencies. Multiple divides separate them, making this especially difficult. The most obvious is one of mandate: on one side are departments tasked with promoting foreign investment—especially Innovation, Science, and Economic Development Canada and the trade side of GAC—while on the other are departments and agencies focused on threats, CSIS and CFINTCOM in particular.

The ICA process also illustrates the different realities of the intelligence and policy worlds. On the intelligence side, there has usually been a good understanding of the threat but a limited understanding of the complex ICA process and of the broader policy context. One interviewee on the policy side described the process as a "source of real frustration." Intelligence analysts, in particular, focus on "threat, not opportunity"; that is, "the skill set they recruit and train." What they have provided, as a result, has not been "particularly nuanced," or helpful. In the words of one interviewee, simply stating "don't go there" cannot be the end of the review process. Threat analysis, in other words, should be weighed against other (economic, financial, political) factors, an exercise the intelligence community has been poorly equipped to accomplish at first. The reverse, of course, has also been true. Especially early on, analysts and their managers "on the trade side were equally unequipped to deal with intelligence." That said, with time, as interviewees aware of this evolution emphasized, these differences have been steadily ironed out, even though tension remains.

The Intelligence Priorities Process

The intelligence priorities process, in theory, sets the framework for intelligence policy dynamics. It is difficult to write about this process in Canada, however, as there is limited open-source information on it. NSICOP's *Annual Report 2018*, in fact, represents the only recent official document discussing it in detail. Our interviewees, as a result, told us relatively little about it. Much about the process is classified, and most of our interviews were conducted in the fall of 2018 and early 2019, before the release of NSICOP's *Annual Report* in April 2019. Before this publication, officials who were willing to talk to us frankly about other issues were therefore (rightly) reluctant to discuss this particular classified matter.

The process for setting intelligence priorities is "the primary mechanism available to the prime minister, Cabinet and senior security and intelligence officials for exercise and control, accountability and oversight of Canada's intelligence production."[5] It is important for four reasons. First, it ensures that the government can hold the intelligence community accountable. Second, it is an essential tool with which the government issues direction and guidelines to the community in terms of its expectations and requirements. Third, it plays a central role in the broader process of determining resource allocation in the intelligence community. And fourth, it helps build a framework to institutionalize a performance measurement system throughout the community, which has traditionally been lacking.

The security and intelligence community must seek approval on the priorities every two years from cabinet.[6] PCO/S&I first coordinates the drafting of a memorandum to cabinet.[7] Since 2018, it has been the Cabinet Committee on Canada in the World and Public Security that considers this memorandum; prior to this, it was the Cabinet Committee on Intelligence and Emergency Management.[8] Not surprisingly, the results of the process are classified. The government redacted all the priorities for 2017–19 in the public version of NSICOP's *Annual Report 2018* (2019, 38).

As our interviews emphasized, the priorities are, by definition, vague and therefore of limited direct utility to guide the work of analytical and collection units. On the basis of those priorities and of subsequent guidance from the ministers of foreign affairs, defense, and public safety, individual departments and agencies therefore produce interdepartmental standing intelligence requirements, which break down broad priorities into more detailed items. Taken together, they represent the requests from clients for specific issues to be analyzed or collected on. According to the NSICOP *Annual Report 2018*, there were at the time over four hundred requirements, ranked into "four tiers by importance and the risk or threat that they pose" (National Security and Intelligence Committee of Parliamentarians 2019, 43).

This more granular stage allows individual departments and agencies to derive requirements adjusted to their own mandates. The result allows, for example, CFINTCOM to have defense-focused priorities (in a document called the *Strategic Defence Intelligence Requirements*) or CSIS to have security intelligence ones (in its *Intelligence Requirements Document*). These "are not plucked out of thin air" but instead "tie back to the government's priorities."

The process has improved over the years. It is now better institutionalized and taken more seriously throughout the community. Whereas it used to be perceived, partly, as an administrative box to tick, it is now more and more understood as necessary to optimize the community's performance. The NSICOP *Annual Report 2018* confirms this view: "The intelligence priorities setting process has improved over the years—an acknowledgement made by every department and agency involved" (National Security and Intelligence Committee of Parliamentarians 2019, 47).

For years, the priority-setting process was "almost exclusively" focused on collection and neglected the analytical side (National Security and Intelligence Committee of Parliamentarians 2019, 39). This made sense; collection using advanced technical means is expensive and can take time to redirect. Analysis, on the other hand, is nimbler; when new issues or threats emerge, it is easier—in theory—to shift individual analysts than the collection apparatus. It was therefore widely perceived that it was more important for the government to give direction to the collectors than to the analysts. While the government's intelligence priorities did serve as yardsticks for analytical units, their impact was, at most, limited. Yet there has been a growing recognition that analytical units would gain from being better integrated into the priorities process. This intensified in 2013, when the IAS and ITAC (the two solely analytical units, with no collection function) started developing their own requirements. In addition, requirements for departments and agencies with a large collection focus but also an analytical function—primarily CSIS and CFINTCOM—now refer to both collection and analytical priorities.

Despite the general belief that a more integrated process is beneficial, the analytical function can and still does operate with a fair bit of detachment from the priorities process, especially on a day-to-day basis for most analysts. Nevertheless, this trend of closer ties between the priorities process and the analytical world represents a positive development, even if its impact has been limited. Better integration, in particular, provides the analytical community with more formal guidance on what the government expects it to write about.

The analytical community faces challenges as it continues its integration into the priorities process. One challenge is the issue of quantification: How does the community rank priorities? Much work remains to be done here to develop and, more importantly, implement a more precise methodology. A second challenge is for the community to learn to better manage risk. By definition, not every threat or issue can be covered; some need to be left out, and others—even if they make it onto the list of requirements, will in practice receive little or no attention. The resulting gaps can be mitigated by relying on international partnerships (especially the Five Eyes), of course, but one interviewee emphasized that the community still has much to improve in terms of its ability to manage such risk. A third important challenge is, as discussed in chapter 1, at the level of the power of the center. PCO/S&I plays a crucial role in coordinating the various steps in the process, from leading the drafting of a memorandum to cabinet on priorities to coordinating development of the requirements. PCO, however, lacks the resources to play a strong coordination role.

Client Relations Mechanisms

Client management implies a range of activities that can broadly be categorized along two axes: whether they are upstream or downstream and whether they are more or less formal. Upstream initiatives seek to better understand the client's needs before a product is written and disseminated; absent such efforts, analysts write in the dark. Downstream initiatives aim to follow up with clients after they have received a product to survey whether it was relevant to their needs. Formal mechanisms consist of bureaucratic bodies tasked with managing relations with clients. These can be embedded in client organizations or remain housed in the analytical unit. In the former case, institutional location allows them to have direct access to clients; they can then share their granular understanding of the needs of client organizations. In the latter case, their strength lies in their proximity to, and therefore understanding of, analysts; they can then actively market their services to client organizations. Informal client management efforts, for their part, incorporate the wide range of actions that analysts and their managers undertake on a daily basis to connect with clients, to become and remain aware of their priorities and needs, and to follow up to survey what was useful and what can be improved. Such efforts are essential. Analytical units "simply cannot achieve success without a dynamic program of informal client management" (Juneau 2017, 253).

Sound efforts to manage relations with clients become a virtuous circle. Feedback from the client should allow the producer to write more targeted analysis, thus better satisfying the client's needs, who will then want more, and so on. The reality, however, is quite different from the theory. As our interviews demonstrated, this feedback loop does not operate effectively. Analytical units have not, traditionally, approached client management in a dynamic and proactive manner, while client organizations have typically not been responsive when asked to provide feedback. It is only in more recent years that the situation has improved.

Indeed, our research identified client relations as a weakness. Interviewees described current or recent initiatives as "too slow and unresponsive." The community's efforts were amply criticized, internally ("we need a better connection to clients"; "we don't play the role of educating clients well") and from the client side ("I was never asked if I got what I needed, even though it would have been super useful," especially given that "we had that kind of interaction with other areas of government"; "I am a senior policy maker in the national security community, and I don't think I've ever been visited by anybody in the assessment community to formally ask me what would be useful"). Interviewees from both sides of the policy-intelligence divide agreed that there needs to be better client management.

That said, our interviewees agreed that to varying degrees, individual analytical units have improved in recent years. Some have experimented with various models of client relations offices, such as CSIS/IAB, which created a position at the deputy director general level with this responsibility. Many interviewees emphasized in particular how the role of the senior leadership of analytical units is key. It is the role of management to translate expert analysis in a way that is digestible and relevant for clients and to seek feedback. While many interviewees criticized the leadership of the intelligence community for not doing enough, they also recognized that there has been significant progress, highlighting notably the work of Martin Green at the IAS. He was described, for example, by one official as the "client manager in chief" for the IAS. He "pushes" IAS products to clients, taking the marketing dimension of his role seriously. He is also viewed as good at leveraging his personal networks. Other interviewees also highlighted the role of Dick Fadden who, when he was director of CSIS (2009–2013), made efforts to market IAB products "downtown." In the words of one interviewee, "Dick was very good and active to put IAB products in front of other deputies and tell them they need to read it." This, of course, harks back to one of the intelligence community's weaknesses, mentioned in chapter 1: how reliant its successes are on personalities as a result of its weak institutionalization.

The client relations officer (CRO) model at CSE is often touted as a model. CSE embeds small teams of CROs throughout client organizations. These officers are then tasked with approaching officials to ask them what topics interest them; they then search CSE databases (to which they have access in their embedded offices), print what they believe to be relevant signals intelligence (SIGINT), and hand deliver it. They then sometimes wait (somewhat awkwardly) while clients sift through packages. The higher an official is in the hierarchy of a client organization, the more attention they can expect. CROs can then receive instant feedback and subsequently adjust the packages they prepare.

Because of this process, CROs are viewed by many clients as nimble in their responsiveness to client needs. In the words of one interviewee, "they make efforts to tailor their products," while another claimed that "some of the raw stuff I get from CSE is spectacular. . . . It can do three things for me: rarely, it is actionable; sometimes, it is a building block in my always developing understanding of a situation; other times, it validates what I already know." CSE also invests significant energy strategizing internally about how to improve its ability to serve clients. The organization constantly tries to assess the impact it is having, according to our interviews, and to understand the needs of the government of the day and whether the intelligence it collects and distributes satisfies those needs. To do so, it keeps extensive statistics on its production, which are found in the classified report it submits to the minister of national defence every year.

Despite its successes, there are problems associated with CSE's CRO model. As many interviewees highlighted, the system works better for senior clients who know and understand what to do with the raw intelligence the CROs provide them. The problem, as detailed previously, is that this is a relatively rare breed in the Canadian system. Interviewees with experience managing analytical units also argued that it was frustrating to them that CROs often monopolize some of their senior clients' limited time to read intelligence. As a result, some interviewees from the analytical side expressed frustration at the CRO system, believing that it can even be detrimental.

More broadly, there are limits to what stand-alone client relations offices can do. They can play the role of messenger between producer and consumer, and sometimes they do it well. But they are not subject matter experts. Even though they can play the role of matchmaker between analysts and clients—a necessary function when done well—their ability to steer analytical production when discussing with either side is limited. That is why the optimal client management approach is one that combines formal channels with deeper informal relations involving everyone on the producer side, from analysts to heads of agencies.

Analytical Support for Whole-of-Government Policy Making

Few challenges that the government faces are the responsibility of one department alone. Whether in the realms of fiscal, economic, environmental, or social policy, decision-making at the most senior levels of the bureaucracy and at the political level can only happen by bringing together and reconciling different institutional points of view. To a large extent, foreign, defense, and national security policy making are not different. Important decisions are made collectively by weighing the often-competing interests and objectives of a range of bureaucratic actors.

Although it is improving, the ability of the analytical community to support whole-of-government policy making remains weak. Indeed, directly related to the weak coordination and centralization discussed in chapter 1 is the tendency of the many analytical units to work in silos. When a crisis hits, the various actors usually manage to more or less force their way through these barriers. That is far less the case in dealing with day-to-day issues outside of crisis scenarios, however. As one interviewee noted, for example, in the wake of the Jamal Khashoggi affair in the fall of 2018, when Saudi agents murdered and dismembered an exiled Saudi journalist in Turkey who had been critical of Crown Prince Mohammed bin Salman, senior clients got "disparate pieces" of the story offering competing assessments.

In the words of one interviewee, the community "is not terribly good at providing information that is not narrowly in their domain." This is true at the analytical level, in the sense that products tend to rigidly stay within the bounds of organizational mandates. It is also the case at the level of community-wide coordination, where officials mostly "wear departmental clothing at interdepartmental meetings, even at senior levels." Analysts and managers, many

interviewees lamented, too often view their role as defending narrow departmental interests; to some extent, this is necessary and unavoidable, but many
interviewees agreed that the analytical community usually stretches it too far.[9]
This was, in fact, one of the criticisms raised by the Air India inquiry, according
to which too much secrecy and too many institutional silos hinder information
sharing.[10] As discussed in chapter 1, this is partly inherent to the system. The
Canadian intelligence community features many agencies with relatively narrow
mandates and, with the possible exception of the IAS, no cross-cutting unit with
a mandate to draw together community assessments.[11]

Yet as interviewees pointed out, bureaucracies are not very good at cooperating; they want to protect their equities and turf. Individuals staffing them are
often territorial and parochial. There has not been, simply put, enough external
pressure to force stovepipes down on a more systematic basis. As one interviewee
put it, "Crises have not driven us to horizontality. . . . When we are galvanized
to cooperate, it is around a big issue; on day-to-day activities, we are very much
siloed." That said, the situation has, here again, improved in recent years. This is
in part the result of the establishment of stronger coordination mechanisms at
senior levels (the triple committee structure at the DM level, discussed in chapter
1), with a steady trickle-down effect through lower-level supporting committees.
These, interviewees agreed, have steadily done a better job of integrating inputs,
which helps push analysis—slowly—in a direction in which it can better support
whole-of-government decision-making.

As noted, Canada's experience in Afghanistan played a catalytic role in driving institutional and cultural change when it comes to supporting initiatives
across departments. Multiple interviewees were critical of the community's inability early on to break down stovepipes as part of its efforts to support whole-
of-government policy making during Canada's combat mission in Kandahar.
Overall, one argued, "we never got a handle" on a whole-of-government approach
for Afghanistan, referring to the analytical community. There was, one interviewee lamented, no cabinet-level process to steer the community to come up
with unified intelligence assessments on the situation. Individual ministers were
briefed, but not collectively. Line departments were virtually all singled out for
intense criticism: DND was "very uncooperative" and "disposed to go it alone,"
while Foreign Affairs provided "weak leadership" and was systematically "short
on staff." As a result, overall, "we could not keep up." The situation did steadily
improve, especially by the end of the combat mission in 2011. The war "acted as
a jolt" to at least partially force down silos. According to one interviewee, the

analytical community deserved "pretty good marks" for in-theater support but not for developing unified strategic assessments to shape and support high-level policy making.

The intelligence analysis community's early inability to work together as part of a whole-of-government approach and then its limited progress during the Afghanistan war mirrors problems observed more broadly in government. The difficulties of the "3 Ds," in particular (diplomacy, development, and defense), in exchanging information and deepening their collaboration were severely criticized by the Independent Panel on Canada's Future Role in Afghanistan.[12] Interestingly though not surprisingly, the limited open-source publications on this topic make virtually no mention of the role of the intelligence community, both at the level of analysis as well as collection and operations, in whole-of-government processes.[13]

Politicization

The politicization of intelligence—the willful manipulation or distortion of data or of assessments derived from data in the pursuit of specific policy, political, or bureaucratic goals—can take many forms.[14] Gregory Treverton, a former chair of the National Intelligence Council in the US, identifies five means to politicize intelligence:

- "Direct pressure": Senior officials coerce others to reach a particular conclusion.
- "House line": An analytic office has a fixed view on an issue, leading to the suppression of other views and thereby shifting the locus of preferred positions from policy (where it is appropriate) to intelligence.
- "Cherry picking": Senior officials choose their preferred one among competing assessments.
- "Question asking": The wording of intelligence questions is manipulated to steer the answer in a preferred direction.
- "Shared mindset": Intelligence analysts and policy makers share strong presumptions (2008).

It is also useful to distinguish between upstream and downstream politicization. The upstream version is rarer; there are few documented cases of intelligence analysts or their managers manipulating the data or the conclusions of their analysis (notably by ignoring, misrepresenting, or inventing facts or assessments) to either support or oppose policy outcomes that they, or their policy clients, prefer. Downstream politicization of intelligence, on the other hand, is more frequent; it occurs when policy makers—the receivers of raw or finished intelligence—commit either of the same three sins of ignoring, misrepresenting, or inventing facts or assessments. It is this second form that—in the US context at least—has come to public light.

Politicization of intelligence can also take hard and soft forms. The hard version is the obviously reprehensible one; it corresponds to a relatively strict interpretation of the definition given, and it is the one that occasionally leads to scandals in the US, notably at the time of the invasion of Iraq in 2003. Yet the hard politicization of raw or finished intelligence, whether upstream or downstream, only describes one part of the universe of possible cases. The mirror opposite of hard politicization is not necessarily soft politicization but rather irrelevance: taken to its extreme, intelligence analysis that is absolutely not politicized, to the point of being rigidly independent of political priorities, is of little or no use to clients. That is why the ideal that analytical communities should aim for is soft politicization: expecting analysts to be aware of and attuned to the political context, without manipulating their analysis on that basis.[15]

Our research turned up no evidence that hard politicization of intelligence analysis in Canada is a serious problem; not one interviewee (and we asked the question to all Canadian participants, serving and retired) could identify a single case. This, arguably, makes the Canadian experience different from that of its closest intelligence partners, the US and the UK.

This seemingly bold assessment must be unpacked. The conclusion that Canada appears to be free of hard politicization of intelligence analysis is not to say that other kinds of politicization do not occur—they do. National security policy making, in particular, is inherently politicized. In a democracy, important decisions are (and should be) taken at the political level and are therefore politicized. It is the prerogative of politicians in democracies to make good or bad decisions (within established legal, financial, and other frameworks). Bad decision-making can be the result of an excessive weighting of partisan considerations relative to technocratic ones, such as policy advice or intelligence analysis by the bureaucracy; that is, again, the prerogative of elected politicians. Such instances are important, but they are beyond the scope of this subsection on the politicization of intelligence *analysis* in Canada. Similarly, we do not make any claim about the politicization of national security at the operational level in Canada (that is, whether partisan political considerations interfere in, and drive or shape, national security operations); that is also beyond the scope of this book.[16]

It is worth emphasizing that the consensus about hard politicization was absolute. In the view of all interviewees, there is no problem with hard politicization of intelligence analysis in Canada. As one claimed, a view echoed by all others, "I cannot think of a single example." Another emphasized that "I saw no evidence that information inconsistent with the assumptions of the government was withheld or massaged.... The content was always politically neutral." This individual further added that they also "never saw any pressure to characterize information in any way.... I would have gone ballistic if I had seen any." Another interviewee specified that even under Stephen Harper's PMO—which sometimes had a tense relationship with parts of the bureaucracy on the policy side—there was never any "pressure to change our assessments." An example illustrates this dynamic of the intelligence community providing unvarnished analysis to the political level. One agency, according to an interviewee, assessed, before the finalization of the 2014 deal that followed, that should Canada sell CA$15 billion worth of light armored vehicles (LAVs) to Saudi Arabia, "our job was to tell [the government] what [the LAVs] will be used for, and we were right," referring to their potential use in combat in Yemen. But, this interviewee highlighted, "of course it is the government's prerogative to sell them, but our job was to tell [them] what we think will happen, even if it contradicts the government's position" at the time.[17]

A critical test of this assessment comes from Middle East issues. The Harper government pushed Canadian foreign policy in a more pro-Israel, anti-Iran direction, leading to some resistance within parts of the bureaucracy, especially at what was then known as the Department of Foreign Affairs (since renamed Global Affairs Canada). Yet during those years, one individual well aware of Middle East intelligence analysis insisted that "we wrote things not jiving with the government's policy," and "it was not a problem"; there was "never negative feedback." According to this individual, there were two reactions to analysis not in line with the government's hardline positions: in some cases, the political level dismissed the analysis, which was its prerogative, and in others it appreciated the challenge function. This is especially important since, as another interviewee pointed out, there were instances of the politicization of the work of other expert communities, such as in criminal justice and drug policy, during the Harper years.

This raises an obvious question: Why is there no hard politicization of intelligence analysis in Canada? Our research suggests that it is the result of the combination of two factors, one relevant to the federal bureaucracy, the second more tied to structural factors beyond the bureaucracy. The federal bureaucracy in Canada, first, has a deeply embedded ethos of nonpartisanship.[18] Within the public service, the intelligence community holds these values particularly strongly. Multiple interviewees agreed that senior clients, in the bureaucracy and the political world, understand and accept that the role of intelligence is to provide unbiased analysis; they even often appreciate it. This, interviewees strongly emphasized, applies to both Liberal and Conservative recent governments. One interviewee from the political world, echoing a point made by others, emphasized the intelligence community's reputation for nonpartisanship: "I assumed it (intelligence analysis) was credible and factually correct, probably more than other" sources of information from the bureaucracy. Prime Minister Harper, according to one interviewee, was "adamant" that intelligence is intelligence; he "never" commented on wanting intelligence to merge with his policy views. Another interviewee emphasized that Harper appreciated the independent analysis he was getting from intelligence agencies. This individual recognized that in other realms, such as social policy, Harper often disliked the advice he received, which led to tension, but this was not the case with intelligence.

The second reason for the absence of the hard politicization of intelligence analysis in Canada is structural. As mentioned elsewhere in this book, Canada's position as a relatively safe country implies that senior public servants and politicians usually believe that they have a limited need for intelligence reporting. They have also been able, outside of rare crises periods, to neglect intelligence issues because the costs of missteps are typically low given the country's secure position. There is, as a result, simply less incentive to politicize intelligence; politicians or senior public servants genuinely believe in deeply embedded norms of the nonpartisanship of intelligence, but this is facilitated by the absence of perceived gains in using intelligence for political purposes. As our interviews confirmed, expert advice in other, more politically charged files typically have a greater likelihood of being politicized.

Case Study: Global Affairs Canada and Intelligence

Global Affairs Canada (GAC), previously known under an alphabet soup of ever-changing acronyms (usually simplified as External Affairs, and then Foreign Affairs), has traditionally had a difficult relationship with intelligence. As our interviews illustrated and as is widely known in the bureaucracy, many diplomats, in Ottawa and abroad and at multiple levels in the hierarchy, have traditionally held intelligence analysis in relatively low esteem and prefer to receive information and analysis from a combination of open sources and internal products (especially diplomatic reporting). Skepticism toward the value-added of intelligence analysis to their work runs deep. In the words of one interviewee, the work of the intelligence community is "usually more interesting than useful," a commonly held view in the department.

Yet GAC, as the primary department responsible for developing and implementing foreign policy, should be, ideally, a major consumer of intelligence analysis. The reality that it is not is one of the clearest indicators of the underwhelming performance of intelligence analysis in Canada. Here again, the situation has improved in recent years. Interviews and multiple informal conversations with retired diplomats show a greater level of resistance or indifference toward intelligence among older generations; GAC officials, especially younger and midcareer ones, generally show more openness and, crucially, a higher level of intelligence literacy. A retired official with broad experience, for example, claimed that they could not recall important decisions at Foreign Affairs "being informed by intelligence," with only limited exceptions such as the campaign for the Security Council seat in the late 1990s. According to this individual and others, reports from missions abroad and the media were, until recently at least, largely sufficient for most senior officials, most of the time.

There are a number of reasons for this disconnect. Part of it is a matter of institutional culture: diplomats, for decades, developed the habit of consuming primarily media and diplomatic reporting. Part of it, as will be discussed in the next chapter, is an issue of classification: it is not always convenient for them to consume highly classified products. Part of the explanation also has to do with the architecture of the national security community in Canada, and it is at this level that there has been most change in recent years. In the words of one interviewee, "most of the intelligence community is not writing for [GAC officials]." According to this individual, GAC tends to fall between the cracks as a consumer: CFINTCOM primarily writes for defense clients, for example, while the IAB aims to support CSIS operations. ITAC products are occasionally relevant, but they are usually highly targeted. The IAS does write products that can be relevant for GAC, but its attention has mostly been focused on PCO and PMO. As a result, "attention for [GAC officials] gets diluted; there are very few [analytical] resources left." If or when GAC officials require a precise analytical product, they cannot task analytical units in other departments, especially when timelines are short. This situation, however, has changed in recent years.

The central unit in GAC responsible for intelligence is the Intelligence Bureau, headed by a director general under the ADM of international security.[19]

The bureau acts as the main liaison for GAC with the Canadian intelligence community and is also responsible for liaising with foreign intelligence agencies (such as the CIA and the British Secret Intelligence Service). Its role, in the words of one official, is to "premasticate" intelligence for the many less educated consumers of intelligence in GAC and to act as a translator or facilitator of dialogue with the rest of the community. Another described the bureau's role as that of an "enabler," to push geographic colleagues throughout the department "to talk to CSE, to build that intelligence culture, to make sure they understand what intelligence is."

The bureau manages four divisions: programs and partnerships, assessments, threat assessments, and countermeasures and intelligence access. Of the work of those four teams, we discuss these especially relevant elements: intelligence liaison offices, the threat assessment unit charged with monitoring the security of diplomatic missions abroad, a recently created assessment unit (the first housed within GAC in decades), and GSRP.

INTELLIGENCE LIAISON OFFICES

Canada has four Intelligence Liaison Offices (ILOs) abroad, in Washington, London, Canberra, and Berlin. They are GAC-funded and fall under the authority of the Intelligence Bureau but perform a whole-of-government function; they represent the entire intelligence community on analytical matters, though not on operations. As such, they interface with the analytical side of the CIA (the Directorate of Analysis) on behalf of CSIS/IAB, for example, but the CSIS Liaison Office in the Canadian Embassy in Washington liaises with the CIA (as well as with the FBI and others) on operational matters. Given that Canada is a net importer of intelligence—its intelligence community receives far more from its partnerships, especially the Five Eyes, than it gives back—the management of these relationships is crucial.

ILOs play a vital role in promoting the work of the Canadian analytical community to the host community, especially in Washington. As our interviews showed, Canadians do not, as a general rule and with only some exceptions, have access to specific data that the Americans do not.[20] Members of the US analytical community are therefore not inclined to spend time meeting their Canadian counterparts to learn facts; they have access to the same information (and far more, given that they do not share all the intelligence they collect with Canada). Instead, the value-added of these exchanges from the point of view of US analysts is to validate their conclusions, to be challenged, to protect themselves against groupthink, and to expect Canadian counterparts to play the role of devil's advocate.

The ILO's role is to manage the logistics of these exchanges and to set them up to best position Canada to leverage these relationships. The ILO in Washington helps manage dozens of exchanges every year. An essential ingredient of its work at this level is to be well aware of the pockets of excellence in the Canadian analytical community—individual analysts or clusters of analysts known in Washington to be skilled and insightful—and to ensure that they participate as much as possible in exchanges. US analysts usually know who they are and expect them to participate; when they do not, there is a cost for Canada as the minor player in the relationship, since with time, US counterparts risk becoming less likely to invest in exchanges. Interviews in Washington, including with US officials, indicated that these pockets of excellence include China and Russia analysts in CFINTCOM, a small group of Middle East analysts in the IAS and elsewhere, as well as specific GSRP officers.

ILOs also receive requests for information from Ottawa almost daily, as officials on the policy or intelligence side need information or analysis right away on specific topics and do not have off-the-shelf products available (which frequently happens, given the relatively small size of the intelligence community). The ILO—especially in the US—can then, in a matter of hours, get products back to Ottawa.

THREAT ASSESSMENT

GAC has increased the resources in recent years of the team responsible for threat assessments relative to mission security. Mission security was not neglected, but it also was not a priority in the day-to-day concerns of the department's leadership. For example, until recently, the department did not collect statistics and trends on threats to personnel and missions abroad. These deficiencies were notably highlighted in a 2018 report by the auditor general that was "scathing," in the words of one interviewee, in its criticism of the department.[21]

The auditor general's report led to the adoption of the "duty of care" agenda, through which the department secured CA$1.8 billion over ten years to invest in the security of its missions abroad, notably in armored vehicles, surveillance cameras, and better physical protection.[22] It also led to a tightening of security procedures, including through enhanced efforts to educate personnel when they travel abroad. The department, according to interviewees, can now provide "better advice," which has "opened many eyes" and helped build greater security and intelligence literacy throughout a department which, in the words of one interviewee, "has not traditionally had a security culture."

The Intelligence Bureau now has a full team doing threat assessments, led by a deputy director. (The other team under the director for threat assessments is responsible for educating and supporting missions abroad.) This team's focus is solely to write and disseminate analyses on threats to missions and personnel abroad; it has thus become a significant consumer of intelligence. Potential terrorist threats represent a large part of the team's focus, though not the only one. This growing focus on mission security assessments is generally perceived in the department as having been, in the view of one interviewee, "quite successful."

ASSESSMENTS

There used to be in External Affairs, as GAC was long known, a "special research bureau," essentially an assessment unit located inside the department but funded by a separate intelligence budget. After the team was the target of budget cuts, the assessment capacity shifted to PCO in 1993, in what became the IAS. The initial plan called for the department to second a handful of employees to the IAS, but this rapidly became difficult given how stretched its human resources were in an era of cutbacks. In addition, secondments to the IAS were not a high-profile career opportunity, unlike career-enhancing stints in other parts of PCO or other central agencies, and mostly attracted officers at the end of their career who wanted a slower pace. By the turn of the century, the relationship between the foreign ministry and the IAS was largely one of neglect. Diplomats abroad and in headquarters were poorly served when they sought analytical support. There was no in-house analytical unit, and units throughout the analytical community did not have the department as their primary client.

It is in this context that GAC decided to re-create an internal assessment unit. It was gradually built up in 2018–19 and has since grown to nearly ten full-time analysts. This new unit is meant to be complimentary to the mission security threat assessment unit (which has more of a tactical focus) and to GSRP (described below) by providing strategic assessments. The department thus chose a format similar to the INR model in the State Department in the US by creating a stand-alone analytical unit within the foreign ministry. This is a different approach from the one taken in the UK, where individual Research Office analysts are physically colocated with the policy unit they work with in the Foreign, Commonwealth & Development Office. The risk with the British model, according to one interviewee, is that analysts need to be sheltered from the day-to-day work of the policy unit so that they can concentrate on assessment work. In the Canadian context, where policy units are overstretched and where there is little tradition of in-house intelligence analysis, there was a well-grounded fear that in practice, efforts to wall off these new assessors might fail.

Initially, the unit primarily focused on key countries, especially Iran, China, Russia, and Venezuela (the last two were priorities for the then foreign minister Chrystia Freeland). Both its areas of coverage and its size have since continued to grow. It is too early to assess this new unit's success, but based on informal conversations, its early days are viewed by some as modestly promising. The leadership of the Intelligence Bureau, in particular, has made important changes to how intelligence is distributed to senior ranks in GAC. Despite the strengths of CSE's client relations model, they believe that "having an officer dropping a package that may or may not correspond to the needs of their clients was not a very effective way of building an intelligence culture." The bureau therefore replaced this model with the preparation of a daily binder, with material organized by themes, that comes with a dedicated intelligence briefer (either the analyst, or the deputy director or director, depending on the rank of the official being briefed; this is similar to the State Department's INR model). The briefer briefs the client, getting to know them and collecting information about their interests and needs. Within two years of its establishment, the assessment team and its managers, by mid-2020, already brief most of its ministers and DMs on a weekly basis.[23]

THE GLOBAL SECURITY REPORTING PROGRAM

The Global Security Reporting Program (GSRP) was created in 2002 in the post-9/11 context when the intelligence community was seeing significant increases to its budgets. This led the ADM for international security (the political director) at the time, Jim Wright, to argue that the department needed, in the words of one interviewee, to get its "elbows in the game." This was, for many in Foreign Affairs, an "opportunity to move," especially given that (albeit limited) efforts to establish a foreign intelligence agency were not progressing, and to acquire the resources to create ten to twenty new security-related positions that had been lost in the cuts of the 1990s.

There is very little public information on GSRP. A rare official public mention came in a testimony by Colleen Swords, then the ADM for international security, to the Senate's Standing Committee on National Security and Defence on May 28, 2007:

In the aftermath of 9/11, the department also established a global security report-ing program, GSRP. There are currently 15 GSRP officers at Canadian missions abroad. This program was created to generate more focused reporting from our posts abroad on terrorism, non-proliferation and similar security issues. These positions are filled by foreign service officers who work as accredited diplomats in difficult and sensitive places including Kabul, Tehran and Khartoum. They are not intelligence operators in a covert sense; they do not run sources, recruit and pay agents . . . What is different about them is their specific mandate to develop non-traditional sources and gain access to information of immediate value to [Foreign Affairs], as well as the Canadian security and intelligence com-munity and the government writ large (Standing Senate Committee on National Security and Defence 2007).

Official documents almost never mention the program. GAC's *Departmental Performance Report* for 2018–19, for example, does not mention it at all (Global Affairs Canada 2019b). Another rare official public reference comes from the *Departmental Performance Report* for 2009–10, which lists a priority from the 2009–10 *Report on Plans and Priorities*: "Increase the availability and timeliness of information on international security and stability issues." The report then quotes an "indicator and target" to assess whether the priority has been achieved as the "degree of expansion of the Global Security Reporting Program." The report assesses that the department "met all" its objectives: "GSRP, designed to collect, evaluate and disseminate overseas security-related information, expanded to 20 officers located in Africa, the Middle East, Europe, Asia and the Americas, who delivered about 800 timely reports on international security and stability issues, which received positive feedback from other government departments and foreign partners" (Treasury Board of Canada Secretariat 2010).

GSRP officers do not operate covertly; they are declared diplomats whose work is in full compliance with the Vienna Convention on Diplomatic Rela-tions and who simply spend most of their time meeting a range of interesting individuals who hold potentially relevant information. It is, in this sense, tra-ditional diplomatic reporting. A few elements distinguish GSRP officers from regular diplomats, however. They are only posted in countries where there is "some degree of instability or a particular interest to Canada," and they report mostly on security-related issues.[24] GSRP officers have also developed, over the years, a particular ethos and mindset that sets them apart from other foreign service officers.

Most importantly, the work of GSRP officers is in theory walled off from the day-to-day activities of the mission in which they serve. The majority of their time is spent meeting contacts from the host government, business, academia, the NGO community, journalists, and opposition parties, and not focusing on high-level visits, consular issues, and other routine or administrative embassy duties. They also have the autonomy and the resources to travel across their host country beyond the capital. When a GSRP officer is posted in an embassy, the head of mission is not supposed to divert their work to day-to-day embassy activities, except for a small proportion of their hours. This has not always been a smooth process. One interviewee recalled how they "had to continually shield them against pressure to pull them into the day-to-day work of embassies." In fact, in one instance a GSRP officer was withdrawn by headquarters because the head of mission kept using that officer for other purposes. Over time, this relative independence of GSRP officers has become broadly accepted. Today, according to interviews, there are about thirty-five GSRP officers in the field. There is no publicly available information on the program's budget, though under the duty of care agenda, it received more resources for new positions in the field, as well as for more administrative and corporate support in headquarters in Ottawa.

GSRP has evolved, after nearly two decades, into a highly respected program, including in allied capitals, for the uniqueness and high quality of its products. Its evolution, however, has not been without controversies. An important point of contention, especially in the early years, is on GSRP's identity. From GAC's perspective, its work is not intelligence but diplomatic reporting, focused on international security issues (proliferation, terrorism, etc.). After 9/11, there was a shortage of this kind of reporting, as the department judged that diplomats spent too much time working on visits, démarches, and other consular or administrative tasks. There was a pressing need, according to one interviewee, to "get out of the cocktail circuit conventional wisdom and go talk to the port operator."

Yet despite reassurances by Foreign Affairs that GSRP officers were not conducting intelligence activities, there was much tension early on with CSIS, which claimed that the program was infringing on its activities. CSIS complained that GSRP officers were not properly trained to "run around," sometimes in hostile environments, gathering information from contacts, and CSIS often dismissed GSRP reports as "rumint."[25] CSIS also believed that this risked duplicating its own work and that it could confuse foreign partners, who sometimes asked where GSRP fit in the Canadian intelligence architecture. Foreign Affairs officials at the time recognized that there was tension—in the words of one interviewee, "old school CSIS hated it"—but, in their view, "it was hard to object to Foreign Affairs doing more" diplomatic reporting, "because they did so little of it." In an example of these early tensions, GSRP announced that it wanted to post an officer in Trinidad. CSIS objected, arguing that it already covered that country, to which Foreign Affairs replied, in the words of one interviewee, that it had "never seen anything" produced by CSIS on this country.

To some extent, both made valid points. GAC is correct in arguing that what GSRP offers is conventional diplomatic reporting. CSIS liaison officers abroad in embassies perform two tasks: liaise with partner agencies and run covert sources, according to section 12 of the CSIS Act. GSRP officers, on the other hand, are diplomats who act overtly, not covertly. They also report on issues well beyond what CSIS covers; in the words of one interviewee, "This is not spook stuff; it is what diplomats do"; it is "open diplomatic reporting on interesting folks." GSRP, as we will emphasize, is "a connecting point on a continuum between foreign policy and intelligence."

Nevertheless, some of the criticism leveled at the program in its early years was fair. According to many interviewees, some GSRP officers, especially early on (and still today, albeit to a far lesser extent), had visions of themselves as more "intelligence-y" than what the program envisioned. Problems arose "when some went beyond their mandate and [thought] they [were] intelligence officers." They then had to deal with far more skilled, better trained, and "less nice" intelligence or counterintelligence agents in host countries. Interviewees confirmed that in some cases, GSRP officers exposed themselves as a result to real risks.[26] According to one critic of the program, some GSRP officers want the benefits of acting like collectors but do not always manage the risks well enough (although this critic recognized that they have improved). Finally, another relevant criticism of the program is—until recently—the limited oversight it operated under, especially when contrasted with the activities of CSIS officers abroad. This, however, is in the process of changing, at least partially. NSIRA is, at the time of writing, conducting a review of GSRP.

Over the years, GAC has worked hard to clarify the program's mandate and to deconflict the activities of GSRP and CSIS officers. Information sharing and coordination between the two has steadily improved, to the point that earlier tensions have largely been resolved at the institutional level. Some tension remains at the operational level, yet this is not only inevitable, it is normal within large bureaucracies. Most GSRP officers now "get it" and are more careful, partly as a result of better training, and focus on their niche of overt sources (though some interviews did suggest that some individual officers are still not careful enough). At the same time, many—though not all—in CSIS have come to appreciate GSRP reports and accept its legitimacy, as long as there is effective deconfliction. Nevertheless, even though institutional tensions are largely gone, there remains lingering frustration within CSIS, where many still view GSRP officers as operating with fewer rules and constraints.

Beyond this turf battle, GSRP is clearly a major success. In the words of one interviewee, "as a consumer, what GSRP tells me is fascinating . . . we acquire astonishing amounts of stuff, directly beneficial to my job." Another one described it as "extremely successful, amazing products; the best I read on Saudi Arabia, Turkey," while a third referred to GSRP writings as "some of the best products I have seen" produced by any Canadian agency. GSRP officers are widely viewed as creative and flexible individuals who have, on average, been skillful at seeking unique and original information and then packaging it in well-written and relevant insights.[27] One interviewee recalled, for example, how the GSRP officer in Damascus (before the embassy was closed in 2012) spoke to Hezbollah members in Lebanon on a regular basis (after "we got appropriate clearance, of course"). Similarly, multiple interviewees highlighted the "phenomenal" work of a succession of GSRP officers in Tehran, before the embassy was closed in 2012, whose unique products were read and appreciated throughout the bureaucracy in Ottawa and, as will be discussed below, also in allied capitals, especially Washington.[28] Illustrating this, GAC recently produced an internal report assessing the value of the program. This report has not been made public, but according to one interviewee, its conclusions were also positive.

GSRP's ability to attract high-caliber candidates is an important dimension of its success. The program has seen, in less than two decades, the emergence of its own microculture. GSRP officers feel, in most cases, strongly attached to their distinct identity, with many serving multiple tours abroad. Many promising foreign service officers (and, in a minority of cases, individuals from other government departments) apply for GSRP postings. Between postings, many GSRP officers also rotate around Ottawa, gaining relevant experience by acting as analysts, team leaders, or liaison officers throughout the national security and intelligence community.

As the program has become increasingly institutionalized, so training for its officers has also become more comprehensive. Departing officers, in most cases, learn the language of their host country. They also receive extensive training in a range of skills, such as networking, elicitation (how to listen), navigating the culture of the host country, writing, and operating in hazardous environments (this last one, which includes a firearms dimension, is provided by the CAF). Some of this training is common to other foreign service officers, but a growing share is specific to GSRP officers.

GSRP reporting is one of the greatest assets for Canada within the Five Eyes community and with other intelligence partners. According to one interviewee, it is "hard to overstate how unique GSRP is, how much Five Eyes partners love it . . . it is a crown jewel." This matters. In the world of intelligence cooperation, good reporting is a currency. Canada is a minor player in this market, and it often finds it difficult to compete. But in the words of a US official, GSRP is "gold"; we "really appreciate its products. . . . We don't read many other Canadian products . . . besides GSRP." This is true beyond the Five Eyes. According to one interviewee, the Germans also "love" its reporting. This is a valuable currency and entry point in liaising with the German intelligence services, who can trade valuable analyses on important topics (such as Russia, Iran, or Yemen).

GSRP's success is in large part due to its unique niche. Its freewheeling nature, with fewer restrictions, gives wide scope for individual initiative and creativity. Few if any other units among Canada's allies similarly straddle the intelligence and diplomatic worlds. It is not covert; it is declared, and contacts are not paid to give information. Yet GSRP officers reach individuals and places and collect information that others, including in many cases Canada's allies, especially the US, cannot.

Overall, GSRP "covers a huge amount of ground" at a relatively low cost. In fact, one interviewee argued that in terms of collection and analysis, "I am not sure there is any better bang for the buck in the Canadian intelligence community." The program is also nimble. One interviewee claimed it was one of the, if not the, most responsive programs within the community of collectors and analysts to respond to requests for information. Indeed, the program has rapidly gained such a strong reputation that intelligence and policy analysts in Ottawa regularly ask questions to GSRP officers, who have become skilled at adjusting their meeting agendas and lists of questions to address these requests.

4 APPROACHES TO ANALYSIS
What Makes a Product Useful?

SHERMAN KENT IS SAID TO HAVE argued that every analyst has three wishes: to know everything, to be believed, and to influence policy for the good (as the analyst understands it; Lowenthal 2017, 213). While knowing everything is certainly impossible, being believed and influencing policy depend on analysts' ability to tailor their message to clients' needs. For that to happen, intelligence analysis must be seen as useful by policy makers. This chapter is based on a series of questions we asked interviewees revolving around such central themes: What makes an intelligence product useful? What differentiates useful from merely interesting analysis?

The chapter builds on the findings of the previous one, which demonstrates that levels of policy literacy among intelligence analysts and intelligence literacy among policy makers remain low. First, we discuss how analysts often prefer to write longer products that go in depth on complex issues, whereas policy makers are pressed for time and usually prefer short notes focused on the implications of current events. We document how the analytical community has steadily adjusted to evolving client demands for brevity. Moving away from a conventional focus on longer assessments, some units have increasingly provided oral briefings, placemats, short daily products, and intelligence profiles, all while exploiting open-source information better. Our interviews demonstrate that, overall, clients receiving such products have become more satisfied.

Second, at the level of content, our research shows that intelligence analysis in Canada does not sufficiently address government priorities but instead too often falls into the trap of producing analysis that is well written and interesting but not sufficiently relevant to justify senior policy makers investing time in reading it. Although there was no consensus, many interviewees on the policy side also called for the analytical community to produce more opportunity analysis (assessing possible courses of action), while intelligence agencies typically prefer to focus on threat analysis.

Third, a large majority of interviewees on the client side confirmed that methodology is, at best, unimportant for them; some went further and expressed their irritation with the frequent use of jargon- and process-heavy analytical techniques and methods. Finally, our research shows that overclassification is a common source of frustration among clients. Among other consequences, it limits the sharing of information to relevant stakeholders with lower levels of clearance and constrains client organizations' ability to use that information.[1]

Product Format

The intelligence analysis community in Canada has made significant progress in recent years at the level of the format of its products: they are, on average, shorter (short daily briefs, in particular, have become important successes); there are more oral briefings; and the use of visual support in written products has grown. Importantly, progress appears to stimulate demand. Clients generally appreciate shorter written products, oral briefings, and placemats and want more.

LENGTH

The intelligence community "absolutely has a problem" in that it still produces too many long papers that consumers, especially more senior ones, are not willing to take the time to read. This criticism came out in multiple interviews. While it applied to the community as a whole, some units were specifically targeted, such as the IAS and the IAB. In the words of one interviewee, expressing a perception commonly held in policy circles, "a six-pager on a country no one cares about is not useful." Another official referred to this as the problem of "overinclusiveness . . . too often I got more than I needed given the limited time I had."

What explains this tendency to write long? As noted in chapter 3, too often analysts have a poor understanding of the time constraints of their senior readers (how limited, if any, time they have to read intelligence) and of where their own area of expertise ranks in their clients' priority rankings (which is variable, but they are usually managing multiple priorities, each demanding attention).[2] Yet as many interviewees noted, managers of analysts deserve an important share of the blame. Ideally, they are the ones who should have a better understanding of the reality of the policy world and should steer analysts toward, in this case, shorter papers. In practice, however, too many mid-level managers—team leads, deputy directors, and directors—do not have the required background to do this (as discussed in chapter 2).

There are consequences to the community's challenges in producing shorter papers. There is primarily a cost in terms of access. Longer papers are simply far more likely to be dismissed by busy clients. This creates a further cost in terms of trust and credibility. As our interviews confirmed, impatience, or a limited tolerance for what is not directly necessary, is one of the dominant personality traits of senior policy clients. When analytical units are perceived as delivering long, meandering products, these individuals may simply choose to ignore or deprioritize the products entirely. As one interviewee diplomatically described it, "the tendency to produce long papers to reflect the full nuance of a situation hinders the impact." In a context where the intelligence community already faces an uphill battle to convince policy makers of its relevance, this is self-defeating.

Nevertheless, the oft-repeated mantra that "shorter is better" should be nuanced in several ways. First, all other things being equal, it should be rephrased as "the higher up the chain the product goes, the more concise it should be"; the DM of foreign affairs has less time to read on one specific country than, say, a subordinate at the director general rank who covers "only" one continent, or part of one continent. Ideal length also depends on importance: the more important the issue is, the more clients will require information. It further depends on clients' prior knowledge of the issue: when a new issue suddenly appears at the top of the agenda, policy makers with little or no background are likelier to ask for longer products, at least initially, to build up their knowledge. Moreover, even though most of the time senior clients have little or no appetite for long products, it does not imply that analysts should never write them. Writing long papers is necessary for analysts to build deep expertise on a specific topic, allowing them to reflect more deeply (provided the topic is an important one, which is not always the case). These products will rarely be read by senior policy makers. Occasionally, however, they may be read by policy analysts also working on the issue.

That said, the situation has been improving. Many interviewees noted that the community is producing fewer long papers than in the past. In the 2000s and into the 2010s, papers produced by the IAS, CFINTCOM, CSIS/IAB, and others were frequently six or eight pages long and often exceeded ten pages. In recent years, most analytical units have been producing shorter papers and products, especially short dailies.

SHORT DAILIES

Soon after he became prime minister in late 2003, Paul Martin found out at a G8 summit, according to an interviewee, that his counterparts received daily intelligence briefings. When he asked why he did not, he was told that his predecessor, Jean Chrétien, did not request them (see chapter 1). In response, the IAS started producing weekly summaries as part of a package that also included longer products. Despite this new weekly product, Martin and his staff did not send much feedback. The situation further changed after 2006 when Stephen Harper became prime minister. Harper progressively came to see its value and even began sending feedback and follow-up questions. To support this growing demand, the IAS established the Current Reporting Unit, charged with drafting and circulating this weekly summary. This was initially somewhat controversial internally, as the small staff in the unit were not subject matter experts but were, nevertheless, tasked with identifying key pieces of incoming intelligence, summarizing them, and then extracting relevant implications.

An existential moment for the IAS came at the time of severe budget cuts in the early 2010s, when it was threatened with disappearance.[3] The IAS survived, but its near-death experience jolted it into action to enhance its relevance. The earlier product was transformed from a weekly to a daily piece, the *Daily Foreign Intelligence Brief* (DFIB). This is a short synthesis not exceeding two pages of, typically, eight key intelligence issues. Rob McRae, then head of the IAS, asked analysts to write about eight lines for each issue: the first four factually describing the issue, and the second four providing an assessment (what is new, why it matters).[4] In managing this transition, the IAS disbanded the Current Reporting Unit and returned the task of drafting DFIB items to analysts.[5] One important innovation as part of efforts to modernize the DFIB and increase its circulation was to include links to longer IAS papers, as a way to advertise them and drive demand. The DFIB's main clients are now PMO and the rest of PCO, even though it is disseminated widely throughout the national security and intelligence community.

Interviewees frequently praised the DFIB; one official labeled it as IAS's "signature product." Another argued that it helped "revitalize the IAS" and that it is a "hit." For most clients, it fulfills a specific need: it provides a quick glance of key issues and offers concise information, which is sufficient for most senior clients. Interviewees confirmed that Prime Minister Harper appreciated it, as did senior officials in his office. In addition, Prime Minister Trudeau's staff find the product useful, although interviewees agreed that, on balance, it is a less avid consumer of intelligence than its predecessor.

A second example of a successful daily product comes from DND. In the 2000s, the director general intelligence (DGInt), subsequently renamed as the chief of defence intelligence (CDI), was producing the *Weekly Intelligence Digest*, a long and unwieldy product that had little impact (see the case study at the end of this chapter for more on the evolution of the organization). Under Linda Goldthorp, the first director general for intelligence production (a position later transformed into the assistant chief of defence intelligence, ACDI), the *Weekly Intelligence Digest* morphed into the *Daily Intelligence Digest*. This was a positive step, although in its early years the daily version remained text heavy, not very user friendly, and poorly connected to senior-level priorities. As will be discussed below, the *Daily Intelligence Digest* has continued to evolve and has now become an effective product.

Our findings strongly show that short dailies are among the most useful products for clients. Their brevity, first, implies that they are more likely to be timely, as opposed to the longer, less standardized products. They also provide a "hook": when an item piques the interest of a reader, provided that the producer agency is sufficiently responsive and that channels are effectively developed, that client is more likely to follow up with additional questions or to ask if longer products are available.

Critics highlight that shorter products come with a cost, in that ideally senior policy makers should spend more time building a deeper understanding of new or complex issues.[6] This is partly valid. It is certainly the case that senior officials in the Canadian national security and intelligence community are usually promoted on the basis of their generalist and managerial skills, not their subject matter expertise. But it is also mostly a false dichotomy. One can lament senior clients not having deeper knowledge of certain issues, but good managers (admittedly not the case for all of them) know how to rely on the expertise of their staff. Moreover, when they really need such depth, they often acquire it over time.

PLACEMATS AND OTHER VISUAL SUPPORT

Increasingly, the intelligence community has moved toward integrating more visual support in its products, including dailies. The idea was, initially, to space out text-heavy reports with various forms of visual products, such as maps, charts, graphs, photographs, and illustrations. In some cases, units have even incorporated editorial cartoons. At the very least, these can serve as a hook to attract attention, which is always a challenge in Canada. Smart or provocative cartoons (including from the regions being written about) can also convey meaning and insight.

The starting point of this evolution was to make the products more visually appealing to clients; it was, in part, a marketing decision. For some analysts and managers, however, especially of the more traditional kind, this evolution represented a step backward. It was, in their mind, "not serious" and a "dilution" of their work. It is easy to counter these arguments. If the products are more attractive and clients are, as a result, more likely to consume them, this gain in terms of access and dissemination is a worthwhile investment. Perhaps more importantly, what has become clear after a few years of the growing sophistication of such visual products is that, when well-constructed, they can contain as much information as text. A graph on missile ranges, for example, or a chart explaining the structure of a terrorist group can convey as much information as a paragraph—and can do it more effectively.

CFINTCOM's Daily Intelligence Digest, in particular, has continued its evolution and has now become widely viewed as a well-crafted and effective product. Among the more recent changes has been the ambitious decision to change its format from standard letter-size paper with only (or almost only) text to an eleven-by-seventeen-inch placemat with graphs, charts, maps, and other forms of visual support, interspersed with text boxes. Of course, this can be resource intensive. To create a more professional look, CFINTCOM, the IAS, and other units have hired graphic artists, integrating them into the work of preparing their analytical products. CFINTCOM has gone further by fostering graphics skills among its analysts. Some have received training, and now many are able to build an increasingly wide range of visual support into their work. (As one official noted, this was born of necessity. Senior clients began asking for more visuals than the new graphics analysts could provide, forcing analysts to learn to do it themselves.)

This recent evolution toward the greater and more sophisticated use of visual support represents an important success for the analytical community. One interviewee recalled how when he was the national security and intelligence adviser (2016–18), Daniel Jean specifically instructed Martin Green at the IAS to quickly make his products "more accessible" to senior clients. Interviewees aware of such recent developments agreed that organizations such as the IAS and CFINTCOM have been fairly successful in these efforts. As one stated, "clients are loud and clear, they love placemats." Another emphasized that Prime Minister Trudeau, in particular, is very visual, as are some of his senior political staff. Many of those interviewees noted that there remains scope for further improvement but that the progress of recent years—especially when remembering how stale most products were until not so long ago—is noteworthy. One official also noted how placemats are the ultimate integrated intelligence product. They include textboxes with background and assessments but can also include imagery, mapping, and open-source intelligence.

The growing use of placemats and other forms of visual support is not without its challenges. Using the work of graphic artists—that is, incorporating it in a coherent and useful way—is a new skill for intelligence analysts, one which remains in development. As one official highlighted, for graphics to be optimally designed, analysts must work in close collaboration with graphic artists, a new habit for most.

Placemats also typically work best when accompanied with an oral briefing, to walk the client through it. This is a strong combination; as we will discuss, the increasingly frequent use of oral briefings allows analytical units to combine the strengths of the two formats. However, the use of placemats without oral briefings may come with a certain cost, notably when placemats carry less text and rely on the client being walked through them. This raises risks of misinterpretation. In addition, some interviewees indicated that products that rely more on visuals and less on text may create problems for institutional memory and corporate records down the road. When an analyst takes over a file, for example, they typically read what their predecessor wrote in the previous year or two. If there are fewer written products, transitions can be more difficult. This can also raise questions from a review and oversight perspective. The National Security and Intelligence Review Agency (NSIRA) and the National Security and Intelligence Committee of Parliamentarians (NSICOP) are meant to have access to intelligence community written records, but if more analysis is disseminated through placemats and oral briefings (see the next subsection), they may face additional hurdles in accessing relevant information. That said, even if these are valid concerns in theory, in practice interviewees emphasized that the IAS and

CFINTCOM, notably, now include fairly elaborate textboxes in their placemats (countering the argument that placemats are too thin as stand-alone products), and that analysts briefing on them now must prepare detailed speaking notes (thus keeping written records).

ORAL BRIEFINGS

Most senior clients interviewed emphasized that in-person briefings by analysts or their managers are very helpful, often as much or more than written products. But a minority disagreed. Some insisted on having their daily or weekly briefing books and were largely satisfied with only written analysis.

As many interviewees noted, there has been a trend in recent years, spearheaded by the IAS and CFINTCOM, to offer more direct oral briefings by analysts (with managers present) or by managers themselves, including to PMO, the clerk of the Privy Council (Canada's most senior civil servant), and the national security and intelligence adviser in the case of the IAS, and the minister and DM and the chief of the defence staff in the case of CFINTCOM.[7]

It was clear from our interviews that this trend of providing more oral briefings is welcome. In the words of one interviewee, "I prefer oral briefings, I get more from them." Oral briefings foster interaction between producer and consumer. This allows clients to identify specific questions and request additional products and allows analytical units to witness the reaction—verbal and often in terms of body language—of clients, providing far better feedback on which questions were answered and which were not, as well as on the preferred modes of information intake (longer or shorter presentations, more or less formal, etc.). One client, for example, expressed a preference for presentations starting with key judgements, briefly, and then letting the discussion flow.

In some cases, senior managers such as the commander of CFINTCOM (or the ACDI) or the head of the IAS provide the entire briefing; in others, the more senior official starts with an introduction (such as key judgements) before leaving the rest of the briefing to the analyst; and in others, the analyst provides the entire briefing. Many clients did not express a particular preference for either model. That said, some did express frustration at briefings by senior managers, viewing the result as diluted by multiple layers of approval or the managers as not having the expert knowledge of analysts. Those interviewees emphasized that oral briefings by analysts, or at least with the analysts present and authorized to answer questions, allow clients to poke deeper by asking precise questions. This provides clients with more detailed answers, and it also gives analysts a better understanding of client needs (the specific questions they have, their baseline level of knowledge, or their preferred briefing style). It also helps build trust between the two sides. According to one interviewee, "the best briefings I got from (defense intelligence) were when I could sit down directly with the analyst, talk through issues, discuss them. Analysts have tremendous knowledge. . . . Analysts typically have very low policy literacy, but by sitting down with them directly, I could prod them, ask specific questions, follow up."

After the creation of the DFIB, the next logical step for the IAS was to start offering oral briefings to senior clients in PCO and PMO. This started under Vincent Rigby, in the early years of Canada's participation in the war in Afghanistan, with weekly briefings to the national security adviser and PMO, and it subsequently steadily picked up momentum. Interestingly, one of the drivers for this initiative was pressure from Susan Cartwright, who was assistant secretary for foreign and defense policy in PCO at the time and who, according to one interviewee, asked "what the hell does the IAS do" and pushed its analysts to get out of the "IAS ivory tower." The IAS decided early on that analysts would do the briefings, with managers present. One interviewee emphasized that this decision did not come without costs, as some analysts were (and still are) poor briefers. In a context where clients are often reluctant to consult intelligence on a regular basis and many are skeptical of its value, mediocre briefings can easily convince them to forego asking for more. This risk was raised by multiple interviewees. The community's leadership is generally cognizant of the risk but calculates that allowing analysts to provide oral briefings is the only way to allow them to gain experience and to identify those who are skilled at it. The key, according to one official, is to minimize the exposure of poor briefers to clients as much as possible (and hopefully provide them with training to help them improve). Over the years, the IAS has entrenched the practice of regular oral briefings. It now provides weekly one-hour briefings to PMO (see the case study at the end of chapter 1).

CFINTCOM has adopted a different approach. Like the IAS, it provides more oral briefings than before. For its daily morning brief to the director of staff of the Strategic Joint Staff (which supports the chief of the defence staff on strategic issues), however, it selects one analyst who becomes the strategic briefer for four to six months. This individual then becomes a full-time briefer, allowing them to develop better briefing skills. This analyst also gains a strong understanding of the needs of senior clients, learns to anticipate questions, and develops more generalist skills (useful assets that are difficult for intelligence analysts to develop). Over time, this helps build a cadre of analysts with strong oral briefing and client management skills.[8] It is in this context that CFINTCOM now offers two verbal briefing courses as part of its set of training modules: how to brief, and how to brief when it is not your area of expertise.

Content

GOVERNMENT PRIORITIES

Many interviewees observed that while analytical products are usually well written and well informed, they are often not directly linked to a specific ongoing policy discussion. In these cases, senior clients will either ignore or lightly skim them. As one interviewee noted, "senior clients do not have time; they will not read it if it is not directly linked to their current priorities."

Consistent with the trends discussed in chapter 3, most interviewees on the policy side, serving and retired, were critical (often heavily so) of the intelligence community's performance at this level. In their view, too many analysts work without knowing why they write, who their target audience is, and what policy or process they support. This is a systemic problem in the Canadian intelligence community. Indeed, a frequent criticism, including by analysts themselves, is that too much analysis is "analysis for its own sake," not directly targeted to government priorities; too often, the intelligence community "wants to go where the intelligence leads them," as opposed to where policy has questions or knowledge gaps. According to another interviewee, "too often, I see (intelligence community) products and I think, who gives a damn, it is so far down in the weeds." The problem, many recognize, is not with the analysis itself; in abstract terms, it is usually quite good. More specifically, the weakness is at the level of its relevance. "We are very good at generic analysis but still weak at digging into Canadian interests, to go from the macro to the specific implications for Canada."

This directly links to the issues of timeliness and of the community's limited ability to adapt to constantly shifting priorities. Many policy officials criticized the analytical community at this level. It "sometimes just can't keep up because events are going too fast." One interviewee criticized the community for chasing "priorities from last year; it takes them time to zero in, even though they are small." Another cited ITAC: its "analysis is typically good, but often my reaction is that it would have been more useful if I had not seen it in the *Economist* two weeks ago; it's often too late to be useful." This is an especially sore point for many policy officials, who must be nimble in their work and who spend a good proportion of their time managing daily fires.

There are valid counterarguments to such criticism. As some of our interviewees note, the policy side typically does not express its priorities and needs clearly, making it inherently difficult for the analytical side to respond—except, as one official noted, in times of crisis: needs are then more precise, making it more straightforward for analysts. Moreover, as another official pointed out, the relatively small size of the analytical community means that it cannot cover multiple countries and topics; when a crisis—such as a coup—suddenly occurs in a country that it barely covers, it can be difficult to respond to sudden requests.

The intelligence analysis community's limited ability to respond to government priorities is a weakness. Nevertheless, the situation has, here again, steadily improved over the years. Until a few years ago, the IAS and CFINTCOM, in particular, were far more systematically dismissed by senior policy makers than today. There is still much scope for improvement, but senior officials would not carve time out of their busy schedules for oral briefings if they did not view them as useful. The DMNS committee (responsible for high-level policy matters, discussed in chapter 1), for example, now makes an effort to circulate its forward agenda to the intelligence community six months ahead to help it plan its work and provide it with opportunities to target its analysis in support of its work.

Interviewees provided examples of this trend of greater success in responding to government priorities. One emphasized that PSC has been properly served by well-targeted CSIS analysis for its work establishing and managing the list of terrorist entities. A few others also mentioned that they viewed the work of FINTRAC—even though its mandate is more circumscribed, so typically more useful in support of law enforcement than high-level policy making—as generally satisfying. Illustrating how the situation has progressed, other officials argued that the analytical community's performance in responding to more recent threats (such as cybersecurity and economic espionage) has not been optimal, but certainly better than its performance in responding to the threats of ten or fifteen years ago (such as the war in Afghanistan).

Another point that came up regularly during interviews was that analytical units often perform better during periods of crises. During these short bursts of acute pressure, Canadian priorities tend to become suddenly far clearer, and higher up the agenda. There is, as such, a precise and pressing need for analysis for specific clients, which is not typically the case under normal circumstances. One interviewee highlighted the role of intelligence analysis to support the resolution of complex cases of kidnappings, where it was "extremely useful." According to this individual, the analysis concretely helped officials on the policy and operational side "to know who to trust, who to talk to, who says what to whom, what could be our leverage, what to ask and not to ask." Similarly, another official cited the example of the aftermath of the major earthquake in Haiti in 2010 where intelligence analysis helped with decision-making.

PESSIMISM BIAS

There is a widespread perception among clients, frequently expressed in interviews, that the analytical community has a systematic tendency to err on the side of pessimism. More precisely, there is, in the words of one official, a tendency to "inflate threats, and also to equate all risks, that is, to fail to segregate or breakdown different components of a broader risk or threat." The community, in the words of another, is often "rigid, it fails to compartmentalize, it fails to assess different degrees of threat." This is an important source of frustration for clients. Risk-averse analysis that assumes the worse is often of less use. Unlike analysts, policy makers cannot simply throw their hands up in the air; they must find solutions, and analysis which merely explains "how bad the situation is" fails to provide support in the identification of solutions and to tell clients something they do not already know.

Interviewees provided multiple examples. On Afghanistan, for example, one interviewee lamented that the analysis was all "doom and gloom. . . . I thought, OK, but what can we do?"[9] On China, to take a more recent example, the Trudeau government had publicly stated its willingness to engage after it assumed power in 2015, but as one interviewee explained, too much of the analysis it received from the community mainly emphasized that "China is bad . . . which is not helpful." As another official argued, it would have been far more helpful for analytical units to identify and frame the real "no-go zones"—areas where they assess the government should avoid engaging with China—and to define and explain the parameters in which engagement would be risky but not off-limits. It is not "sustainable," in this official's view, to keep on repeating "you can't go there" without damaging the relationship with clients.

OPPORTUNITY ANALYSIS

This debate on the community's pessimism bias highlights the reality that threat analysis in a conventional sense is sometimes of limited interest for senior policy makers, especially because it is rarely actionable. It matters much more in a context where analysis supports law enforcement or military operations, but for high-level policy making, it is of less frequent use on a day-to-day basis. Would the production of more opportunity analysis (also referred to as *options analysis, scenarios analysis,* or *competitive political analysis*) help the community provide a better service? Interviewees provided different answers to this question. Many said yes, but a smaller number were less enthusiastic.

Opportunity analysis can take a variety of forms.[10] At its most basic level, the analyst defines a problem and then analyzes a small number of options to deal with it, without taking the last step of recommending one. One official described this kind of analysis as providing "tiered courses of actions with costs and benefits for each; the client can then manage risk" by being better informed in choosing one option. This is, admittedly, a more expansive conception of the role of intelligence analysis, defining it more broadly than being focused only on threat. According to this view, intelligence analysis is most useful when it is multiphased; if it is focused on a single point, it narrows its impact. The ideal intelligence report, as such, is "phased in time." It first provides a "factual snapshot of current conditions" (the capabilities and intentions of the adversary). It also asks, "How will the conditions change if I intervene? How will adversary intent evolve? How will the balance of costs and benefits for me and the adversary evolve on the basis of my, and its, actions?"

Does the Canadian intelligence community conduct opportunity analysis? According to our interviews, there have been some attempts over the years, but they have mostly been limited and *ad hoc*. The IAS has dabbled in the practice, for example, deciding to make it more of a priority in its range of analytical products. (It labels it "competitive political analysis"). Nevertheless, opportunity analysis remains relatively rare in Canada compared to some of its allies. Multiple interviewees emphasized that they had seen it done by Five Eyes partners, especially the US, and found it appealing. One official spoke of "a cultural shift" in the US intelligence community that has led it to increase its use of opportunity analysis in recent years, even if there still remains much resistance. This, the official noted, has been accompanied by the development of training courses to support analysts.

Many policy officials we interviewed expressed a wish to receive more opportunity analysis. One of them, for example, insisted that "I like it and think we could do more of it"; another, from the political world, argued that it would be "absolutely welcome." As one interviewee emphasized, the leadership of the intelligence community is "said to think about" doing more. But, this official emphasized, "we are not there yet; analysts need a much better understanding of the policy context and connections to policy counterparts, which we simply do not have."

There are advantages and disadvantages for analytical units going down this road. In our interviews we found three general positions: those in favor, those who saw its appeal but felt it would be too resource intensive or that it would steer analytical units away from their core mandates, and traditionalists opposed to such initiatives. Arguments in favor note that it provides what is often a missing link between threat analysis (actor *x* is bad) and the government's response (what to do about *x*). For many policy makers, intelligence products focused on threat analysis are usually "an FYI," as one interviewee described it: "That's the state of play, that sounds bad, but that's it. . . . It's not helpful on what we could do to change the issue or protect or promote some interest." More useful would be products combining the state of play with an analysis of possible responses. Policy makers regularly use such analysis in multiple sectors; from their perspective, the oft-heard argument that "this is not intelligence's job" is neither convincing nor relevant.

The major challenge, which proponents recognize, is that calling for more opportunity analysis is easy to say but hard to do. It is, first, labor intensive. Good opportunity analysis takes time; in a context of scarce resources, asking for more means, in practice, getting less of something else. One interviewee on the management side of the analytical community, who was sympathetic to the idea in principle, offered this note of caution: "We cannot institutionalize it and make it automatic—we simply would not have the human resources for that, because it is time consuming and requires much more skill and expertise." The latter point matters because opportunity analysis can only succeed if the analytical unit is closely linked to its client organization(s) and is deeply aware of the policy context. As one interviewee familiar with the necessary methodologies emphasized, analysts need "a real link to the government's agenda and priorities." This raises two important obstacles: first, limited policy literacy in the intelligence community would need to be improved and, second, the frequent lack of clearly defined objectives of Canadian foreign policy would make the development of concrete options challenging in many cases.

To be relevant, moreover, opportunity analysis must flirt with the policy line without being prescriptive; in practice, this is a difficult balance to strike. Asking the Canadian intelligence community to do this would be difficult. As interviewees pointed out, the culture of the community is risk averse. Many analysts are so convinced of the need to refrain from crossing the line into policy prescription that they typically commit the opposite mistake: they stray too far from it. Highlighting that it is a difficult balance to strike should not, however, be a definitive counterargument. Policy units in the bureaucracy have learned to strike difficult balances on a daily basis, providing politically sensitive but nonpartisan advice.

This, of course, raises the objection that it is the job of policy, not intelligence, to conduct opportunity analysis. This is partly valid, but not entirely. Policy units indeed perform analysis of options; it is central to the policy development process. But policy units are frequently overstretched, and often do not have time to conduct systematic and in-depth options analysis. In addition, intelligence analysts often have subject matter expertise and analytical tradecraft lacking in policy units. Senior policy makers, moreover, frequently insist that they want more. A middle course leveraging the strengths of each side could, as such, see intelligence analysts analyzing the likelihood of success of policy options developed by the relevant policy unit.

A third view emerged in our interviews from a small but significant minority, those who strongly opposed experiments with opportunity analysis. This opposition was largely rooted in a defense of the status quo and a traditional view of the role of intelligence. Those who hold this view raised valid concerns about the consequences that might follow from getting closer to policy. One official firmly said no: "Not having it reinforces the 'just the facts' strength of intelligence analysis. . . . Others do it in the government." Another made a similar point: the intelligence community should "absolutely not" do it because the job of intelligence analysis is to "agree upon a set of facts; anything more, and products become distrusted." Similarly, critics argued that it would raise risks of politicization, of telling politicians what they want to hear, skewing the pros and cons of the analysis to favor particular outcomes.

Should intelligence analysis units increase their efforts to conduct opportunity analysis, part of the answer to such criticism is that their work would have to remain carefully scoped. One official proposed such a compromise: the community should provide opportunity analysis, but it should focus on relatively well-circumscribed policy problems, not "meta-issues." Its opportunity analysis should not aim to represent the definitive answer but rather to propose one input among others. It should, in particular, not forget the distinction between evidence and advice. To be able to do this, analysts and their managers would need to become more comfortable entering the grey zone between threat analysis and policy prescription, while always refraining from actual prescription.[11] This does not come without risk, but there is an important distinction between analysis and advocacy that, if well understood, can be workable. As one interviewee argued, advocacy asks "what levers should we pull," whereas analysis looks at "what levers do we have, and what are the pros and cons of using each."

BLUE FORCE ANALYSIS

The Canadian intelligence community has traditionally been reluctant to do blue force analysis (that is, to analyze the capabilities and intentions of allies and friends). This is a frequent source of frustration for policy clients; in the words of one of them, "That is often what we need." Yet for many in the Canadian intelligence community, this is a red line, in part as a result of a traditional "we don't spy on allies" mantra. But analyzing the intentions and actions of allies and partners is not the same as clandestinely collecting information on them.

It is true that, to some extent, it is the work of policy (and operational) units to look at the intentions, capabilities, and actions of partners and allies. The dynamic here is similar to the one previously described with opportunity analysis. Policy units do incorporate this in their work, but they often lack sufficient time and resources. Senior clients, moreover, frequently lament that the intelligence analysis they receive is too narrowly focused on "red forces" (adversaries) and ignores allies and partners. This, from their point of view, is problematic and means that often many consider that they do not receive an optimal service. To address this tension, there is a potential compromise whereby intelligence analysis better incorporates the capabilities, intentions, and policies of allies and partners as a secondary priority, with the top one remaining its focus on adversaries. This would better serve clients and would be complementary, not redundant, to policy work. This is especially true with regard to the US. Canada has no greater foreign policy interest than managing relations with the US, which directly implies that optimal decision-making requires a heavy input analyzing US capabilities, options, decision-making processes, and strategies.[12]

INTELLIGENCE PROFILES

Analytical units in Canada have traditionally been reluctant to write intelligence profiles—short documents focusing on a foreign leader, such as a head of state or minister, or other prominent figures, such as terrorists, describing their background, politics, ideology, and character. Some analysts derisively refer to profiles as "glorified journalism" and do not consider it as part of their mandate. We found, however, a near consensus among clients that they are useful and that they would appreciate receiving more. Many interviewees reported, for example, finding them especially useful before meeting counterparts.

OPEN SOURCE

Multiple interviewees emphasized how slow the community has been at adapting and improving its skills to exploit open-source intelligence (OSINT).[13] As one interviewee noted, we "badly need better skills at exploiting OS. . . . There are so many answers to our questions that are available in OS and are more available than through classified means." This individual added that "we put too much emphasis on covert sources of information and not enough on open sources. What do covert sources tell me that I cannot know otherwise?" As this individual and others pointed out, the community invests exponentially fewer resources in OS than in clandestine collection.

There are still many negative perceptions throughout the intelligence community on the value of OSINT. Many still condescendingly believe that it is not much more than browsing the newspapers and that, as one interviewee put it, "if the data is not classified, it is worth less." This is, in the eyes of most senior clients we interviewed, a significant problem which has a negative impact on the quality of analysis and on productivity. That said, one official who reviewed a draft of this chapter in the late spring of 2020 made the interesting observation, which would benefit from further study in the future, that the COVID-19 pandemic is "shak[ing] the cobwebs from the last redoubts in the Five Eyes who devalued OSINT," including in Canada, as many analysts are forced to work from home without access to classified systems.

As many interviewees emphasized, senior clients have access to multiple sources of information. This is an important point often misunderstood in the intelligence community. As one explained, policy makers are willing to consume intelligence to keep abreast of important developments, but "we (also) have our own information channels," such as social and traditional media, other government analysis, and other stakeholders. Moreover, from the clients' perspective, "OS is much faster."

We heard similar arguments from interviewees in the US. During the Arab uprisings in 2011, for example, the situation was moving extremely rapidly. Intelligence often could not keep pace, forcing officials on the policy side to seek information from open sources. One official, for example, explained how the intelligence community was not providing analysis suggesting that the Libyan opposition was about to take Tripoli in August, while they could find this information on Twitter. Part of the problem is a slow approval process, which leads analytical products to be outpaced by the more flexible social media. More broadly, as new actors emerged and old ones fell, the entire process of requirements, collection, source recruitment, analysis, and so on was slow to adapt. That being said, this individual emphasized that even though there remains scope for improvement, the US intelligence community is steadily getting better at incorporating OS in its work.

One interviewee from the policy world estimated at 95 percent the amount of information provided by intelligence that they could get from OS. Another argued that "a study I did showed that *The Economist* was as good as SIGINT except for the most operationally focused analysis"; in this official's view, 80 to 90 percent of the information relevant to their needs is available in open sources. Some in intelligence would disagree with such numbers. Part of the disagreement can be explained by what is measured. While the intelligence side would rightly claim that more than 5 or 10 percent of the information they collect cannot be accessed through open sources, some on the policy side would reply that while that may be true, what matters, from their perspective, is that much of that unique information is too detailed to be relevant for their purposes. Ultimately, what matters is that it is a common perception on the policy side, and this inevitably leads many prospective clients to focus on consuming open-source information.

An ideal process is to build as comprehensive a picture as possible using OSINT, which is less costly and often nimbler, and then to fill in gaps and validate the preliminary picture with classified intelligence. This is a balance that Canadian intelligence does not achieve well, though interviewees agreed that the situation is steadily improving. In the words of one, "we worked hard to convince the intelligence community to increase its use of OS"; there has been "much resistance but slowly but surely it is more accepted." A number of organizations, such as CFINTCOM, have established OSINT cells, though work remains to fully integrate them into the work of the intelligence analysis enterprise. Many challenges remain for the community to more systematically incorporate OSINT into its work. One obstacle is cultural: many analysts and their managers still view OSINT as less reliable and useful. As one official highlighted, there are important generational differences at this level, such as younger analysts tending to favor social media. There are also technical obstacles; in some workspaces, such as CFINTCOM, many websites are still firewalled, preventing analysts from accessing them.[14]

Similarly, the analytical community often fails to make optimal use of external knowledge. Multiple interviewees agreed that the community underexploits external expertise and that it would gain by doing it more, even though they recognized that it has improved over the years. In particular, some interviewees mentioned the Academic Outreach Program at CSIS, renamed the Academic Outreach and Stakeholder Engagement Program in 2019, as a successful initiative to leverage external expertise. Established in 2008, the program established itself as a model emulated by other intelligence services in allied and partner countries. It has developed an extensive network of contacts in academia, think tanks, and other circles with potentially relevant expertise. It has also emerged as nimble and creative in its ability to set up events—workshops, lunchtime briefings, and informal discussions with various levels of the chain of command—to bring the universes of external experts and of the intelligence community together. Importantly, it has become, over the years, valued by analysts elsewhere in the community outside CSIS. The program is not without its critics, however. There are some inside CSIS, in particular, who view it as primarily geared toward supporting the executive and of limited use for analysts and intelligence officers.[15]

A successful outreach program can bring important benefits. Even though there is significant subject matter expertise throughout its agencies and departments, the community inevitably faces limits, either because of its small size or the inherent limitations to its ability to gather information. Some academics, journalists, and nongovernmental organization workers, for example, have access to people who would not normally open up to intelligence services, while business people can bring a different perspective and access to competing data sets. Even when they do not bring original data to the interaction, external experts can provide a useful challenge function. This is necessary to counter the inevitable tendency toward groupthink. In the words of one interviewee, too often the intelligence community's default assumption is "things are muddling along, slowly getting worse . . . it has a hard time analyzing and foreseeing disruption." Another interviewee pointed out that the intelligence community also has a tendency to over-rely on intelligence about the capabilities and intentions of rulers, and to neglect other sectors of society. This was a weakness, in particular, at the time of the Arab uprisings, when new actors emerged in civil society in countries such as Egypt and Libya on which there was little or no intelligence but on which external experts—notably in academia, civil society, and the media—had expertise.

The Role of Methods

A large majority of interviewees on the client side of the intelligence policy nexus confirmed that methodology (discussed in chapter 2) is, at best, of limited importance to them. A number went further and openly expressed their irritation with the frequent use of jargon and process-heavy analytical techniques. As one argued, "sometimes products are so heavily caveated, they are difficult to understand." Some interviewees were scathing and blunt: most methods are "boring and useless, and they make clients flee." Analysts should use instead, according to this official, "clear and precise language." This official, like others, was particularly annoyed at the tendency for analysts to hedge by using "almost certainly" as opposed to "will" when anticipating actions or events. This, in their view, muddles the analysis and makes it heavier and less precise. As one interviewee summed up, "methodology matters, but it can be dangerous. . . . It can hamper the ability to be effective and relevant." Because it is also time consuming, it can hamper analysts' ability to deliver products on time; a late product based on a rigorous methodology, this individual insisted, is useless.

Interviewees, with only a small number of exceptions, were especially hostile to the use of probability ratings, levels of confidence, and other forms of conditional language, with one referring to these as "utterly useless" and only managing to irritate senior readers and drive their attention away. Referring to degrees of confidence, another stated plainly, "I hate that. . . . It does not mean anything to too many people outside the intelligence community. Analysts are better off using plain language." Many interviewees singled out for particular scorn what they viewed as the excessive use of the word "likely," which makes the analysis "clunky." Too much conditionality, interviewees agreed, makes the analysis "less fungible and usable."

As some interviewees noted, this is a challenge common to many, and probably all, expert communities in government. Senior officials who had rotated in policy positions in, for example, the economic, social, or health fields reported similar frustrations; one, only half in jest, said that "stuff produced by lawyers is even more incomprehensible." The challenge for every expert community is to know the audience and adapt its products. Yet too often, many analysts view this condescendingly as dumbing down their work. This, our research showed, is an area where there remains significant scope for improvement (see the conclusion for more on this).

Despite these misgivings, interviewees on both the policy and intelligence sides recognized that methods can be useful and perhaps necessary—provided they are used discretely and with plain language.[16] ITAC, for example, has developed methodologies to evaluate the terrorism threat to Canada.[17] Interestingly, some of the clearest examples of the relevant use of methodologies provided by interviewees referred to instances of analysis in support of operations rather than policy. CSIS, for example, has developed a matrix to determine whether or not to appraise the minister of public safety of high-risk operations, taking into consideration political, diplomatic, and security risks. When the operation meets a certain threshold of high risk, the minister usually gets read in. The National Fisheries Intelligence Service (the unit within Fisheries and Oceans Canada tasked with providing intelligence analysis to support fishery officers in enforcing the Fisheries Act) has also developed a rigorous methodology to determine which targets to prioritize. To do so, it weighs different factors, such as the threat on the resource, the scarcity of the resource, and the degree of criminality of the target. Analysts fill a grid and then prioritize targets. This is labor intensive in terms of the human resources required to "populate" the grid, but it is necessary to ensure that scarce resources are allocated optimally.[18]

Overclassification

As noted in the section on open-source information, a common perception inside the intelligence community is that the higher the product's classification, the better it is. Yet this is another hindrance to the community's ability to provide an optimal service to clients.[19] Our research clearly shows that there is a strong belief on the consumer side—but also an understanding on the producer side—that this is a significant problem. Interviewees, for example, said, "Yes, it's a problem . . . products are way overclassified"; "as a policy person, I am frustrated by that"; "on a five-page report on a cyberattack, three or four small points made it top secret . . . [that] unnecessarily restricts" the impact. Another official argued, "Most products going to policy should be at secret or less. There is rarely a need for more." There is, importantly, similar criticism among clients of the US intelligence community. Policy officials in the State Department, for example, often find it unnecessarily complicated to work at the top-secret level.

Higher classification comes at a cost, and sometimes a significant one. It makes distribution slower and logistically more complex, constraining the ability to access senior clients in a timely manner. As many interviewees explained, it also reduces the usability of intelligence products. For senior policy makers, it is often an unnecessary irritation to have to wonder whether they can use a certain piece of information in a specific setting or not. It is especially costly because senior clients, notably those from the political world, move at a fast pace, and overclassification makes dissemination unwieldy and slow. As a result, for many of our interviewees from the policy and political side, "intelligence is constantly behind the curve."

A majority of interviewees highlighted this as "definitely a problem." Products at high classification levels—typically top secret and above—are especially difficult to consume for political staffers, who often do not work in spaces with the required facilities to discuss and store them and who are often reluctant to take the time to reach secure areas and be locked into them without access to their phones. Often, the higher classification adds little or nothing from the client's point of view but comes at a serious cost in terms of usability and dissemination. One interviewee from the intelligence world agreed that this is a major problem: "I confess I tried very hard (to change this) but it is a battle I lost. . . . There is huge resistance within the intelligence community."

It is also problematic for policy clients, notably at GAC or DND, because many in those organizations do not have high-level clearances. This is even more the case with nontraditional partners, those agencies and departments that have not historically played an important security role but are increasingly called upon to help counter emerging threats, such as foreign meddling (Elections Canada) and foreign investment by state-owned enterprises in sensitive fields (Innovation, Science, and Economic Development Canada). In those organizations, even fewer staff have top-secret clearances, while access to secure zones and computer systems is scarce.

Moreover, policy people—especially senior officials but even junior analysts—are reluctant to spend time going back and forth between their offices and secure areas (known as sensitive compartmented information facilities, or SCIFs), especially when, as discussed throughout this book, there is limited appetite to consume intelligence to begin with. In GAC headquarters in Ottawa in particular, in most of the building, conversations and documents can only be held up to the secret level. Missions abroad have similar limitations; some do not even have SCIFs. As one interviewee explained, the logistics of dealing with top-secret information and products in GAC is a "nightmare." It is also problematic on the political side. Many political staffers in ministerial offices and in PMO do not have top-secret clearances. The prime minister and ministers also travel a lot, including inside Canada, implying that even getting low classification products to them can be complicated, let alone top-secret ones.

The intelligence community's difficulty in working in unclassified or low-classification environments makes engagement with nongovernmental stakeholders far more complex. Such engagement has become increasingly frequent in recent years, notably to address emerging threats such as elections meddling and foreign investment. The community, for example, has increased its engagement with universities and industry. This requires adaptation, especially to share unclassified information—what one interviewee referred to as the "unclassified privileged space." Some individuals working with nongovernmental stakeholders have received clearances over the years, but only a small number (and few have secure spaces anyways). Yet despite the government's commitment to such engagement, there remains resistance and risk aversion in the intelligence community to work at the unclassified level and to share information with uncleared, nongovernmental partners.

"Slowly but surely," as one interviewee assessed, there has been progress as the intelligence community steadily better understands the trade-off between classification and usability/dissemination and learns to make more effort to provide analysis at lower classifications. One interviewee, for example, emphasized how CSE has made considerable efforts recently to declassify more. It extracts secret portions from top-secret documents so that they can be circulated more, and it also more frequently offers different classifications for individual paragraphs. CSE has also invested in more training for its analysts to help them learn how to lower classification levels. This individual specified that the establishment of the Canadian Centre for Cyber Security has forced CSE to accelerate these efforts as its products generally have to be unclassified.[20] ITAC has, similarly, made efforts to evolve in this direction. It now has a portal for first responders, for example, on which it posts unclassified assessments; ITAC aims to be "quite liberal" on access to this portal. It has also named a "champion of releasability," who is the deputy director general for production management (in charge of making sure requests for information are actioned on time). This has allowed ITAC to increase the dissemination of its products.

Case Study: Canadian Forces Intelligence Command

The defense intelligence function in Canada has undergone major organizational and cultural changes in the past two decades. As of September 2001, it was led by the director general intelligence, or DGInt. The organization (also then referred to as DGInt) was widely viewed as dysfunctional, with major human resources problems. It was mostly focused on military operations, viewing operational commanders as its main clients. It had few contacts with the policy world and limited influence with the senior levels of the department. Within the broader intelligence community, DGInt was a marginal player. In the words of one interviewee, it was "seriously broken."

With the support of the Defence Management Committee, then the highest-level internal body, the DM and the chief of the defence staff launched a comprehensive top-to-bottom review. The goal was to overhaul not only DGInt but also the defense intelligence function as a whole (that is, intelligence activities conducted by other DND/CAF units outside DGInt, notably by the three services and by operational commands). The effort led to the *Defence Intelligence Review* (DIR). Completed in 2003, the DIR highlighted major problems and vulnerabilities with the defense intelligence function and made a range of recommendations to overhaul it.

The DIR's most visible recommendations were to change DGInt's name to the Chief of Defence Intelligence (CDI) and make its head a two-star officer instead of a one-star. Whereas DGInt did not have authority over parts of the defense intelligence function, CDI would now be the functional authority over the entire function throughout DND/CAF. And whereas in the past DGInt reported to the deputy chief of the defence staff (a position abolished in subsequent reforms, chiefly responsible for operations), CDI would now report to the Chief of the Defence staff and the DM. The objective was to give greater visibility and access to defense intelligence at senior levels on both the military and civilian sides.

The DIR called for the creation of the role of director general for intelligence production, a new position held by a civilian reporting directly to CDI.[21] The objective here was that a senior civilian responsible for analysis would be better able to steer the organization to look more to the civilian side of the department, which had previously not been much on its radar, and to enhance defense intelligence's status within the intelligence community in Ottawa and with allies. The DIR further recommended—even though some interviewees were reluctant to use the term—a certain civilianization of CDI, an increase in civilian representation from the director general for intelligence production down to mid-level managers and analysts.[22] The organization also cleaned house. According to one interviewee, it pushed into retirement a generation of colonels who were resisting change and had been, in some cases, responsible for the internal dysfunction.

The DIR encouraged CDI to continue providing analytical support to operations, but also to increase its focus on senior-level decision-making in DND and the CAF and to better promote its products. As a result, the first director general for intelligence production, Linda Goldthorp, canceled DGInt's flagship analytical product, the *Weekly Intelligence Digest*, which was long and unwieldy and, according to interviewees, not viewed positively in senior circles. Instead, she established the shorter—and more frequent—*Daily Intelligence Digest* (discussed previously).

In 2013, CDI was renamed the Canadian Forces Intelligence Command (CFINTCOM). This implied that the commander of CFINTCOM, notably, gained greater authorities and autonomy. The role of director general for intelligence production was renamed the assistant chief of defence intelligence (responsible for a steadily broader remit) and formally became the civilian second-in-command for CFINTCOM. This emulates the model of allies, such as the US (the Defense Intelligence Agency) and the UK (the Defence Intelligence Staff), where there is a similar burden-sharing.[23] According to interviewees, the defense intelligence function as a whole employs close to four thousand individuals, both civilian and military, with about one thousand working in CFINTCOM. The others mostly work in the intelligence units of the three services (army, navy, and air force) and of the two operational commands (Canadian Joint Operations Command and Canadian Special Operations Forces Command). The defense intelligence budget is not publicly available; the NSICOP *Annual Report 2018*, for example, redacts the section where it is discussed (National Security and Intelligence Committee of Parliamentarians 2019, 61).

The mandate of the commander of CFINTCOM, who is still also the chief of defence intelligence, is to oversee the provision of "credible, timely, and integrated defence intelligence capabilities, products, and services" in support of Canada's national security objectives (Department of National Defence 2018). CFINTCOM collects more types of intelligence than any other agency or department in the federal government (human, signals, open-source, imagery, geospatial, medical, meteorological, among others, while it also has counterintelligence responsibilities). As such, it is, by some measures, the organization in the intelligence community with the broadest mandate. CFINTCOM has two specific tasks. First, to support military operations, it collects intelligence, including with deployable capabilities, through the Joint Imagery Centre, the National Counter-Intelligence Unit, the Mapping and Charting Establishment, the Joint Meteorological Centre, and Joint Task Force X (which collects human intelligence). Second, it provides analysis, strategic warning, and threat assessments to support decision-making in DND/CAF and the broader government of Canada, as well as in support of CAF operations.[24]

The commander of CFINTCOM is a two-star/flag officer, and is supported in his or her duties by the ACDI, a civilian with the rank of EX-3 (director general). This position is responsible for the analytical function, with two teams, each led by a civilian director, one for transnational and regional intelligence and one for scientific and technical intelligence. More recently, the ACDI also became responsible for review and compliance, leading a team in charge of coordinating defense intelligence remits to the new review and oversight bodies (NSIRA and NSICOP) and conducting compliance evaluations of intelligence activities throughout the CAF. A fourth team, the Directorate of Intelligence Production Management, also falls under the ACDI's responsibility. It manages, among other issues, the editing and dissemination of analytical products as well as training and professional development.

While the quality of defense intelligence analysis was "abysmal" two decades ago, in the words of one official, it has since significantly improved, according to every interviewee who spoke on this issue. There was, however, no firm consensus on the extent of this improvement. Though all agreed that more can be done, some believe that it is now "in the big leagues," while others still believe that CFINTCOM "punches below its weight." The command now views the DM, the Policy Group (led by the ADM for policy, broadly the equivalent to the undersecretary of defense for policy in the US), and the ADM responsible for procurement as important clients. This was not the case in the past. As one interviewee recalled, the Policy Group often had a dysfunctional relationship with CDI, largely because the latter focused its energies toward the military, not the civilian side. The creation of the position of the ACDI, in particular, has helped rebalance this.

The core regional analysis team, the directorate of transnational and regional intelligence, today is far better connected outside the defense intelligence function, both in DND/CAF and throughout the intelligence community. Its analysts and managers regularly provide oral briefings to senior officials, on both the civilian and military sides, and beyond throughout senior levels of the government, and their written products are disseminated and read far more than in the past. The unit still faces challenges including, as discussed in chapter 2, on the human resources front. The Directorate of Scientific and Technical Intelligence provides a capability that is genuinely unique in Ottawa; as one interviewee put it, "no one else does" what it does. Its experts on topics ranging from missiles to chemical and biological weapons, in particular, are widely respected, even among Five Eyes partners. One interviewee recalled, for example, how its expertise on chemical weapons, when used in Syria in the first years of the war in the country that began in 2011, was a "great asset" that "really increased CDI's exposure."

One interviewee cited the close collaboration between the Policy Group and CFINTCOM in the drafting phases of the Liberal government's defense policy— Strong, Secure, Engaged—released in 2017, as a good example of intelligence successfully supporting policy (Department of National Defence 2017c). Before the government formally launched the process of developing the new policy, defense officials correctly planned that it would be necessary to start preliminary analysis in anticipation of the work to come. They wanted the eventual policy to be premised on a long-term assessment of Canada's strategic environment. The Directorate of Strategic Analysis, the unit in the Policy Group charged with leading this effort, consulted CFINTCOM (and others in the intelligence community) and came up with a global view of threats to Canada; one official described this cooperation as "fantastic" and fully agreed that intelligence "shaped" the result. The resulting long paper, which was even discussed by a committee of DMs (GTFAD, for Global Trends, Foreign Affairs, and Defence), eventually became the fourth chapter in the policy, which analyses the global context.

5 RECOMMENDATIONS AND THE WAY AHEAD

OUR RESEARCH MAKES IT CLEAR that there has been an improvement in the performance of intelligence analysis in supporting policy making in Canada since 2001. Nevertheless, there is much that can still be improved in the intelligence policy nexus. On a positive note, the Canadian intelligence and national security community is increasingly aware that the nature of emerging and evolving threats and the uncertain international environment mean that it needs to provide better and more timely analysis to support policy makers. Some, such as PCO/IAS, CSE, and CFINTCOM, have been making gradual improvements over the past decade. Others, like CSIS/IAB, are coming later to the game but are increasingly finding their footing with new products and modes of delivery. Yet there is still room for improvement when it comes to the governance and structure of the analytical community as a whole, human resources management, the management of the intelligence policy interface, and in delivering the kinds of products that policy makers need.

The literature on improving analysis is overwhelmingly dominated by the US experience. In addition, this literature tends to focus on analysts and the techniques they use more than on the environment and context they find themselves in. Therefore, this last chapter adds to the literature on managing intelligence policy dynamics. Our focus remains on the Canadian context, but many of the suggestions and lessons offered here are applicable elsewhere.

A final caveat is warranted. We conducted our interviews in 2018–19 and finished writing this book in the summer of 2020. It would be naive to believe that government budgets will be similar to what existed prior to the COVID-19 pandemic. Some initiatives may not be financially possible in the years ahead. At the same time, the pandemic has resulted in new and evolving threats in terms of cybersecurity and violent extremism, while the international environment continues to shift. Although outside the time period of our study, senior members of the intelligence community have noted to us throughout 2020 and early 2021, as we were finalizing this manuscript, that there is more, not less, demand for their products, including with nontraditional partners and consumers. In this sense, it is possible that the intelligence community may exit the pandemic with a clientele that has never been more diverse and educated in the use of its products—meaning there may be more of a willingness to invest. Regardless, many of our recommendations, particularly around product delivery and community coordination, are of little or no cost. The key issue is whether or not there is enough will to enact change.

Governance and Structure

STRENGTHENING THE CENTER

Most interviewees agreed that the Canadian intelligence analysis community needs a stronger center, but there was much divergence on the extent to which the center should be strengthened and on precisely how to do this. Suggestions ranged from forming a US-style, powerful center combining some of the functions of the National Security Council and the Office of the Director of National Intelligence, at one end of the continuum of views, to marginally strengthening the role of the national security and intelligence adviser (NSIA) by only tinkering with the current system.

In our view, there is a strong case in favor of a moderately more powerful center. This would allow for an enhanced coordination and community-building function and would better position PCO to support cabinet and relevant DM-level committees. A stronger center would help prioritize collection and analysis, foster closer cooperation between intelligence and policy, encourage the development of higher literacy on both sides of the intelligence policy divide, and ensure better communication throughout the system. A stronger center would also gain a better ability to challenge other actors across the community. But to do this, the center—that is, PCO/IAS and the NSIA—need an enhanced ability to work horizontally across the community, and thus both need more resources as well as a stronger mandate. Critics of proposals to strengthen the center rightly highlight that too much centralization can stifle the autonomy of individual departments and agencies and that the concrete benefits are unclear.[1] This is a valid concern, but this is one of many areas where the Canadian debate differs from the US one. In Canada, despite the strengthening of the office of the NSIA in recent years, the position remains relatively weak, in terms of the size of its staff, budget, and authority (as noted in chapter 1). The office has not, in our view, reached the tipping point where added responsibility and capacity would bring diminishing or negative returns.

The first step to strengthen the center of the analytical community should be to boost PCO/IAS's role. At the level of analytical coordination and leadership, a stronger IAS is a necessary condition for the development of better community-wide standards, as well as enhanced professionalization, training, and professional development. These improvements, discussed in greater detail below, simply cannot be achieved without a greater level of central leadership. A number of interviewees raised parallels here with the Office of National Intelligence in Australia, which in many ways resembles the IAS. The Office of National Intelligence, widely respected in the Five Eyes community for the high quality and relevance of its analysis, plays a stronger coordination role in the Australian analytical community than the IAS currently does.

The IAS's new powers should focus on analytical coordination and leadership, and on policy development with regard to the analytical function across the intelligence community. The IAS performs this role now, but in an ad hoc manner and with very limited resources. To a partial extent, a stronger IAS would mirror some of the functions that the director of national intelligence plays in the US. More specifically, it would partly resemble analytical leadership and coordination responsibilities under the director of national intelligence's Mission Integration directorate. This would send a strong signal to the rest of the community that intelligence analysis is important.[2]

Organizationally, this stronger role for the IAS should primarily be located under the current director of operations, the number two official in the secretariat. Four separate teams should be established under his or her authority:

- A community-wide excellence center for human resources, training, and development. The director of operations is already responsible for the Intelligence Analysis Learning Program (IALP), as discussed in chapter 2, but this team would have a stronger leadership role, notably to better coordinate between the IALP and individual training units throughout the community, and to develop and enforce community-wide standards. The IALP, as discussed below, would also increase the quality and quantity of the courses it offers. This team would, in addition, work to develop and enforce community standards on hiring and retaining high-quality analysts.

- A new intelligence analysis policy coordination function. This team would be responsible for providing more systematic support for cabinet and DM committees (especially DMIC, and others when necessary), and their subaltern committees at lower levels. To do so, the team would liaise more robustly with other actors throughout the analytical community, as well as with the other secretariats in PCO (Foreign and Defence Policy as well as Security and Intelligence). More broadly, it would provide a coordination function for the analytical community as a whole, chairing director-level meetings on a monthly basis to ensure, in particular, that choices of topics are harmonized and that possibilities for cooperation are maximized.

- Third, all production management functions in the IAS (including the recently created graphics position), which includes editing and disseminating products, would be located here.

- Fourth, as discussed below, the IAS would create and host an open-source excellence center.

Finally, given the emergence of new threats to the security of Canada, the IAS should receive additional funding for a small number of analytical positions, in addition to the policy and corporate functions suggested previously. That is, the IAS has diversified its analytical focus in recent years away from traditional geopolitical priorities, notably by writing products on climate change, but this is a trend that needs to intensify. It should, as such, create positions focusing on the transnational aspects of right-wing extremism, technology (cybersecurity, artificial intelligence, big data, etc.), health (especially in the context of the COVID-19 pandemic), and the interplay of economics and security (particularly as it pertains to investments in Canada by Chinese state-owned and state-championed enterprises). As with its other priorities, the IAS should analyze these topics from a comprehensive, whole-of-government perspective, encompassing multiple perspectives and combining both open and classified sources. This would allow other units such as CSE, CSIS/IAB, and CFINTCOM to focus more on threat-focused security and defense intelligence, which better suits their mandates.

The IAS, however, might be unable to secure new funding for these additional positions, especially if government finances prove tight in the aftermath of the pandemic. Should this be the case, we recommend that perhaps five to eight current analytical positions in the IAS be transferred to perform at least some of these new policy and coordination responsibilities. This would decrease the IAS's capability down from the current level of about thirty analysts, but the cost could be limited if its leadership manages risk appropriately by transferring analyst positions working on lower priority topics. These costs would, in the big picture, be more than outweighed by the gains these new positions would bring.

CABINET COMMITTEES

In terms of structure beyond the IAS, we recommend the creation of a national security committee of cabinet, similar in some ways to the Australian model that the Office of National Intelligence supports. This committee would be chaired by the prime minister, with the ministers of foreign affairs and public safety as deputy chairs (or stepping in as cochairs when the prime minister does not attend). Other members would include the ministers of national defence; international trade; justice; innovation, science, and economic development; transport; health; finance; and environment (and others as required, depending on the agenda). Senior bureaucratic officials, especially the clerk of the Privy Council and relevant DMs, would also be full members (unlike other cabinet committees). The NSIA would be secretary to the committee, supported by the IAS and other PCO secretariats.

Over the years, across successive governments, a wide range of cabinet committees have been primarily or secondarily responsible for national security and intelligence, often in combination with other related issues such as foreign affairs, defense, and emergency management. As of 2020, two committees can include discussions on national security and intelligence, the Cabinet Committee on Global Affairs and Public Security, and the more recently created Incident Response Group, an ad hoc committee bringing together relevant ministers to deal with emergencies, with membership and frequency of meetings adjusted as required (Lapointe 2020).[3]

The addition of the Incident Response Group represents an improvement. It is a privileged forum where members of cabinet, including the prime minister, as well as senior officials can exclusively focus on national security issues. It remains insufficient, however; a permanent National Security Committee would represent a further improvement. The Incident Response Group's ad hoc–ness, in particular, may prevent it from addressing deeper and longer-term challenges. A permanent committee with regularly scheduled meetings—even in the absence of crises—would provide more stability, and it would institutionalize and routinize discussions and decision-making on national security.

Another step to optimize its use and relevance at the cabinet level should be, as some interviewees suggested, to make intelligence analysis a formal part of the cabinet process, as opposed to its more informal and ad hoc contribution until now. This could come, for example, through the institutionalization of a section in memoranda to cabinet (the main decision-making document at this level) going to the proposed National Security Council, when necessary, on the view of the intelligence analysis community. The IAS would be the lead drafter of this text but would have to extensively consult the rest of the community— just like the rest of a memorandum to cabinet is also the product of widespread consultation and negotiation throughout the bureaucracy. This would force the community to come up with a consolidated view to a greater extent than it does now in the National Intelligence Assessment (NIA) process discussed in chapter 1. Such a reserved space for intelligence would not be unique; other themes, such as communications, often also have a reserved box in memoranda to cabinet.[4]

A stronger IAS, more closely connected to the cabinet process, would also be in a better position to support the three DM committees that form the core governance architecture of national security and intelligence. The IAS, in particular, would be in a better position to support the DMIC. This committee should continue its positive evolution of recent years, during which it has gone from being a backwater ADM-level committee with a poor attendance record to a DM-level body with monthly meetings and, on average, higher attendance and good participation. Yet as some interviewees noted, much can still be improved. Deputies still sometimes spend a portion of the committee's scarce time discussing the details of assessments, and even in some cases suggesting editorial changes. They should leave it to lower-level committees to argue about the assessments. At the DM level, assessments should, ideally, be accepted and serve as a starting point. DMIC would then be more productive as a senior body if it focused more on the implications of particular assessments, using NIAs as springboards for policy discussions. It would, in other words, be a more formal and concrete link between intelligence analysis and policy. This appears to have been the NSIA's intent in 2020 when the committee was reformed and renamed, as discussed in chapter 1; time will tell if these objectives are met. To optimize its impact, moreover, the IAS should strictly limit its NIAs to a maximum of three to four pages; as interviewees lamented, many NIAs reach DMIC still exceeding ten pages, making it unlikely that deputies read them entirely.

NATIONAL SECURITY AND INTELLIGENCE ADVISER

Another recommendation in terms of structural reforms revolves around the issue of the NSIA's portfolio. Until early 2020, the NSIA was responsible for the three relevant secretariats in PCO: IAS, Foreign and Defence Policy (FDP), and S&I. A minority of our interviewees suggested that this should be broken up, usually on the logic that "you can't have the person reporting to the prime minister on opportunities and on constraints being the same person." For advocates of this view, the NSIA should be responsible for security and intelligence functions in a narrow sense (that is, the IAS as well as the S&I secretariat), while the foreign and defense policy adviser should report directly to the clerk of the Privy Council (the prime minister's DM and the civil service's top bureaucrat), without going through the NSIA. This is, in fact, the structure that was adopted in early 2020, when Vincent Rigby replaced Greta Bossenmeier as NSIA after she retired. The FDP secretariat was then removed from the NSIA's portfolio to report directly to the clerk.

We believe that this decision to split the NSIA's main functions represents a step backward. A majority of interviewees agreed that there had been much progress in the past ten years or so in integrating the various streams—intelligence analysis, security and intelligence policy, and foreign and defense policy—through the office of the NSIA, providing comprehensive advice to the prime minister and cabinet with one voice. Splitting the office of the NSIA into two positions has instead weakened the system's ability to use intelligence directly in support of policy. We therefore recommend that the FDP section be returned to the NSIA's portfolio.

INTELLIGENCE PRIORITIES

Our research also detailed how there has been much progress in the intelligence priorities-setting process in recent years, notably on the analytical side. That said, we concluded that the weakness of the center in PCO prevents it from playing a stronger leadership and coordinating role in developing and implementing a more optimal process. As such, our recommendation here dovetails with the ones previously described: a stronger center under the NSIA is necessary to reinforce the priorities process. This is essential for governance reasons (better performance measurement and stronger accountability) and to formalize and institutionalize links between the requirements of clients and the production of analytical units. This implies a stronger role for both the S&I secretariat (to coordinate and exercise leadership at a general level) and for the IAS. For the IAS, the enhanced policy and corporate function we have proposed would also put it in a position to play a stronger role in coordinating the development and monitoring of Standing Intelligence Requirements for the community as a whole.

IMPLICATIONS FOR OTHER ANALYTICAL UNITS

If PCO/IAS's coordinating role is to be strengthened, where does this leave the rest of the analytical community? It is important to recognize that analysts within these other organizations also write for audiences beyond policy makers; they are expected to produce analysis that helps inform and drive intelligence collection and various kinds of operations as well. This may include writing products for operators (on the military side) or for collectors to help them refine their targeting practices, or strategic pieces for the leadership of their organizations. While principles of good writing and analysis always apply, the need to support a range of consumers means that analysts in these other assessment units within collection agencies often have to choose which audience they are focusing their efforts on, operations or external/policymaking clients.

Yet it is essential for agencies collecting foreign and security intelligence to have their voices heard at the center of government. As such, analysts in these organizations need to maintain a 360-degree view understanding the operational, executive, and external needs of their clients. Therefore, they need leadership that can help with prioritization, time management, and networking to improve in figuring out what consumers need, the best format to provide this information, and obtaining feedback to make the most of the resources each analytical unit has.

Overall, our findings show that CSE and CFINTCOM have done well in recent years to better navigate these challenges. CSE was often described in our interviews as a model for managing client relations, and it continuously reassesses and adjusts its practices as necessary. CFINTCOM has hired managers with policy experience, designed new products (such as placemats), and implemented an ambitious training agenda for its analysts. CSIS is behind these other organizations, with much (though not all) of its analysis traditionally oriented toward operations. However, as discussed in the case study in chapter 2, there is increasing recognition internally that it must make better efforts to have its voice heard outside its own building, particularly on emerging threats like investments by state-owned/championed enterprises in sensitive sectors. As such, it is also introducing new products and emphasizing policy relevance in the work of the organization as a whole.

To support this, collection agencies need to maintain a roster of 360-degree analysts, as policy/operations specialization is not likely or practical given their small size. Therefore, as noted previously, managers need to help administer the responsibilities of analysts. This means that the community should ensure that managers have policy experience and better training in understanding the needs of clients going forward. While bringing managers with policy experience into these units has proven beneficial, ensuring at the same time that managers with limited prior intelligence experience receive support and training in this area would also provide for a smoother transition.

Additionally, in an ideal world, a stronger PCO/IAS could play a role in better coordinating product topics, helping to streamline the demands on other analytical units. While joint products take time to produce, an institutionalized practice through PCO/IAS might ultimately prove beneficial. Analysts working in operational environments can learn from those working in more policy-focused environments and vice versa. If regularized, such a joint products process would become easier to manage over time, alleviating some of the burden on analysts in the long run.

Finally, a few caveats must be kept in mind. As one interviewee reminded us, there is a tendency in Ottawa, whenever there is a perceived problem, to suggest boosting PCO's role; as this individual sarcastically put it, "if it is important, put it in PCO." This should not automatically be the case; PCO, like the White House in the US system, must remain lean and relatively small (at least compared to line departments). Burdening it with too many responsibilities risks distracting it from its core priorities. Duplication, moreover, would be a waste of scarce resources, set the bureaucracy up for additional and unnecessary conflict, and weaken ministerial authority. In addition, it is important for intelligence analysis units within collection agencies and line departments to ensure that their own views are heard. It is only natural that different agencies with different mandates and niches disagree over the nature of a threat. A stronger PCO/IAS should not mean "one voice," but a more coordinated conversation.

There is, however, a case to be made that moderately boosting the IAS's resources and authority is justifiable. If anything, it would bring IAS responsibilities to the level of those of other secretariats throughout PCO. Even if they are small, they are more powerful relative to their respective line departments than the IAS is relative to the intelligence analysis community. The challenge would be to strengthen the IAS so that it can better serve the prime minister and cabinet and accomplish its broader coordination function without duplicating what other departments, especially Global Affairs Canada and Public Safety Canada, do.

Foreign Intelligence

As noted in chapter 1, there was no consensus among our interviewees as to whether or not Canada should have a foreign intelligence collection agency. Those opposed argued that there is no obvious place to put such an organization, it would be expensive to set up, and it is not clear that there would be an audience for its products. Others, however, argued that more foreign intelligence would help better support Canadian foreign policy.

Overall, despite the mixed reception, we are inclined to support the creation of a Canadian foreign human intelligence agency. If that is not possible under current fiscal and political circumstances, we believe it is necessary for Canada to collect more foreign intelligence under its current arrangements, for several reasons. First, given the positive reception of GSRP products (discussed in chapter 3 and further ahead), taking the next step and moving toward more formalized foreign intelligence collection makes sense. There is a strong audience for foreign political reporting, suggesting that those who argue there is not enough appetite are mistaken.

Second, both Canadian and non-Canadian interviewees indicated that allies would welcome such a move. Offering more and better intelligence would give Canada greater leverage with its allies and partners, particularly the US. It is clear that other states would take Canada and Canadian interests more seriously if Canadian officials could bring more valuable assets to the table. While allies and partners generally view Canada as reliable, they also often view it as something of an afterthought. Foreign intelligence collected and assessed by Canada would provide Ottawa with a greater voice, particularly among its Five Eyes partners.

A third reason was not so much discussed by our interviewees, but it is hard to avoid: the world order is changing in ways that have serious consequences for Canada. While cooperation with the US continued during the Trump era, Canada's main allies—particularly the US and the UK—are likely to be focused on domestic issues post–COVID-19. While UK politics will be distracted by the aftermath of Brexit, US politics may continue to be impacted by Trumpism, including a staunch anti-multilateralism, for some time. In this sense, the institutions upon which Canada has traditionally depended upon, especially NATO, the North American Aerospace Defense Command (NORAD), and perhaps even the Five Eyes, may come under continued stress. Better foreign human intelligence collection would provide Canadian policy makers another tool as they navigate the uncertain waters of the twenty-first century.

A final argument for establishing a Canadian foreign human intelligence agency is that it would focus on Canada's national interests. Intelligence from the US, UK, and Australia reflects the priorities of those countries. They pick and choose what they share with Canada, and while they are close allies and partners, their priorities are not automatically fully aligned with Canada's best interests. Episodes such as rising tensions with China over Huawei and the Meng Wanzhou case, aggressive actions by Saudi Arabia against Canada and its dissidents, and Russia flexing its muscles in the Arctic suggest that we are entering a world where Canada needs more, not less, intelligence that reflects its own priorities.

Realistically, however, it is not clear that any Canadian government will pursue this option in the short-to-medium term. Setting up a new foreign human intelligence collection agency, in particular, will be expensive, and the time and human resources required will be significant.

We therefore propose a two-fold halfway step for Canada as a second-best solution. The first phase would be to increase the collection and reporting currently undertaken by existing agencies. CSE, in particular, could be tasked with collecting more SIGINT on Canadian priorities. While CSIS is limited in its capacity to collect information only on threats to the security of Canada, there is no reason why it cannot increase its footprint abroad to collect more information about these topics overseas. In 2016, CSIS's then review agency, the Security Intelligence Review Committee, noted that "CSIS has developed a new foreign collection platform model to refine and enhance its collection capacity abroad to better meet intelligence requirements" (Security Intelligence Review Committee 2017). In this sense, the government could carefully foster CSIS's efforts to collect more security intelligence abroad. Additionally, the government could augment GSRP by continuing the trend of its growth and task it with producing even more reports in countries of interest.

The second step would be to further Canadianize analysis. As discussed in chapter 1, Canadianization is an approach to analysis that critically assesses foreign intelligence in such a way that better highlights Canadian perspectives and interests, focusing on the audience, what they need to know, and what the Canadian angle is on a particular issue. It ensures that Canadian viewpoints are not lost in the volume of information Canada receives from allies and partners. It also ensures that information and assessments, which may be tainted by the different perspectives or capabilities of other countries, do not get in the way of understanding how information applies in a Canadian context.

Even if Canada does eventually create a foreign human intelligence collection agency, Canadianization should be pursued in the meantime. Ensuring that analysts better understand Canadian perspectives and interests is fundamental to this process (we discuss approaches to training in this area below.) While it does not make up for the lack of a foreign intelligence service, it at least ensures more rigorous critical thinking on some of the key issues Canada faces.

In addition, Canadianization should be complemented with greater institutional support to build networking capacity internationally with key allies and partners. As a start, a liaison position for the NSIA in the Canadian embassy in Washington, DC, should be created to play a coordinating role for the Canadian intelligence and national security community in its relations with its US counterparts. At present, the Canadian embassy in the US features a large number of officials from throughout the intelligence community. Every agency has liaison officers, often more than one. These individuals talk to each other, but our interviews showed that there is a lack of coordination, with efforts being ad hoc and decentralized. In addition to providing this coordination function, this new office would also provide a direct contact to the Office of the Director of National Intelligence.

THE INTELLIGENCE BUREAU IN GAC

Finally, we propose recommendations for the Intelligence Bureau in GAC. GSRP, in particular, has been a success, and it now has now about thirty-five officers posted abroad. It is certainly possible to conceive of five to ten additional countries that the program could cover, and for which there would be a market at headquarters and in the broader government. Yet in a context of scarce resources at GAC, especially in the post-pandemic world, it is not clear that posting additional GSRP officers abroad is realistic. At the very least, our hope is that the gains of recent years—the surge up to thirty-five officers and the growth of corporate and analytical support for the program in Ottawa, which is necessary to sustain it—are not walked back. Its unique niche, which we described in chapter 3, has allowed the program to become, in the view of some interviewees, a "crown jewel," respected in Canada and by partners. The program's leadership should, nevertheless, continue the steady professionalization and institutionalization of its management, notably to ensure that candidates are adequately vetted and trained. Efforts to increase deconfliction and coordination with other government departments, especially CSIS, have partly succeeded in solving earlier tension at the institutional level (though some opposition remains at more operational levels in CSIS). This momentum should continue, to consolidate those gains and maximize cooperation. Finally, it is important that the two new review and oversight agencies, NSICOP and NSIRA, look into the work of GSRP. Scrutiny and accountability will undoubtedly be a difficult process for a program and a department not used to it, but they are essential in the longer term.

The creation of the strategic assessment team nested alongside GSRP is a promising evolution. Its analysts are closely connected to the work of GSRP officers, and early indications are that its work is increasingly valued in headquarters, even if questions about its relevance remain. We therefore recommend that its modest growth continue, and that efforts to make the work of its analysts better known in Ottawa continue and intensify. This is a point that also applies to GSRP. Even though it has succeeded, in less than two decades, in building a valuable and recognizable brand, GAC can do even more to aggressively market its products in Ottawa and abroad to better leverage their strong value. That is, although it is political reporting, its products are an important asset that GAC underexploits in a global intelligence market in which Canada has a limited range of assets.

This should be, in particular, the role of GAC's Intelligence Liaison Offices, of which Canada has four (in Washington, London, Canberra, and Berlin). Canada should consider opening more (in France, in particular, and eventually in nontraditional partner states), or at least to increase the size of existing ones to allow them to better cover broad geographic areas. Beyond their size, they should be more dynamic and aggressive in viewing themselves as marketing agents who exchange Canadian products for those of allies and partners. In the words of one interviewee, "we don't do a good enough job of injecting ourselves in the US system . . . it prevents us from maximizing the benefits of the relationship." To do so, there should also be better coordination with the other intelligence liaison positions in embassies, notably those of defense intelligence.

Managing Analytical Units

EXCHANGES AND SECONDMENTS

Exchanges and secondments between the intelligence and policy worlds are by far the most effective tool to foster greater policy literacy. Training and shadowing are useful, but ultimately it is only by "doing" policy that intelligence analysts and their managers can gain a granular understanding of its requirements. This is often easier said than done, however. Human resources processes often lack the flexibility to allow or encourage such movement; in other cases, managers are reluctant to see their best analysts leave for one or two years on secondment. Given the relatively small size of the Canadian intelligence analysis community, "bench strength" is usually thin. As a result, approving the secondment of, say, a strong China analyst is likely to create real short-term costs for the home agency. A secondary issue is that some analysts are reluctant to leave their home department because they do not trust that the system values exchanges or secondments, or because they have a fixed idea of what their job is and prefer not to leave it.

And yet it is essential for the top leadership to focus on the big picture and work to better institutionalize exchanges and secondments for the longer-term health of the community. This means accepting the temporary loss of some of their best talent and establishing incentives for analysts to take an exchange/secondment and devoting resources to ensure these programs succeed. Making these programs more permanent and institutionalized in the long run will also make them seem less risky for analysts who feel the pay-off is uncertain. The Security and Intelligence Policy Program, discussed in chapter 2, represents an extremely positive step in this direction.[5] It should be protected and fostered. Ideally, the DM of public safety should keep a direct interest in the program and occasionally brief the DMNS committee (the main policy committee for the community) to ensure high-level buy-in and coordination, which remains a challenge. The program should be continued and expanded so that with time, it will allow for the build-up of policy and intelligence literacy on both sides; as these young analysts move up the hierarchy, the potential benefits should only grow.

JOINT DUTY FOR PROMOTION

An even stronger step would be to make stints in the policy world prerequisites for promotions. Although common practice in the US, this proposition is controversial in the analytical community in Canada, as it effectively blocks from promotions those analysts who have been around for years but who do not have policy or other experience. Since gaining policy experience has not been traditionally valued by analysts (and in many cases, their own organizations), some see this as unfair. For example, a recent competition in the IAS for two director positions did exactly this.[6] As a result, many experienced analysts were disqualified, causing significant frustration. That said, the best response here, and the one senior management in the IAS took, is to accept that this resentment is the necessary result of its refusal to promote career analysts with little or no understanding of policy. This is difficult, but it is the right decision, and it is essential to build in the longer term the organization's ability to be more relevant.

HIRING AND CAREER PATHS

Human resources are crucial to the operation of intelligence and national security departments and agencies. Yet in recent years there has been more emphasis on the collection and storage of intelligence (as well as legislating and reviewing these practices) than on who actually assesses the information gathered.

We have already made several recommendations in this area: intelligence and policy analysts working in national security should be encouraged to do exchanges and secondments, and to some extent to require them for promotions. However, there are limits to what steps the community can take in this space. Human resources management is difficult and plagued with problems across government, not just in national security. Moreover, some organizations have more control over their hiring practices than others. That said, agencies can take some steps to improve their analytical units.

First, more often than not, our interviewees supported approaches to hiring that—to some extent—emphasize generalist skills over more specialized knowledge. Analysts, in this view, need to be flexible and able to adapt. This suits a smaller intelligence community, in which analysts are often required to cover several countries or a large thematic area such as energy or foreign investment. Moreover, highly specialized analysts have a stronger tendency to focus more narrowly on their immediate area of expertise, which those with less specialization and a broader focus will be, on average, better positioned to avoid.[7] Specialization is important for highly technical areas (such as cybersecurity, missiles, or nuclear programs) and key countries of interest (notably China and Russia); we are not recommending that it be ignored. But it is important for units to also hire and develop analysts who can adapt to rapidly emerging and evolving threats. In this sense, senior management in analytical agencies should continue moving in this direction.

It is also important for units to ensure their analysts have a diverse set of perspectives. Countering groupthink and echo chambers is key to avoiding bias and stagnation. Importantly, many interviewees emphasized diversity of experience over diversity of representation in hiring decisions. In our view, however, both kinds of diversity are important (Momani and Stirk 2017). This is also the view of the NSICOP study on diversity within the intelligence and national security community (National Security and Intelligence Committee of Parliamentarians 2020a). This was not, however, a central focus of our study; as such, diversity in the intelligence and national security community remains an important avenue for future research.

Finally, as discussed in chapter 2, there was no consensus over whether the community should take a more formalized stance toward career paths or even the development of a specialized "analyst" occupational group. Although the formal creation of a group may go too far, having weighed the evidence, we believe a more coherent approach toward defining flexible standards would be beneficial, coordinated through a stronger NSIA and PCO/IAS. For example, such an approach could set clearer guidance for education and training, rotations/secondments, and qualifications for promotion. In addition, based on this more coordinated approach and guidance, a strengthened NSIA could organize more community events on issues related to analysis and the intelligence and national security community generally, bringing analysts together to improve community networking. While there will always be a need for specialized agencies to have their own human resources policies, the current lack of guidance means that there have been inconsistent standards, making much needed initiatives, such as exchanges and secondments, more difficult. A more coordinated approach would lead to the enhanced professionalization of intelligence analysis in Canada.[8]

Managing the Intelligence Policy Interface

One of the core themes in our research was that policy literacy in the intelligence community—the general level of understanding of the policy process by intelligence analysts and their managers—has improved over the years but remains insufficient. In this context, what can be done to ensure that the recent positive trend of greater policy literacy can continue, and be strengthened? Training and professional development are essential. Intelligence analysts must receive better and more training on what policy is, and is not, and how they can better support it. An additional set of initiatives can help foster a culture of stronger policy literacy throughout the intelligence community. Some of them are already being implemented; they should continue, and ideally intensify. For example, shadowing programs, in which junior intelligence analysts spend time—days, possibly more—following senior officials, can shape their understanding of the role and needs of policy before they become entrenched in traditional views. This, in the words of one interviewee, can help analysts develop an "anticipatory capacity," not in the conventional sense of anticipating developments on the topic of their analysis but rather in anticipating the requirements of clients.

EDUCATING CONSUMERS

Our research also strongly highlighted the reverse problem: intelligence literacy in the policy world is similarly weak. This is, largely, also an inherent feature of the Canadian system. As long as national security issues remain of limited importance, policy makers face fewer incentives to invest time and energy in better understanding intelligence. That said, some initiatives could help improve the situation.

The first and most obvious step is for the intelligence community to invest more effort in educating its consumers. Indeed, the need to educate clients came up as one of the most popular answers when we discussed training with interviewees. There is a sense that improvements in analysis will have a limited impact if consumers do not appreciate enough what they are reading. Fortunately, this can be done at little cost. In the words of one interviewee, "I did a brief to a minister once on Intelligence 101. It was useful. It would be beneficial to do the same to others." Such briefings—to ministers all the way down the chain to policy analysts—can be useful not only to introduce clients to the topic but also to build bridges and open channels of communication. Intelligence 101 briefings do already occur, a positive trend of recent years that many interviewees pointed out, but there is scope to offer more. Similarly, the community could offer policy clients the reverse course that it already offers to its own analysts. In parallel to a Policy 101 for intelligence analysts, it should offer an Intelligence 101 training course for the policy world. Ideally, it would be for the Intelligence Analyst Learning Program in PCO or the Canadian School of Public Service to coordinate and offer such a course. It would be specifically designed for policy analysts (and a different version could be offered to their managers) to explain what intelligence is, what it can do for them and what it cannot (to counter frequent misperceptions and misaligned expectations), the types of products it offers, how its analysts come up with their conclusions, and how to communicate with them.

INCREASED POLICY-INTELLIGENCE INTERACTION

Another tool to boost intelligence literacy would be to organize, on a regular basis, roundtables, more or less formal opportunities for policy and intelligence analysts working on a similar issue, across the bureaucracy, to get together and exchange views. Such exchanges already occur. The IAS, for example, organizes interdepartmental expert groups on a regular basis, but they tend to be irregularly attended by policy analysts. At more senior levels, such exchanges have become increasingly frequent and institutionalized in recent years, especially through the subordinate-level committees in support of DM-level committees. These exchanges provide opportunities for analysts and managers to learn about the other's priorities and knowledge gaps, and more broadly about the other side's culture and ways of doing business. They are also essential to establishing personal ties and building trust. The challenge in setting up such events is of course the availability of individuals on the policy side, who usually need some prodding and convincing to invest their time. Possible solutions for the intelligence world to make these more appealing can include focusing the discussion on the "so what" as opposed to solely the "what," inviting external experts to broaden the discussion, inviting nontraditional partners to the table (e.g., from the economic side, to hear different perspectives), and being careful not to hold the discussion at high classification levels (which prevents many in policy from attending, and even if they are cleared, it makes it less useful to them).

CLIENT RELATIONS

Formal client relations efforts—bodies set up to manage relations with clients—by various units in the analytical community have ebbed and flowed over the years, especially as many met with limited success. The chief of defence intelligence organization (the predecessor to CFINTCOM), for example, briefly had a client management office in the mid- to late 2000s. It will be interesting to follow, in the coming years, the evolution of new client relations functions in CSIS/IAB and elsewhere, and to determine whether they can genuinely support the organization's ability to serve clients.

In the meantime, some of the most effective client relations processes are the more informal ones: direct relations between intelligence and policy counterparts, from analysts all the way up to DMs and heads of agencies. It is at this level that there is significant scope for improvement in the Canadian intelligence community, even if the situation has already improved in recent years. Senior management in analytical units should emphasize more strongly to their analysts that they need to invest more time informally contacting their policy counterparts to get to know them better: to be included more frequently in some of their communications, to be invited to their meetings, to regularly meet them to remain updated on their priorities, and to more proactively promote their analyses. After delivering a written product or oral briefing, they should follow up to survey whether it was useful and if the client has pending knowledge gaps or questions. Management, put differently, needs to help analysts "market" their products, something for which they are traditionally ill-equipped.[9]

The prevailing culture throughout the intelligence analysis world does not value enough this type of commitment. When hearing such recommendations, many intelligence analysts and their managers answer that they do not have time. But this is indicative of senior management's inability to foster in their staff a better prioritization calculus. Even if it comes at the expense of other activities, it is a necessary long-term investment for analysts to spend more energy trying to understand the policy process. It is the role of management to foster this change in culture.

Yet as discussed in chapter 2, managers often find themselves in their positions with limited policy experience. Moreover, in the same way there are few community-wide standards for analysts, there is even less when it comes to being promoted into management. This often puts managers in a difficult position, as they are increasingly asked to build bridges between the intelligence and policy worlds, even though many of them have limited familiarity with one of them, usually policy. Therefore, in the same manner we suggest intelligence analysts should have basic training in policy and in communication skills, their managers (especially in intelligence collection agencies) should also be required to do such training, especially if they have not served in policy positions before.

POLITICIZATION

There is, finally, relatively little to improve in terms of the hard politicization of intelligence analysis, since our research found a strong consensus on its absence in Canada. If anything, as discussed throughout this book, the community needs to develop a stronger and more nuanced ability to engage in the soft politicization of its products, by being more sensitive to and aware of the political and policy contexts while not bending to political pressures. One element, nevertheless, is worth keeping in mind. Recent efforts to increase oversight of and transparency in the national security and intelligence community could, with time, increase the risk of politicization, as the US experience demonstrates.[10] This is by no means an argument to reverse or even slow down current efforts to enhance transparency; we firmly believe that such efforts should continue. It is, simply, a note of caution to be aware of the eventual implications of reforms. Recent progress starts from such a low bar, in any case, that this risk remains far in the future.

What Makes a Product Useful?

As one interviewee put it, "we need better analysis, not more analysis or more collection" in Canada. That is, even though there is a need and an appetite for more analysis on specific emerging or evolving threats, such as foreign online electoral interference, overall the thrust of reforms should focus more on the quality of analytical support to policy making than on its quantity. There is, arguably, not enough bandwidth among senior readers for significantly more analysis. This last section thus provides a series of recommendations to provide better analysis, focusing on the granular aspects of format, content, sources, methods, and classification.

FORMAT AND DELIVERY

The analytical community, first, has progressively instituted major reforms in terms of the format of its products in recent years, leading to significant progress. There remains, nevertheless, scope for further improvement.

In terms of product length, first, the community has been performing better, steadily moving away from long papers. The community regularly produced papers of more than five or even ten pages in the decade after 9/11 and often seemed oblivious to the absence of virtually any readership outside the small immediate circle of other analysts working on the same topic. The situation has gotten much better. Long products are rarer today, even though they still occur, while short ones are more frequent. Nevertheless, interviewees on the policy side who are currently in service still lamented the frequency of papers of more than five pages, even while they recognized improvements, criticizing what they perceive as the analytical community's inability to evolve further.

This is all the more striking given how common the recognition is today that there is a fast-declining marginal utility of drafting products of more than two or three pages. It is, indeed, this growing awareness that has led the community to increasingly focus on producing short daily products that have triggered positive reactions among clients. Our main recommendation at this level, in this context, is simple: the IAS and CFINTCOM should continue devoting an important proportion of their resources to these short products, while seeking to improve them.

ORAL BRIEFINGS

Similarly, as discussed in chapter 4, the analytical community has significantly increased, in quantity and quality, its provision of oral briefings in recent years. Interviewees on the policy side clearly labeled this as an important success. Our main overall recommendation is, therefore, again to ensure that this positive trend continues.

One specific area where there is scope for improvement is at the level of oral briefing skills. As one interviewee noted, when a very senior policy maker retired recently, he specifically emphasized this point in his farewell speech to employees. CFINTCOM and the Intelligence Analyst Learning Program at PCO recently started offering courses on oral briefings, a positive development. These courses should be improved, including through the development of more advanced versions, and made more widely available. Professional development modules can also organize workshops to allow analysts to practice and update their briefing skills, where they could receive feedback from other analysts and from policy officers. Informal training on oral briefings, on a day-to-day basis, can also be improved, notably by filming briefers and allowing them to watch clips of their presentations while receiving feedback from experienced briefers and clients. Another possibility is to more regularly bring junior analysts along with senior ones providing oral briefings, allowing them to watch and learn. There is also a need to enhance the skills of briefers and managers to help them better translate complex issues, especially emerging and technical ones, into digestible language for policy makers, who are nonexperts. This is difficult but essential. Few things decrease client appetite for intelligence as much as technical briefings full of jargon. Finally, a tool to further institutionalize the importance of oral briefing skills is to include them as an essential requirement in competitions for promotions to senior analyst positions, a trend which has already begun but which could be more generalized.

PLACEMATS

A third, related area of major improvement and success in recent years is the growing use of placemats and other forms of visual support. As with short daily products and oral briefings, our main recommendation is to ensure that this trend continues and becomes institutionalized and more widespread. Again, small additional steps can be taken. The community can hire more qualified staff with graphics skills, and it can still better integrate their work in analytical products. A recent, surprisingly positive development has seen analysts themselves develop graphics skills, allowing them to build and integrate appealing and user-friendly, but also information-rich, visual support (charts, maps, etc.) in their products; this has been the case, notably, within CFINTCOM. The community should continue encouraging this by providing analysts with more training and software tools. Finally, to ensure that institutional memory remains strong (and that, as a result, responses to review and oversight requests, as well as transitions when personnel move on, can occur appropriately), analytical units should continue making sure that sufficient written records are kept when they provide oral briefings.

GOVERNMENT PRIORITIES

One of the most frequent criticism of intelligence analysis in Canada is that it is interesting but not always sufficiently focused on supporting government priorities. As with the other gaps and weaknesses identified in the previous four chapters, there is no easy recipe for success. At the broadest level, the most important remedy to position analytical units to better support government priorities is to increase policy literacy. Analysts simply cannot be expected to write directly and concretely in support of government priorities if they do not intimately understand the policy context. As such, our previous recommendations to enhance policy literacy are equally applicable here. The onus, again, is on management in the analytical community to foster and encourage a work environment in which this is possible.

Other initiatives would help. The management of analytical units should hire more generalists, as those with a broader focus and skillset are, typically, better able to respond to quickly shifting priorities. Similarly, a few interviewees suggested that analytical units should create more positions focused on thematic as opposed to regional topics, such as economic security, cybersecurity, climate change, and global health. Such positions exist (the IAS tasked an analyst to focus on climate change, for example, and CSIS/IAB has had thematic analysts focusing on economic security, energy security, and cybersecurity for well over a decade), but there is a strong case that more are needed.

Too often, the production of intelligence analysis in Canada also fails to fully reflect the reality that high-level policy making occurs in a whole-of-government context. That is, intelligence analysis is too often plagued by the same kinds of silos as other sectors of government. This is, again, an area where there has been some improvement recently but also where further improvement is possible but difficult given the permanence of bureaucratic realities. This is an issue that primarily, though not exclusively, concerns the IAS: as the analytical unit housed in PCO, it is responsible more than others for providing more comprehensive analysis. Nevertheless, as many interviewees emphasized, other analytical units such as CFINTCOM and CSIS/IAB, while respecting their primary area of focus (defense and security intelligence respectively), can and should better situate some of their analytical products in a whole-of-government context.

To achieve this, analytical units should continue to improve the training they offer analysts to help them better understand how the policy process they support works. The intelligence community, moreover, has learned to circulate its draft products and to consult far more extensively in recent years, but too often those consultations still primarily take place within small circles of intelligence analysts working on similar issues. Instead, consultations should be systematically broadened to include policy counterparts, other analysts working on similar issues (for example, a China analyst could consult more extensively with other China analysts working on the trade side), and external experts.

OPPORTUNITY ANALYSIS

The question of whether intelligence analysis units should provide opportunity analysis remains a matter of debate. Given the appetite by many on the client side to receive some, we recommend that analytical units continue to cautiously move forward with building the capacity to provide opportunity analysis, mindful of the risks and concerns. Ultimately, these are manageable; what matters is that when asked, consumers indicated they want this type of product. Analysts need careful mentoring and support by management since, in most cases, they are not familiar with the technique and do not possess the necessary understanding of the policy context, without which opportunity analysis is not possible.

For the community to move forward, there is, as such, a need for training specifically on this approach. There is also a need to integrate this training into the necessary broader efforts to improve policy literacy among analysts and their managers. As some interviewees pointed out, the CIA provides training on opportunity analysis; Canadian analysts could follow courses in the US, if possible. Even better would be for a designated Canadian individual to receive sufficient support so that they could be trained to become the trainer in Canada. This would reduce the costs and simplify the logistics of sending analysts to the US for training; it would also allow the training to support Canadianization (i.e., tailoring to the needs of the Canadian context). More broadly, managers of analytical units need to enable their analysts to be less risk averse; without a clear license from the chain of command, such a culture change cannot be implemented more than very partially.

BLUE FORCE ANALYSIS

Our interviews showed that clients want more blue force analysis (that is, products incorporating analysis of the capabilities and intentions of allies and partners). They understand that the dominant focus of intelligence analysis is, and should be, the "bad guys," yet at the same time they are sometimes frustrated by the absence in the intelligence products they receive of any focus on Canada's allies, especially the US. To address this gap, we recommend that intelligence analysis units— especially those in support of foreign policy (the IAS and the new assessment unit in GAC) and defense policy (CFINTCOM)—establish (or reestablish, in the case of the IAS) positions for analysts focusing exclusively on US foreign and defense policy toward countries or themes of interest, as well as on domestic politics in the US. These products, in many cases, could be jointly written with regional or thematic analysts focused on the issue in question. This would not represent spying on the US—the inevitable criticism that many in the intelligence community use in response to this recommendation—since no information would be collected clandestinely in the US. Rather, these analysts would utilize open-source information on the US (and the vast diplomatic reporting coming out of Canadian missions in the US), as well as classified information on US foreign and defense policy.

METHODS

Our interviews provided a mixed picture on the utility of methods in intelligence analysis. All interviewees on the policy side agreed that they want to be confident that the analysis they receive is based on sound and rigorous work.

Most, however, argued (in some cases quite forcefully) that they do not want to see those methods, especially if they involve the heavy use of technical jargon. There is a mismatch here, as many analytical units, and especially many in the training community, still put much emphasis on methods. As such, there is a good case to be made that the intelligence community should decrease its focus—in its training modules especially—on labor-intensive, process-heavy techniques and methods, which are of limited value to clients, and focus more on quality of writing and policy relevance. Training should emphasize that methods should be used with a lighter touch. This also implies that the heavy emphasis in the US intelligence studies literature on the importance of the sound use of methodologies has limited bearing on the reality of intelligence analysis in a smaller intelligence community like Canada's.

AVOIDING OVERCLASSIFICATION

Overclassification, finally, is a significant problem for the Canadian intelligence community. It was one of the most prominent sources of frustration among our interviewees on the policy side. It is of course far easier said than done, but a product that loses, in schematic terms, 10 percent of its accuracy by decreasing the level of classification (because key details are removed) but gains 20 percent in dissemination (products at a lower classification can be disseminated more widely and become more usable) is ultimately a better product. Or, in the words of one interviewee, the intelligence community "needs to get better at extrapolating and generalizing upward to be able to classify downward." This can come only as a result of better training that supports analysts in making these judgements. It is also ultimately the role of management to push analysts to write at lower classification levels, when possible. There is, in other words, no magic formula. It is for analysts and their managers to strike the ideal balance between analytical specificity and product dissemination and usability.

Another option is to release multiple versions of the same product, at both lower and higher classifications. This, however, is again far easier said than done. It is time consuming and labor intensive. As multiple interviewees emphasized, especially those on the management side of analytical units, producing multiple versions of the same product is a luxury that the often overstretched analytical community cannot always afford. In addition, as one interviewee highlighted, sometimes the organization writing the product does not own some of the more highly classified information (it may come from another organization or, quite frequently in the Canadian case, from another country). In those cases, it often has limited or no flexibility to change the level of classification without sacrificing significant analytical accuracy.

OPEN SOURCE AND DATA ANALYTICS

Our research shows that the analytical community underexploits open-source intelligence (OSINT), although it has made much progress in recent years—a trend almost certainly accelerated by the fact that many analysts have been working from home during the COVID-19 pandemic. Nevertheless, there is still a dominant culture of viewing OSINT as inherently inferior to classified intelligence. A number of initiatives could help the community improve its ability to exploit OSINT. The most obvious one is to improve training on how to access and exploit OSINT. The work of open-source organizations such as Bellingcat clearly shows the potential benefits here.[11] Beyond technical aspects, this strikes again at the notion of the need to enhance policy literacy. Intelligence analysts need to better understand how they de facto compete with publicly available analysis for the attention of senior clients, and that this is often a battle in which they start with a disadvantage. Similarly, training, and more broadly a cultural change, needs to emphasize that OSINT is not inherently inferior to classified information; data is data, however it is obtained. What matters—beyond its reliability, which needs to be ascertained whatever the level of classification—is how relevant for clients are the insights produced on its basis.

Enhancing the use of open-source information needs to come at two levels: analysts must learn to better integrate OSINT into their analysis, and dedicated units should be created in agencies where none already exist. The Australian counterpart to the IAS, the Office of National Intelligence, for example, has a thirty-person OSINT-dedicated unit. One apparently small but in practice necessary step here would be to remove the many firewalls that, absurdly, still today block the access on unclassified computer systems to many crucial websites, ranging from Twitter—without which OSINT research is sometimes practically impossible—to password-protected websites providing news, to various databases.

As one interviewee emphasized, the Canadian analytical and policy communities need to be "all over the US" in exploiting OSINT. Managing relations with the US is by far Canada's most important foreign policy priority. As such, gaining a detailed, refined understanding of US politics is essential to the optimal management of bilateral ties, and of foreign policy more generally. The

Canadian embassy in Washington, DC, already does this—and does it quite well. That said, there is scope for the broader machinery to enhance its efforts not to spy on the US but to collect more and better open-source information. Again, similar to the earlier discussion regarding blue force analysis, many in the intelligence community are reluctant to do so, mostly on the basis of the notion that "we don't spy on allies." This is self-defeating, as we are not calling for clandestine efforts focused on the US but for greater (transparent) efforts to collect OSINT and analyze it—on what is, and will remain, by far Canada's most important foreign policy priority.

Our recommendations with regard to more and better exploitation of OSINT fit into a larger trend discussed by our interviewees: the Canadian intelligence community needs to improve its ability to use, assess, and understand different kinds of data more generally. As outlined in chapter 2, numerous interviewees stressed the need for intelligence analysts to have, either through learning or as a condition for their hiring, greater skills in working with data, including the abilities to "bring meaning" to data and to exploit it. While analysts will always need to be proficient in writing and critical thinking skills, the ability to assess and find trends in "big data" are important skills for the future.

Yet finding individuals who are proficient in both written and oral communication skills and data analytics is a challenge. To supplement this growing need, we recommend that the intelligence community develop data analytics and open-source exploitation courses to help transform and, in the words of one interviewee, "deepen the bench" on these skills. While not all analysts will want or need to participate in such courses, they will appeal to those who wish to enhance their skillset or take on new challenges. To support these and other initiatives, as mentioned previously, we recommend the establishment of an open-source intelligence center hosted by the IAS to coordinate, build expertise, and educate the community.

EXTERNAL EXPERTISE

A related area of improvement would be for the analytical community to enhance its ability to benefit from external expertise. There has been, here again, much progress in the past ten years. Nevertheless, there is scope for the intelligence community to further increase its gains from the knowledge and insights of external experts. This is essential for analysts to be challenged and avoid groupthink, to test or validate their assumptions, to hear from different perspectives on specific problems, and, in some cases, to meet individuals who have access to data to which intelligence organizations do not (e.g., journalists or business people who travel to interesting countries or meet specific individuals).

Existing programs in CSIS and DND (the Mobilizing Insights in National Defence and Security, or MINDS) are well funded and should continue, given their value, as discussed in the previous chapter.[12] GAC, however, lost its equivalent years ago, the now defunct International Security Research and Outreach Program. Comparable efforts in the foreign ministry have since been informal; the department should establish a new program, with stable funding. The skill set needed to manage these programs is in some ways unique. DND, for example, has simply asked policy officers to rotate through assignments in managing the MINDS program. This is not ideal, as these individuals, even though they are usually skilled policy officers, do not have the knowledge or background to optimally connect the supply (external expertise) with the internal demand (intelligence, operations, and policy units who may benefit from this expertise).[13]

Another option to assist the national security and intelligence community in optimizing its access to relevant external expertise would be to revive the foreign ministry's interview program. There is very little publicly available information on this unit. In testimony to the Senate's Standing Committee on National Security and Defence in 2007, Colleen Swords, then the ADM for international security, referred to "a long-standing government interview program at [the Department of Foreign Affairs and International Trade, as it was then known] which draws on the experience and knowledge of Canadians and others who have particular insight into developments abroad with specific knowledge of interest to Canada and its close allies. This interview program operates entirely on a voluntary basis" (Standing Senate Committee on National Security and Defence 2007). Two of our interviewees said that this program has since been discontinued.

This program was located in what is now the Intelligence Bureau. Its purpose was to debrief Canadians returning from travel or stays abroad who had access to relevant and unique knowledge and insights. This, as interviewees recalled, included business people, NGO workers, and academics. The transcript of their interviews would then be synthesized and circulated inside the department and the broader intelligence community. This was valuable, as some of these individuals had unique perspectives. One especially useful benefit was that many of those individuals could provide a uniquely Canadian perspective on developments in a specific country, which would be consistent with efforts to stress the

Canadianization of intelligence analysis. Locating such a program inside GAC and not CSIS—which of course has its own programs to access comparable information—may make some Canadians less reluctant to meet with, and open up to, foreign ministry officials. Should this program be revived, it would of course need to be deconflicted with similar programs—at CSIS and elsewhere within GAC (as diplomats and GSRP officers, in particular, regularly hold such meetings abroad).

Measuring Success

How would we be able to assess if the recommendations we offer in this chapter have made a positive difference after five or ten years?[14] Measurement of success is naturally easier if it focuses on process. A future evaluation of progress in the intelligence and national security community could, for example, count the number of new training courses offered, the number of analysts hired, or the amount of reports that use a novel approach such as opportunity analysis. This would be useful as a starting point, but it would also be incomplete, as it measures output not outcomes. The more useful, but less quantifiable and more difficult to assess, measure of success is to assess impact by finding out whether, for example, opportunity analyses or new training courses contribute to better policy making.

An especially difficult element to monitor here is cultural change. As argued throughout this book, for the intelligence analysis community to succeed in better managing the overclassification of its products or to become more transparent, deep cultural shifts are necessary. Measuring this is complex and should be done through extensive case study research—by academics or potentially by review and oversight bodies like NSICOP. Our goal in this concluding section is therefore to very preliminarily lay the groundwork for what would have to be done.

On the governance front, one of the most important indicators to monitor in coming years is the continued evolution of the deputy minister committee structure in a more sophisticated and institutionalized direction. As previously discussed, the recently renamed Deputy Minister Intelligence Committee, in particular, now aims to focus more on the "so what" of intelligence assessments and less on the "what," as its predecessors too often did. An essential ingredient for this evolution will be the strengthening of the NSIA's function, both in terms of capacity and responsibilities. This would contribute, ideally, to greater coherence, more information sharing, and enhanced interagency collaboration. At the institutional level, we will also monitor the evolution of foreign intelligence collection. If a new stand-alone agency is not created, will there at least be greater efforts to gather more intelligence and then to incorporate its output into broader foreign and national security policy making? Finally, for the analytical community to evolve toward greater relevance, it will need to further Canadianize its analysis, putting more emphasis on linking it to Canadian interests.

Many indicators on the human resources and management front are straightforward, and perhaps here is where outputs can be more clearly linked to outcomes. Ten years from now, students of the Canadian intelligence community will want to assess the dissemination of best practices in human resources matters and measure the number of secondments and exchanges. Beyond the numbers, it will be especially useful to monitor whether those who benefited from those programs in the 2010s and early 2020s, having been promoted to positions of greater responsibility, are better able to act as bridges between the policy and analytical worlds. On the training front, a tempting mistake would be to merely aim to enhance the quantity of courses offered, but this would be a trap. Instead, the leadership of the community must make sure that improvements come as much in terms of quality as of quantity. Finally, as NSICOP has already begun to report on issues of diversity (as discussed in chapter 2), monitoring how successful departments and agencies are at hiring a more diverse workforce should also be relatively easy to monitor.

Policy and intelligence literacy, on the other hand, are challenging to precisely quantify. Nevertheless, a central element to monitor in the development of the intelligence policy interface in the coming decade will be whether the positive trend of greater policy and intelligence literacy that we described throughout this book continues and is strengthened. Intensive interview-based research will be necessary to make this assessment. To push this research further, efforts to refine our ability to define and measure policy and intelligence literacy would be highly valuable—and this, notably, would be relevant in national contexts other than Canada.

There will be other important factors to monitor in the long term as well. As intelligence takes on a steadily more prominent role in senior levels of government and as review and oversight mechanisms lead to enhanced transparency, it is likely that pressures and incentives to politicize intelligence will grow. We will therefore stay acutely interested in whether our assessment regarding the question of hard politicization of intelligence analysis in Canada (our research found no evidence) eventually changes.

Finally, the improvements of recent years in terms of product format will hopefully be sustained. It will then be important to study in greater depth what, precisely, are the gains and costs that accrue from shorter and more user-friendly written or oral briefings, and from the enhanced use of visual support. One interesting initiative here would be to launch in-depth surveys of client satisfaction with these products.

THE FUTURE OF THE CANADIAN INTELLIGENCE AND NATIONAL SECURITY COMMUNITY

IN WRITING THIS BOOK, we have been extremely fortunate to spend time with almost seventy individuals from all levels of the intelligence and national security community in Canada and from allied national security communities. Ultimately, it is impossible to capture everything from the wide-ranging conversations that we had. Therefore, this forward-looking conclusion highlights themes and questions that emerged and that have important implications for the future of intelligence and national security in Canada. The first section looks at the nature of the intelligence and national security community. Can we even say there is a community? Or is it merely a bunch of agencies and departments operating in silos? Should we consider that intelligence analysts form an "expert community" like any other and foster it to develop this way? Next, we look at future challenges and opportunities. We briefly examine the nature of the Canada-US intelligence-sharing relationship in the Trump era and discuss the implications should "Trumpism" survive Trump. Finally, we focus on issues that could shape the future of the community itself: increasing professionalization, learning from allies (especially Australia), and increasing levels of cooperation between the intelligence community and nontraditional partners.

The Nature of the Canadian Intelligence Community

IS THERE TRULY AN INTELLIGENCE "COMMUNITY"?

The relative weakness of institutions in the intelligence community and the immaturity of Canada's national security culture raises the question of whether there truly is an intelligence "community" in the federal government. Ideally, the intelligence community should consist of a sum greater than the total of its parts, but in reality that is not the case; it has not truly reached "community" status. There is, in particular, still too much competition between agencies, and work is too often done in silos (see chapter 4). There are also no common standards in human resources (hiring, training, promotions, or performance evaluation). As many interviewees emphasized, more broadly, there is no strong sense of belonging uniting its members.

There is also no assessment community but instead, in the words of one interviewee, "a series of little outposts" who do not coordinate enough. Some competition between analytical units is both necessary and inevitable, as it pushes them to perform better. But many interviewees insisted that there is "too much competition," which is "not particularly healthy." Perceptions of others within the community are often tense. The IAS is viewed as too academic, detached, and arrogant, while the IAS views others as too tactical and not of high quality. Views of CSIS/IAB are often negative, and its peers almost systematically describe ITAC in critical terms. For many interviewees, "we need to do a better job of joint products, coordinating topics, pooling resources (for analysis but also training, etc.), and generally working together."

This raises an interesting parallel: some of the other functional communities in the federal public service have a greater sense of community. Auditors, communicators, and human resources officers, for example, have common standards and enforce them more or less rigorously for hiring and training, performance measurement, and so on. They manage their affairs at least partly collectively and collaboratively.

There have been a number of initiatives over the years to try to build such a sense of community, with some success—in the sense that even though there is a long way to go, there is definitely a greater sense of community today than ten or twenty years ago. It was, in particular, one of the objectives behind the establishment of the Deputy Minister Intelligence Assessment Committee (recently renamed the Deputy Minister Intelligence Committee). It is also why Greg Fyffe, the head of the IAS in 2000–2008, supported the establishment of the Canadian Association of Professional Intelligence Analysts to stimulate cross-community conversations and networking. It was also one of the objectives of the review tasked in 2016 to Linda Goldthorp, a long-standing member of the community who had previously been in the IAS and in defense intelligence. Her goal was to help better define the community and propose recommendations to help it build a stronger sense of itself. The exercise, however, became difficult and bitter, and the report was largely shelved—to some extent, an apt analogy. In taking steps to further build this sense of community, senior officials would benefit from continuing their already deep exchanges with close intelligence partners, especially from the Five Eyes, to learn about their efforts at this level.

INTELLIGENCE ANALYSIS, AN EXPERT COMMUNITY LIKE ANY OTHER?

This parallel between the role of other expert communities and of the intelligence community is an important point to keep in mind when thinking about intelligence policy dynamics. It is, in theory, the role of the leadership of these communities to translate their expert knowledge into a product that is digestible, relevant, and comprehensible for policy clients. It is then the role of policy to incorporate these multiple inputs into the policymaking process. In practice, however, expert communities—engineers, lawyers, accountants, auditors, human resources specialists, and others—each have their own specialized knowledge, processes, vocabulary, and culture. Too often, their understanding of the reality of the policymaking process outside of their own sphere is limited, as senior interviewees with experience in multiple policy fields emphasized.

Indeed, interviews with the most senior policy makers—those with significant experience in other fields, such as economic or social policy—showed how their frequent frustrations with the dynamics of intelligence policy relations are similar to those they frequently harbor toward other expert communities. In their view, experts are often similar in that too often they have difficulty understanding the needs of policy clients and tailoring their work (notably their language) to support those needs.

That is, the Canadian intelligence community's limited policy literacy is comparable to the limited policy literacy found among other expert communities such as scientists and engineers. This is a general problem throughout the federal bureaucracy, and to varying extents in other countries, and one that causes constant frustration at the most senior levels. Intelligence, in this sense, is not unique; it represents one expert input into the policymaking process, like multiple others, and the fundamental nature of its interaction with the policy realm is broadly similar to that of those other inputs.

In the Canadian public service, senior executives rotate through multiple assignments, with the objective of forming leaders and generalists who can manage the bureaucratic process. Expertise is less privileged at higher levels. A DM of foreign affairs or public safety, for example, will likely have had senior postings in economic or social policy prior to reaching this position. This is often criticized, as it implies that senior officials in the foreign, defense, and national security policy worlds sometimes come to their position with limited subject matter expertise. Low-level staff in the intelligence community, in particular, are frequently critical of superiors they see as parachuted with little or no background. The upside, however, and the justification for this approach, is that officials at the most senior levels—DMs, ADMs, and their equivalents—are managers of people and process, and they can and should rely on the expertise of their staff.

Among serving or retired senior policy makers we interviewed, many emphasized how policy making in the national security community can and should be done in the same way it is done in the economic or social worlds. In their view, national security policy making suffers because too many in the community perceive it as more unique than it is or should be. Policy making in other realms is more transparent and open to scrutiny, and policy makers consult more widely, while many in the intelligence community are reluctant to adhere to such practices. But in the words of one interviewee, strictly from a process perspective, "developing an antipoverty strategy is not, or should not be, different, from developing policy in the national security world"; procedures to handle specific information are different, but the process should not be.[1]

The absence of transparency and openness in national security policy making too often creates a closed feedback loop, and the resulting absence of scrutiny contributes to suboptimal decision-making. Indeed, a core element of drafting good policy is a collaborative approach, which is necessary to obtain buy-in throughout the bureaucracy and from external stakeholders. The intelligence and national security community, in the words of multiple interviewees from senior policy ranks, poorly understands this and does not sufficiently have the reflex to think in a broad, whole-of-government policymaking approach. They are, however, slowly improving. As mentioned elsewhere, there is now, in particular, a growing number of senior intelligence positions occupied by individuals with policy experience.

The drafting of Bill C-59 represented an effort to move away from this closed model, as the process was opened up to an unprecedented extent and involved significant internal and external consultations.[2] Yet the intelligence and national security community lacked the skill set to play along. This matters: the ceiling for intelligence analysis to shape policy making is inherently low because too many in the national security community still lack the necessary skill and experience to understand how their work fits into broader policy processes. Put differently, a precondition for intelligence to optimize its impact on policy making is stronger internal policy literacy.

How Structure Shapes Outcomes

One of the most important conclusions of this book is that structure matters: the international security environment that Canada has navigated over the past decades has deeply shaped its intelligence community.

This structural context helps explain the low intelligence literacy in the policy world, and in particular among Canada's politicians. Because Canada is a relatively safe country, there is only limited incentive for senior policy makers to use intelligence. They can use it if or when they choose to, but they can also make do without it most of the time. In other words, they typically suffer little to no cost if they ignore or make limited use of intelligence in their day-to-day work. This is not to say they suffer no cost, but, on average, there are fewer consequences than in many other countries, where the costs of ignoring intelligence in foreign and national security policy making is typically higher. The result is a political and bureaucratic reality in which the government is rarely focused on files for which intelligence makes a significant difference. Intelligence, in other words, is simply not a priority, most of the time, for DMs and the political level. This has a profound ripple effect throughout the system.

Canada's closest allies and partners face different sets of structural incentives: the US is a superpower with global interests while the UK is a former imperial power with a deep tradition of engagement abroad and the experience of violence in Northern Ireland. Australia (discussed further on) is smaller than both but has strong interests in its immediate area in southeast Asia, since developments there immediately affect it in a way not comparable to Canada. These three countries, because of their tradition of global engagement and/or their clearer interests, have a deeper culture in their policy establishments of requiring intelligence analysis; their policy makers far more often need intelligence and know how to use it. These structural realities matter for comparative purposes: because of these differences, lessons learned in one national context may not be applicable in another one, or only partly so.

This structural reality has other implications that help explain some of the dominant features of the Canadian intelligence analysis community. It makes reform more difficult. Because the system as a whole perceives only limited incentive to improve, reform initiatives face a higher threshold, as it is more difficult to mobilize political and bureaucratic constituencies in support of change. As we intend to explore in a future project, reform thus tends to occur mostly in fits and starts, often as a result of external shocks to the system. When a new threat emerges for which the community is unprepared (such as recent foreign electoral meddling or the COVID-19 pandemic), the system is at first unable to deal adequately with the new threat and is then jolted into making the necessary adjustments.

This importance of structure in shaping the nature of the intelligence analysis community also implies that its weaknesses and deficiencies are, fundamentally, not the responsibility of its individual analysts. This is not to say that they are completely blameless. As our interviews showed, some—especially among those who have been around for longer—are resistant to changing bad habits. But for every such "bad apple" in PCO/IAS, CFINTCOM, and CSIS/IAB, there are many younger and dynamic or experienced and knowledgeable midcareer analysts who, on the contrary, are constantly frustrated by their own immediate management's inability to provide them with the tools to achieve greater relevance. Yet, collectively the Canadian polity has decided, for the mostly sound and enviable reason that the threat level has been relatively low in recent decades, that the intelligence analysis community does not require more resources and that its contribution is not systematically essential to high-level policy making.

The system has therefore created a relatively low ceiling for the intelligence analysis community's success. To put it bluntly, if senior policy makers had wanted better intelligence analysis over the years, they would have fostered the conditions to develop it. Senior management, in particular, would have provided mid-level management with more resources, better tools to manage human resources in more productive ways, and stronger license to innovate and develop higher quality products. Individual analysts can try their best to change this, and some do, but there is relatively little they can do in the absence of greater will several levels above their pay grade.

That said, the situation has changed progressively over the past years, and we expect this trend to continue: this structurally induced ceiling for success has been steadily rising, as our book has documented, and the quality of analysis has followed. Starting with the aftermath of the September 11, 2001, terrorist attacks and then the difficult episode of Canada's deployment to Kandahar in Afghanistan (2005–2011), followed by the emergence of a series of new threats in the 2010s (foreign investment by Chinese state-owned enterprises, foreign electoral meddling, economic espionage, and cyberattacks), and culminating since

2020 with the COVID-19 pandemic, the intelligence analysis community has seen the demand for its products steadily grow. The community has responded, albeit with a lag and unequally, by reforming many of its ways of doing business. Even though the average view among our interviewees is that the intelligence analysis community's performance remains underwhelming, all agreed that it has also steadily improved. As one said, "it is night and day" when comparing its performance in 2001 and in 2021.

Trumpism

A question that seemed to hang in the air during many of our interviews was the impact of the presidency of Donald Trump on the Canada-US relationship generally—but also as it applies to intelligence sharing. That Trump had a difficult relationship with his intelligence and national security community has been well established in media reporting. His transactional and skeptical view of multilateralism also raised questions about the future of NATO and of the Five Eyes partnership.

But deeper and more concerning issues go beyond the man himself. It is the forces that Trump has unleashed, a unilateral "America First" nativism, that is as disruptive inside the US as it is outside. While Trump left office in January 2021, it is possible that "Trumpism" will survive him—that is, future Republican politicians could take up this mantle (perhaps more effectively) with a view to abandoning America's traditional Western leadership role. In this sense, the risks of Trump's presidency are not likely to go away when he leaves office.

In the meantime, our findings make it clear that despite Trump, working-level cooperation has continued largely unabated among the Five Eyes and, more directly, Canada and the US. The two countries continue to share intelligence, hold meetings, and otherwise exchange information. Nevertheless, sustained Trumpism in the long run may have two important impacts on Canada. First, Trumpist policies have created a certain level of instability within the US population, including in the US intelligence and national security community, and particularly in agencies such as the FBI and the Office of the Director of National Intelligence. While operations have (mostly) continued unabated, if senior management is disrupted by bureaucratic infighting, it means it is less focused on the mission. Given that Canada is a net consumer of US intelligence, there could be an effect on the quality and/or quantity of the intelligence Canada receives. The Capitol Hill riot of January 6, 2021, often referred to as an insurrection, also raises the possibility that US intelligence and national security agencies will be consumed with far-right or "domestic" extremism for years to come. Importantly, this is an area where Americans have not traditionally shared as much intelligence with allies, including Canada. Second, and more generally, a Trumpist America is destabilizing for the international community. Oscillations between retrenchment and unilateralism can cause something of a whiplash for foreign policy makers among traditional US allies and partners. Moreover, it gives opportunities for belligerent and authoritarian states, such as Russia, China and Saudi Arabia, to unleash wars and aggressive policies on their neighbors and other targets—including Canada.

While all of this may seem far removed from how intelligence analysts can better support their policymaking colleagues, Canada's dependency on US intelligence means that the ability of these analysts to do their job will be affected by the future course of US domestic politics. This is a trade-off Canada faces in its close relationship with the US. It may impact the international environment, the quality of information they receive, and the future existence of the international arrangements and alliances Canada depends upon for its security. The question then becomes what Canada should do to prepare. In chapter 5, we made the case that while Canada should ideally move to establish a foreign human intelligence service, it is more likely that it will have to adjust how its current departments and agencies collect and assess intelligence, particularly with an enhanced Canadian national interests perspective in mind. Better informed policy makers receiving Canadian or Canadianized intelligence will, ideally, be better equipped for the foreign policy challenges of tomorrow.

As it has already begun, Canada can also continue steadily building up its relations, in intelligence and other matters, with allies and partners beyond the US. Canada and the UK, for example, intensified their already close diplomatic and security relations in 2019 and 2020, as witnessed notably by the frequency of contacts between their foreign ministers. More broadly, in diversifying its partnerships, Canada—as the country closest to the US—can leverage its proximity to share lessons learned with others on how to live with an increasingly unpredictable Washington.

The Evolution of the Intelligence Analysis Community

PROFESSIONALIZATION

A constant theme of this book has been that when it comes to intelligence supporting policy making, the Canadian intelligence community has improved, but much more work still needs to be done. In chapter 5, we offered advice on how some of these improvements could be made. But on top of this, interviewees consistently brought up the idea of the need to "professionalize" the Canadian intelligence and national security community. Overwhelmingly, they said this in the context of advocating reforms that would turn intelligence analysis into a profession like other areas of expertise in the federal government, such as auditors, human resources professionals, lawyers, and engineers.

When speaking about how professionalization may come about, interviewees mentioned accreditation, training standards, the creation of a "stream" within the public service, improved coordination between analytical units, standardization of human resources practices, and the fostering of a sense of coherence that is currently lacking. While some noted that this would improve the way the intelligence analysis community performs its work, others also emphasized that a more professionalized approach would help save money in the long-term through a better rationalization of resources.

But perhaps most importantly—and the reason for raising these issues here—is that the national security and intelligence community wants more professionalization. As one interviewee noted, "there is a desire to turn this sort of odd craft that we do into something with some professional standing." Although interviewees differed in their approach, few argued for keeping the status quo. While professionalization is likely to be tricky—requiring input and agreement from both the core and periphery departments and agencies in the community, as well as from central agencies, notably the Treasury Board—the fact that most interviewees see the very tangible benefits suggests that it could meet with success.

AUSTRALIDEALIZING

Interestingly, when it came to examples of countries that get the relationship between intelligence and policy making right, interviewees often pointed to Australia. They spoke favorably about the Australian approach to intelligence and national security in several ways. First, many admired the way that Australian officials look at national security problems through an Australian lens and make their perspectives clearly known in Five Eyes meetings. Second, many pointed to the reality that Australia puts effort and resources into its allied relationships, especially with the US. Many interviewees noted that the Australians are better represented in Washington and frequently bring useful and actionable intelligence to the table. They are also more proactive in cultivating the relationship. Third, interviewees praised Australia's intelligence culture, noting there is "total integration" with policy making, an appetite for risk-taking, and a constant updating of the national security architecture to meet evolving threats. In addition, interviewees noted that there is a willingness to critically assess strategy and priorities through "white papers." In other words, intelligence is central to policy making and integrated into larger decision-making processes, and the community is willing to engage in reflection on whether its strategies meet current challenges. The underlying theme in these comments is clear: Canadians could and should learn more lessons from their Australian counterparts.

There are, however, two qualifications to this praise. First, many interviewees speaking favorably about Australia also noted that it has a very different threat environment than Canada. In this sense, Australians have been forced to step up their intelligence game because, geopolitically, they live in a more challenging threat environment. Second, idealizing the Australian experience needs to be done with some caution. As Andrew Pickford and Jeffrey Collins argue (writing in the context of national defense), there is an "Australidealizing" trap where Canadians see their Five Eyes allies and partners at being better at all things national defense and security (2016).

And yet there are reasons to believe that many interviewees were making comparisons that went beyond such idealizing. Many have worked in Australia or closely with Australian counterparts. Their favorable evaluations of the Australian intelligence and national security community are more grounded in observation than wishful thinking. While there is not enough room here for a full comparison with Australia, its similar size, system of government, and shared interests through the Five Eyes suggest that Canadian officials wishing to bring about change have a good starting point for thinking about reforms by looking at that country.

NONTRADITIONAL PARTNERS

A third theme emerging from our findings is that there has been, in recent years, increased cooperation between the traditional members of the Canadian intelligence and national security community and nontraditional partners elsewhere in the federal government, as well as in other levels of government, the private sector, and academia. Perhaps the most stunning example of this is the support that CSE provided to Elections Canada in the run-up to the 2019 federal election. Just a few short years earlier, the idea that cyberspies would be near, let alone actively involved in, an election was unheard of. This example illustrates how evolving threats cause some of the traditional walls between intelligence and many areas of the policy world to come down.

In reflecting on our discussions with interviewees, it seems clear that this process of cooperation has been ongoing since at least the late 2000s, when the government created the Afghanistan Task Force in PCO. This task force brought officials from across the government together to try to improve the management of Canada's efforts on the ground in that country. This has accelerated in recent years, driven by a requirement for unprecedented cooperation to meet the challenges of emerging threats, particularly with departments that have traditionally been outside the intelligence and national security community: foreign fighters (involving Transport Canada and Passport Canada), foreign investment by state-owned and state-championed enterprises (Innovation, Science, and Economic Development, formerly Industry Canada) and threats to democratic institutions (Elections Canada, Canadian Heritage). Given changes in the international context, cooperation between the intelligence and national security community and these nontraditional partners will remain, and likely intensify, for some time to come. Indeed, when finishing this book in early 2021, intelligence officials speaking under the Chatham House rule confirmed an unprecedented demand for intelligence products as a result of the COVID-19 pandemic. These requests were coming from cabinet, as well as from nontraditional partners who have not "pulled" intelligence analysis in the past to help them make decisions. This would not have been possible without key changes on the intelligence side. According to one interviewee, the community realized that "nobody was listening to them"—in other words, they were sitting on valuable information relevant to key challenges but lacked a strong voice around the many tables outside of the intelligence community where decisions are made.

Nevertheless, as these relationships are evolving, challenges remain. The first is that the policy community often does not have the infrastructure necessary to receive intelligence in a timely way. For example, setting up sensitive compartmented information facilities is expensive. It requires secure computers, often in a remote room, far removed from a person's place of work, where they do not have access to their normal phone. Second, as discussed in chapter 2, there is a lack of training for individuals in the policy community to help them learn about intelligence. As one interviewee noted, "we don't know how to educate a (policy) person who is coming into this sort of protected space and say this is the kind of information you are going to receive, this is the network." A third issue relates to the second: if the intelligence and policy worlds still do not understand each other well, there will continue to be communication problems. For example, one interviewee noted that within the policy world, the "challenge function" (rigorous scrutiny of assumptions and plans) is a critical part of policy development. But this function is not performed in the same way in intelligence—analysts can provide assessments but they must protect sources. In this sense, a cultural divide remains between the two worlds. These are challenges that Canada's allies and partners also face. As we will explore in future projects, the integration of these budding nontraditional relationships in Five Eyes and other networks, where both information and lessons learned can be exchanged, will be essential.

We have discussed some of the solutions to these challenges : better training, more secondments and exchanges, better networking, and more frequent meetings with clients. But there are other options as well. First, in the words of one interviewee, there is a need to somehow "demystify" intelligence so that people understand it better. But it also takes a willingness on behalf of the Canadian intelligence community to recognize that the community is larger than what its members have traditionally believed. It has to take proactive steps to cooperate with nontraditional partners—a difficult task given that cooperation within the traditional community itself is often still a challenge. Indeed, the idea that there has to be willingness by people at all levels of government for more exchanges between traditional and nontraditional partners seems to be increasingly accepted, but now it must be better put into practice.

APPENDIX

A Guide to the Canadian Government and to the National Security and Intelligence Community

To help readers unfamiliar with the structure of the Canadian national security and intelligence community, we present here a short overview of the Canadian government. It will also assist those wishing to make comparisons between the Canadian and other intelligence communities (particularly that of the US), which is a key goal of our project.[1]

The Canadian Government

Canada is a constitutional monarchy and parliamentary democracy that operates under the conventions and customs of the Westminster system that originated in the UK. Canada and the UK share the same monarch in a personal union, but the office of the Queen of Canada and Canadian Crown are legally separate and distinct from the Queen of the UK and British Crown. Queen Elizabeth II therefore serves as Canada's head of state in a distinct capacity from her role as the British monarch. The Queen is represented in Canada by the governor general, who exercises nearly all of the Canadian head of state's functions.

In a Westminster system, government authority formally flows from the Crown, as the executive power. In practice, nearly all executive authority is exercised by the prime minister and ministers who belong to cabinet. According to binding constitutional conventions, the prime minister and cabinet must be parliamentarians and are held to account for affairs of government by the houses of Parliament. Unlike in the US, therefore, the Canadian executive and legislative branches are fused, owing to the rule that the prime minister and cabinet should be parliamentarians.

Canada has a bicameral parliamentary system with a lower chamber (the House of Commons) and an upper chamber (the Senate). The lower chamber is comprised of elected members of Parliament (MPs) and the upper chamber of appointed senators. All Canadian legislation must pass both chambers, but by constitutional convention the Senate will not block legislation that has the support of the Commons.

While the monarch is the Canadian head of state, the head of government is the prime minister, who is almost always the leader of the party that holds the confidence of the House of Commons.[2] The office of prime minister is not defined in Canada's Constitution. The role and functions of the head of government are largely defined by constitutional conventions that have evolved over the centuries, first in the UK, then in Canada itself. Today, the prime minister is the most powerful political figure in the country, with the ability to appoint cabinet and control its decisions. The prime minister exercises core executive authorities, such as the conduct of diplomacy and the deployment of the armed forces on operations overseas, and they largely control the legislative agenda and the life of Parliament.

While the prime minister and cabinet ministers are supported by a set of partisan advisers in the Prime Minister's Office (PMO) and in ministerial offices, the Canadian public service is composed of permanent employees of the state who are expected to be politically neutral. The prime minister, however, has the power to appoint public servants at the highest levels of the executive, which gives the head of government some influence over the executive branch. In addition, the highest-ranking public servant, the clerk of the Privy Council, is understood to be the prime minister's bureaucratic deputy, helping the head of government manage all executive departments and agencies.

All heads of Canada's national security agencies are appointed by the prime minister on the advice of the clerk of the Privy Council. Most of them will have previously served in high-ranking roles in different departments and agencies across government. In some cases, they will also have had experience outside the national security and intelligence community.

As noted previously, the prime minister has considerable power in the area of foreign, defense, and national security policy. The prime minister and cabinet can exercise the Crown's prerogative powers to deploy the Canadian Armed Forces (CAF) and do not require parliamentary approval. The executive also exercises these prerogative powers to negotiate, sign, and ratify treaties. Parliament is only involved in the treaty process to scrutinize international agreements and pass enacting legislation. For the purposes of this book, these are the most important ministers in terms of national security:

- Minister of foreign affairs, the senior minister responsible for Global Affairs Canada (GAC)
- Minister of national defence, with responsibility for the Department of National Defence and the Canadian Armed Forces (DND/ CAF) and Canada's national cryptologic agency, the Communications Security Establishment (CSE)
- Minister of public safety and emergency preparedness, with responsibility for most of Canada's national security agencies, including the Canadian Security Intelligence Service (CSIS), the Canada Border Services Agency (CBSA), the Integrated Threat Assessment Centre(ITAC), and the Royal Canadian Mounted Police (RCMP)

Canada's National Security Agencies

In many respects, Canada's national security architecture is similar to that of its allies; there are several agencies that are specifically devoted to security and intelligence as well as departments and agencies that have security as a part of their broader functions. For the purposes of this appendix, we have divided these into four core functions: central agencies; collection and analysis; operations, enforcement, and community engagement; and larger departments with national security functions.

Canada's national security architecture does differ in some respects. Until 2018, Canada was one of very few democratic countries to have no legislative review of its national security agencies. But perhaps the biggest difference between Canada and its allies is the lack of a foreign human intelligence service. Canada has no equivalent to the US CIA, the British Secret Intelligence Service, or the Australian Secret Intelligence Service. Whether or not Canada should develop such an agency has been a matter of scholarly debate (Collins 2002; Farson and Teeple 2015; Tierney 2015; St. John 2017).

CENTRAL AGENCIES

Within the government of Canada there are three central agencies, departments with a coordinating function and involvement in the highest order of decisions of the executive: the Treasury Board of Canada Secretariat, the Department of Finance, and the Privy Council Office (PCO). The Treasury Board is a committee of cabinet ministers who provide spending authority to government departments and set regulations within the executive. Its work is supported by the Treasury Board of Canada Secretariat. The Department of Finance drafts the federal budget and macroeconomic policies. PCO, which is headed by the clerk of the Privy Council, is effectively the prime minister's department, coordinating the implementation of the government's agenda across the executive and supporting cabinet decision-making. PCO houses the prime minister's national security and intelligence adviser (NSIA) and foreign and defense policy adviser, as well as the Security and Intelligence (S&I) secretariat and Intelligence Assessment Secretariat (IAS). The NSIA has direct access to the clerk of the Privy Council, and by extension the prime minister. The NSIA also supports cabinet committees involved in national security decisions, and works closely with the heads of Canada's security and intelligence agencies. It is supported by PCO/S&I and PCO/IAS.[3]

PMO is composed of partisan loyalists whose job is to provide political advice to the prime minister. Beyond this, however, it is difficult to precisely outline PMO's roles and functions in the national security space as each prime minister uses and structures the office differently. Each minister also has their own political staff who help in their decision-making and coordinate with PMO and other ministerial offices. Given their central role in decision-making, some political staff in PMO and in ministerial offices receive high-level clearances and therefore access to classified information.

PCO/S&I provides overall support on policy coordination and direction for the government in the area of national security and intelligence. It is also responsible for the prime minister's and cabinet's security. Its staff is largely comprised of seconded individuals from other departments and agencies across government.

PCO/IAS is an analytical body within PCO focusing on international issues; it is similar to the Office of National Intelligence in Australia and to the Joint Intelligence Committee in the UK. It is managed by an assistant secretary to the cabinet who is responsible for the analytical assessments produced within the secretariat. PCO/IAS plays a limited coordinating function, often bringing subject matter experts from multiple departments and agencies together to write community-wide assessments on a particular issue. While the IAS produces intelligence assessments for the broader intelligence and national security community, it is increasingly focused on supporting the needs of the prime minister and cabinet (Fyffe 2021). Although PCO/IAS provides intelligence assessments, it has no collection capacity. Instead, it receives raw and finished intelligence from other government of Canada agencies and from allies and partners.

The Privy Council's Foreign and Defence Policy secretariat, which was under the NSIA's authority until 2020, provides advice on foreign policy to the clerk and to the prime minister. The foreign and defense policy adviser tends to be an experienced diplomat and travels with the prime minister on foreign visits.

CORE COLLECTION AND ANALYTICAL AGENCIES

Within the Canadian government there are four agencies with intelligence at the heart of their functions: CSE, CSIS, ITAC, and FINTRAC.

The Communications Security Establishment (CSE), the signals intelligence and national cryptologic agency, is one of Canada's oldest national security institutions, with its origins in the Second World War. Today, CSE has four major functions: collecting foreign intelligence from the global information infrastructure; information security; assisting domestic law enforcement (with a warrant); and, as of 2019, foreign active (offensive) and defensive cyber operations. Importantly, CSE is not allowed to collect intelligence on Canadians. This can only be done if a law enforcement or national security agency is able to secure a warrant from a federal judge that allows CSE to obtain this information on behalf of the requesting agency. CSE regularly exchanges information with its partners in the Five Eyes: the National Security Agency in the US, the UK's Government Communications Headquarters, the Australian Signals Directorate, and New Zealand's Government Communications Security Bureau. CSE falls under the responsibility of the minister of national defence.

The Canadian Security Intelligence Service (CSIS) was created in 1984 in the wake of several scandals. These led the Commission of Inquiry Concerning Certain Activities of the Royal Canadian Mounted Police (known as the McDonald Commission) to advise the government to remove national security functions from the RCMP and to create a civilian intelligence agency. CSIS now collects security intelligence within Canada and is responsible to the minister of public safety. As a civilian (not a law enforcement) intelligence agency primarily focused on domestic threats, it has no direct US counterpart. Instead, its international equivalent is the UK's Security Service. CSIS's mandate is to collect information and advise the government on threats to the security of Canada, defined as espionage, foreign influenced activities, terrorism, and subversion. Investigations surrounding subversion, however, have been suspended since 1986 (Whitaker,

Kealy, and Parnaby 2012 242). While CSIS is primarily domestically focused, under Canadian law it may collect foreign intelligence within Canada (i.e., on foreign targets within Canada's borders) at the specific request of the minister of foreign affairs or minister of national defence. Within the Service, the Intelligence Assessment Branch (IAB) is responsible for providing analytical products.

The Integrated Terrorism Assessment Centre (ITAC) is housed within CSIS but exists as a separate agency. ITAC was created in 2004 in the wake of Canada's first ever national security policy, reflecting a trend across Western governments, including Five Eyes countries, to create integrated analytical bodies composed of representatives from across government. Ideally, such centers would break down silos and improve interagency coordination and the flow of information and intelligence (Carvin 2021a). ITAC therefore brings together its own analysts as well as secondees from multiple agencies. At approximately forty to fifty employees, it is one of the smallest national security institutions in the Canadian government. Its Five Eyes equivalents include the National Counterterrorism Center in the US, the Joint Terrorism Assessment Centre in the UK, and Australia's National Threat Assessment Centre.

ITAC is managed by its own director, appointed by the NSIA in consultation with the director of CSIS. The director of ITAC is responsible to the CSIS director as well as to its Management Board, chaired by the NSIA and attended by DMs from participating organizations. ITAC's mandate has changed over time and now mostly focuses on providing intelligence assessment to senior policy makers. ITAC does not collect its own information but has access to CSIS and CSE databases.

The Financial Transactions and Reports Analysis Centre of Canada (FINTRAC) is Canada's financial intelligence unit. It was created in 2000 in response to various international initiatives and United Nations Security Council resolutions that required governments to take steps to stop the funding of violent extremism. Exceptionally among Canada's national security agencies, FINTRAC reports to the minister of finance. FINTRAC's US counterpart is the Department of the Treasury's Financial Crimes Enforcement Network (FinCEN).

FINTRAC investigates money laundering and counterterrorism finance in line with Canada's domestic laws and international obligations. It does this through the use and production of financial intelligence. FINTRAC operates at arm's length from police, law enforcement, and other national security agencies to which it is authorized to disclose financial intelligence. Its national security responsibilities include receiving suspicious reports and voluntary information from financial institutions; producing financial intelligence relevant to investigations of money laundering, terrorist activity financing and threats to the security of Canada; and researching and analyzing trends and patterns in money laundering and terrorist activity financing (Financial Transactions and Reports Analysis Centre of Canada 2018; Pyrik 2021). FINTRAC carries out its mandate by disclosing threat activity financing via disclosures to law enforcement as well as strategic intelligence about various financial intelligence trends and developments.

FINTRAC seems to have struggled with its mandate since its creation in 2000. In the last eighteen years it has issued relatively few financial fines (totaling CA$6 million) compared to FinCEN (US$7 billion). Further, during this time there has been only one conviction on strictly terrorism finance grounds in Canada that resulted in a six-month sentence for a man who provided CA$3,000 to the Tamil Tigers. (Although there have been several cases where terrorism financing was part of a larger suite of facilitation charges.) International bodies, such as the United Nation's Counter-Terrorism Committee and the Financial Action Task Force have noticed this poor track record and suggested recommendations for improvement (Roach 2011, 382–84; Berman and Pellegrini 2016).

OPERATIONS AND ENFORCEMENT

While these organizations have responsibilities for collecting intelligence and producing analysis, they are separate from law enforcement bodies. Therefore, community relations and the prosecution of threat-related activity are conducted by separate agencies, both within the portfolio of PSC: the Royal Canadian Mounted Police (RCMP) and the Canada Border Services Agency (CBSA). PSC was created in 2003 as a direct result of the 9/11 terrorism attacks to create a federal coordinating body managing the nexus between intelligence, police, and government responses (Wilner 2021). It is similar to the UK Home Office and, to a lesser extent, the Department of Homeland Security in the US.

Although its portfolio includes agencies that collect intelligence and prepare analytical products, PSC itself has no intelligence gathering capabilities; its focus is on policy and operational coordination. It is also responsible for producing a limited number of national security related documents, including the annual *Public Report on the Terrorist Threat to Canada*. It is primarily a consumer of intelligence used in the development of national security policy and operations.

The RCMP is responsible for criminal investigations leading to the prosecution of individuals linked to threat-related activity. The RCMP is Canada's federal police force, with its origins dating back to 1873. While the closest comparison in the US context is the FBI, the RCMP is no longer the investigatory lead on national security threats.[4] However, once CSIS has determined that a threat-related activity has reached the point where it should be prosecuted, it sends an advisory letter to the RCMP, which will then open a separate, parallel investigation for the purpose of pursuing criminal charges, although this can be a cumbersome process fraught with difficulties (Forcese 2018; Forcese and West 2021, 465–68).The RCMP has four main functions as it relates to national security: (1) preventing, investigating, and prosecuting national security offences; (2) protective policing of internationally protected persons (heads of state, diplomats, the prime minister, select ministers, Supreme Court and Federal Court judges, and the governor general); (3) providing advice to departments and agencies on protective security measures; and (4) consolidating threat assessments from the national security community to provide appropriate protection of internationally protected persons, foreign missions, and special events (Forcese and West 2021, 106; Roach 2021).

To complete these functions, the RCMP maintains analysts at all levels of the organization. While some provide tactical support for police investigations, analysts within the National Security Division and the National Intelligence Coordination Centre generate products based on domestic and foreign intelligence to support high-level strategic decision-making within the RCMP. Importantly, to prevent Canadian or foreign intelligence being brought into courtroom trials as evidence, these intelligence units within the RCMP ensure sensitive intelligence is "walled off" from the regular police force and kept out of investigative files that may be disclosed as part of the trial process. In this sense, most of the RCMP's collection activities are centered on gathering evidence for prosecution, with analysis providing strategic support to that end rather than support for policy making across the rest of government.

Although Canada has always maintained a border security force, the creation of CBSA in its current form dates back to 2003. Concerns about border security in the aftermath of 9/11 saw the government bring together the enforcement functions of the Canada Revenue Agency, Citizenship and Immigration Canada, and the Canadian Food Inspection Agency into one force, which today stands as Canada's second largest law enforcement agency after the RCMP (Leuprecht et al. 2021). CBSA's US counterpart is Customs and Border Protection. Similar to the RCMP, CBSA is mostly an intelligence consumer, although it can exchange information with other national security services. CBSA has its own analysts who mostly prepare internally focused products to assist border officers. Of necessity, CBSA works closely with its US counterparts along the Canada-US border.

GOVERNMENT AGENCIES WITH NATIONAL SECURITY FUNCTIONS

Canada's defense, foreign affairs, and justice departments have important national security functions. On the defense side, command authority for the CAF flows down from the Queen, who holds the powers of command in chief, while the governor general is granted the ceremonial title of commander-in-chief. In practice, the CAF are under the direction of the prime minister and minister of national defence, and under the command of the chief of the defence staff, who is appointed by the prime minister. As the head of government, the prime minister is responsible and accountable for all affairs of government, including national defense, while the minister of national defence is legally responsible and accountable for the defense portfolio under the National Defence Act (Juneau 2021). DND/CAF collect, produce, and consume intelligence and intelligence assessments to fulfill their mandate. At the core of this is Canadian Forces Intelligence Command (CFINTCOM). It prepares analytical products for both internal and external consumers and is responsible for a range of units charged with collecting human, geospatial, and imagery intelligence, among others.

GAC is responsible for foreign relations, making it the equivalent to the State Department in the US and the Foreign, Commonwealth & Development Office in the UK. Formally, there is nothing relating to national security in GAC's legislative mandate, but in practice the department plays an important role in this realm. First, as noted previously, the minister of foreign affairs may request from other national security agencies that they collect information that will help it with its mandate. Some actions by national security agencies such as CSE and CSIS also require consultation with or approval by the minister of foreign affairs, especially when Canada's foreign relations could be affected. Second, since 9/11 GAC's mandate has expanded to include a role in countering terrorism and the proliferation of weapons of mass destruction (Nesbitt 2021). Although it played an important role in producing foreign intelligence during the Cold War, today GAC is more an intelligence consumer than producer. It is therefore largely dependent on intelligence-sharing from other government departments and from allies and partners (Nesbitt 2021). In recent years, however, GAC created and then expanded its Global Security Reporting Program (GSRP), which tasks diplomats with gathering open-source information and political reporting abroad that is shared within GAC, with other federal departments, and with allies and partners. In addition, GAC recently established its own intelligence analysis unit to support internal decision-making.

In Canada, the minister of justice has several roles to play in national security. First, the minister, as the attorney general of Canada, conducts litigation for or against the Crown (in this context the federal government) or any department within federal jurisdiction, including national security agencies. The minister is also responsible for the Department of Justice, which includes providing advice as the government's "law firm" (Forcese and Poirier 2021).

There are major differences in how the departments of justice operate in Canada and the US when it comes to national security. Many of the types of law enforcement responsibilities that fall under the US Department of Justice (FBI, Bureau of Prisons, etc.) are regulated by separate departments and agencies in Canada (particularly PSC). In this sense, the role of Canada's Department of Justice is more limited in the national security space. In addition, whereas in the US each national security agency has its own lawyers to litigate in court (and fight interagency battles), in Canada all government lawyers are Justice Canada employees who are embedded in departmental legal service units. As Forcese and Poirer (2021) note, this allows the Justice Department to "speak with one voice" in terms of policy and advice given.

Justice Canada employees embedded in departmental legal service units within national security agencies have access to intelligence analysis products, but many legal documents, such as warrants, must be based on facts (intelligence information) as opposed to assessments. These lawyers write legal assessments regarding various cases and issues, but these are mostly for internal consumption within their agencies and Justice Canada. As they may involve highly sensitive issues, they are not widely shared across the intelligence community.

The final institutions of importance here are the new national security review bodies established by the Justin Trudeau government. As noted previously, Canada has lagged behind its Five Eyes counterparts when it comes to national security oversight and review.[5] There was no parliamentary body with access to classified information that could monitor the activities of Canada's intelligence and national security community, and most institutions and departments discussed previously did not have independent review agencies. Where there was independent review (over CSIS and CSE, in particular), the bodies were stovepiped and restricted to only a specific department or agency. In other words, review bodies were unable to take a pancommunity perspective because, for example, the body that reviewed CSIS was unable to look at how these activities impacted CSE and vice versa. This meant that review bodies were unable to follow the thread to see how intelligence, including intelligence analysis, was used once it had been passed on to other departments and agencies.

This changed between 2017 and 2019, with the creation of three new review bodies. First, the National Security and Intelligence Committee of Parliamentarians (NSICOP) was created as an executive body composed of members of Parliament and senators with access to all national security information within the government, save for cabinet confidences. Although the remit of NSICOP has not been fully clarified in law, the body has so far focused mostly on efficacy issues. Second is the National Security and Intelligence Review Agency (NSIRA), an independent review body managed by civil servants with the ability to review the work of any agency that has access to intelligence. Unlike its predecessors, it is able to see how intelligence moves across the community and how it is used. Finally, the Office of the Intelligence Commissioner supports a retired or supernumerary judge who serves an oversight function in approving certain cyberoperations and the collection and use of datasets.

For the purposes of this book, the first and second new review bodies are the most important. Both have the remit to review analytical products and how they are used and shared within the national security and intelligence community. It also means that departments and agencies that have never been subject to independent review before, especially GAC and DND/CAF, now have their intelligence functions—including the production, consumption, and sharing of intelligence products—scrutinized.

NOTES

Introduction

1. In this context, the book does not focus much on the Royal Canadian Mounted Police (RCMP), where the bulk of the analytical work supports law enforcement operations. To be clear, this does not imply that there is no strategic analysis within the RCMP: analytical work to support operations does not have to be solely tactical and operational in its nature. In addition, the RCMP has, in recent years, boosted its strategic analysis capacity to support policy making within the force. This analysis, however, has by its nature a limited impact outside the RCMP and, as such, largely remains outside the scope of this book. (Interestingly, the RCMP has chosen to colocate its strategic policy and strategic analysis teams to ensure the close integration of their work.)

2. This difficulty in measuring success is also highlighted by Canada's National Security and Intelligence Committee of Parliamentarians in its *Annual Report 2018* (2019, 51). See the report for details on a draft framework developed by the Privy Council Office (but eventually discarded as too unwieldy) intended to measure how effectively the intelligence community was delivering on the government's intelligence priorities.

3. As one official reviewing this chapter pointed out, this is largely true in the policy-making context but not in an operational one.

4. For an early explanation of the changes in Bill C-59, which created the act, see Forcese and Roach (2017).

Chapter 1: Governance and Structure

1. For more on PCO's role in security and intelligence issues, see Fyffe (2021).

2. On PSC's role and mandate, see Wilner (2021).

3. The Washington, DC, station is one of three publicly declared CSIS offices abroad, the others being in France and the UK.

4. There is also a range of lower-level committees to support these deputy minister committees.

5. In the wake of the failed attack by Umar Farouk Abdul Mutallab (known as the Underwear Bomber) in 2009, senior officials realized they were poorly equipped to coordinate a response. The assistant secretary for S&I (Rennie Marcoux) and an assistant deputy minister (ADM) at Public Safety, Linda Claremont, decided to set up a weekly ADM committee for national security operations, ADM NSOps. This body, which still

meets today, brings together the main players (Privy Council Office, Canadian Security Intelligence Service, Royal Canadian Mounted Police, Global Affairs Canada, Department of National Defence, Communications Security Establishment, and others) to share information on threats and operations. More broadly, it aims to build trust and relationships, which were weak back then; they have improved, though far from enough. In the words of one interviewee, ADM NSOps does "simple, but necessary things." Initially, after its meetings the committee debriefed the national security adviser, Stephen Rigby, who saw value in it and subsequently created a deputy minister–level equivalent, the Deputy Minister Operations Committee (DMOC).

6. There were, over the years, numerous predecessor committees to DMIA/DMIC, such as the ADM Intelligence Assessment Committee (IAC). The IAC was usually poorly attended and low on the list of priorities of its members. One individual, who was a member in the 1990s, claimed that he did not regularly attend and that, even when he did, it was not a priority; from his perspective, notably, it was too operationally focused. Interestingly, this individual recalled that the very existence of the committee could not be disclosed. DMIA was subsequently eliminated by Morin's successor as national security adviser, Stephen Rigby, but it was later reinstated at the request of deputy ministers.

7. Some interviewees criticized the IAS for not taking other views seriously enough when it drafts NIAs.

8. This interviewee made this point regarding DMIC but emphasized that it also applied to DMOC and the DMNS committee.

9. In the words of one interviewee: "And this was fascinating to observe in the Prime Minister's Office (Harper's), how the public service . . . tries to adapt its working methods to the particular styles and personalities of the prime minister and the people working for the prime minister." For more on PMO and intelligence, see Lilly (2021).

10. One senior policy official who reviewed a draft of this chapter reacted to this paragraph by arguing that "this is a massive failure on the part of senior public service leaders, not the prime minister . . . the fact that the prime minister did not read (intelligence) should have made those working for him even more assiduously attentive to this material."

11. One interviewee recounted an episode during which an analytical unit wrote a piece on an international leader. Harper disagreed and sent the unit a written note in which he wrote that the paper "totally mischaracterized" this leader, which elicited a "mix of sheer terror and excitement" among management and analysts: excitement that Harper had read their product and cared enough to respond, and terror that he had disagreed. To its credit, the unit stood by its assessment.

12. According to Philippe Lagassé, "Prerogative powers are discretionary authorities of the Crown as recognized by common law and the Constitution of Canada in sections 9 and 15 of the Constitution Act, 1867. Crown prerogative was originally the source of all governing authority but has been gradually reduced as parliamentary statute has expanded. A core set of Crown prerogatives, however, have been kept in place, reflecting their importance for the head of state and head of government functions, and the need for discretion and flexibility in areas of executive competency. Prerogatives of an

executive nature are exercised by the prime minister, cabinet, and in certain cases, individual ministers, reflecting the constitutional functions and responsibilities of the political executive." Correspondence, May 12, 2020. For a discussion of DND's intelligence authorities, see the National Security and Intelligence Committee of Parliamentarians *Annual Report 2018* (2019, 57–121).

13. Available in Appendix A of National Security and Intelligence Committee of Parliamentarians (2019).

14. Proceeds of Crime (Money Laundering) and Terrorist Financing Act, s. 40 (b).

15. Under section 55 (3) (where "designated information would be relevant to investigating or prosecuting a money laundering offence or a terrorist activity financing offence") and 55.1 (1), (Threats to the Security of Canada) of the Proceeds of Crime (Money Laundering) and Terrorist Financing Act, FINTRAC is able to disclose information to "the appropriate police force," Canada Border Services Agency, Canada Revenue Agency, Revenu Québec, Communications Security Establishment, Canadian Security Intelligence Service, and Department of National Defence.

16. Canadian Security Intelligence Service Act, s. 12(1): "The Service shall collect, by investigation or otherwise, to the extent that it is strictly necessary, and analyse and retain information and intelligence respecting activities that may on reasonable grounds be suspected of constituting threats to the security of Canada and, in relation thereto, shall report to and advise the Government of Canada."

17. Communications Security Establishment Act 2019, s. 17: "(a) provide advice, guidance and services to help protect (i) federal institutions' electronic information and information infrastructures, and (ii) electronic information and information infrastructures designated under subsection 21(1) as being of importance to the Government of Canada; and (b) acquire, use and analyse information from the global information infrastructure or from other sources in order to provide such advice, guidance and services."

18. The authors wish to thank Philippe Lagassé on this point.

19. It is worth noting that this does not differ from broader government of Canada practice on how analysis is coordinated and legislated generally. However, it is interesting to contrast how responsibilities, authorities, and operations are increasingly detailed in statutory authorities.

20. For more on ITAC, see Carvin (2021a).

21. An official who reviewed this chapter added, "Analysts benefit from having someone else to talk to; someone with related expertise but a different organizational orientation is a useful foil. Many analysts are already too entrenched in their own views; knowing someone else from within the community might call them out is good for them."

22. See also Canadian Security Intelligence Service Act 1985 s. 2.

23. The Royal Canadian Mounted Police is able to go abroad to collect information that supports its criminal and national security investigations, although it does not tend to produce analytical reports for government or policy makers outside of its own organization and, as such, is not discussed here.

24. It is not clear the extent to which Barnes is suggesting that these incidents of what he calls "behind-the-scenes bureaucratic push-back" represent a kind of politicization. It is noteworthy that Barnes does not use the term. In our view, there are at least two reasons to suggest this is not a case of politicization as we understand it here. First, the "push-back" seems to have come from other agencies within the bureaucracy, not from the political level. Another important factor as well is that, as discussed later in this chapter, it appears that intelligence did not play a major role in the Chrétien government's decision to stay out of Iraq; at best intelligence provided support for Chrétien's instinct against Canadian involvement but was not the deciding factor. In this sense, the incentive to politicize was limited. We further discuss politicization in chapter 4.

25. See also the discussion in West (2021).

26. See also National Security and Intelligence Committee of Parliamentarians (2020b, 13).

27. Three interviewees noted that the federal court increasingly plays an oversight and review function through issuing or quashing warrants and in court trials. As these activities do not touch upon the intelligence policy nexus, we will not discuss the impact of the federal court here. See Forcese (2018).

28. In the early hours of November 5, 1995, a man broke into 24 Sussex, the prime minister's residence. Chrétien's wife locked their bedroom door, with the man right on the other side, and called the police. For details, see Fisher (1996).

29. Even though it was initially modeled on the Joint Intelligence Committee, in some ways the IAS is similar to the Bureau of Intelligence and Research in the State Department in the US. The bureau has a good track record, but its relatively small size implies that it is not a major player in the US intelligence community as a whole. We thank an anonymous reviewer for suggesting this comparison. See King (2017).

30. According to one interviewee, "Chrétien was known to read *The Economist* and *The Globe and Mail*, but not intelligence."

31. This reconstruction of the role of intelligence in shaping Chrétien's decision is based on multiple interviews with individuals involved with the process. See also Sayle (2017, 210–27) and Barnes (2020).

32. One interviewee emphasized that the intelligence community understood that the consequences of refusing to participate in the invasion were serious. Indeed, after Canada declined to participate, the US reduced intelligence-sharing with Canada (though as one interviewee nuanced, DGInt, as Defence Intelligence was then known, lost significant access, but not CSIS). Many in the community feared this would be permanent, but it subsided. The consequences, as such, were minor in both scope and duration.

Chapter 2: Managing Analytical Units

1. See for example Gannon (2008); Gentry (2016, 154); Gentry (1995); Juneau (2017, 249–53); Marrin (2011, 2); and Moore, Krizan, and Moore (2005, 211).

2. DRDC's mandate is to support "defence and security operations at home and abroad with knowledge and technology; provide S&T to forecast, cost, and deliver

future readiness levels to meet operational requirements; and, generate knowledge and technology for a robust, connected and multi-jurisdictional security and intelligence environment." It is in some ways similar to the US government's Defense Advanced Research Projects Agency, although there are key differences between the two. See Smith (2014).

3. In particular, these studies were conducted with the explicit purpose of "identifying human capability challenges in the Canadian intelligence community, with a particular view toward identifying how behavioural science might help to respond effectively to these challenges" (Adams et al. 2012, iii).

4. Although they document the trend toward hiring more generalists, Roi and Dickson are critical of it (2017, 237).

5. According to an individual who reviewed a draft of this chapter, CSIS took its first steps toward hiring managers with policy experience at this time to help manage the impact of several official inquiries into actions of the intelligence and national security community that may have led to torture (especially the Arar and Iacobucci inquiries), as well as court challenges to certain counterterrorism measures, such as security certificates to detain certain individuals believed to be engaged in threat-related activities.

6. This was also a finding in Derbentseva, McLellan, and Mandel (2010, 62).

7. The Treasury Board of Canada Secretariat is the central agency in the federal government that approves how the government spends money on programs and services. It thus has a lot of say over how the intelligence community administers itself. See the appendix.

8. See, for example, Derbentseva, McLellan, and Mandel (2010, 42–44); Moore (2005, 29–43); Moore, Krizan, and Moore (2005).

9. In the Advanced Policy Analyst Program, recruits serve in four six-month rotations through a line department and three central agencies (Department of Finance, Treasury Board of Canada Secretariat, and the Privy Council Office). See Government of Canada (2017b). The Policy Officer Recruitment Programme "is a three-year program created to recruit, develop, and train talented individuals from entry to working-level in the Policy Group at the Department of National Defence." See Department of National Defence (2019b).

10. Marrin borrows these terms from Folker (2000).

11. See also Lowenthal (2013). For a similar, if more critical view, see Gentry (2016, 165).

12. Training at GAC/GSRP is discussed in the case study in chapter 3.

13. We discuss bridging the intelligence policy gap in Canada in the next chapter, so only a brief summary is provided here.

14. See for example Pherson and Heuer (2011, 49–50).

15. Some organizations, like CSIS, do not follow the federal government's occupational groups for analysts, using other job classification systems inherited from the RCMP.

16. Following a series of revelations about domestic surveillance of Canadians by the RCMP, CSIS ended its subversion investigations in 1986. It does, however, remain a part of the CSIS Act.

17. A detailed account of the events of the 1970s, the McDonald Commission and the establishment of CSIS can be found in Whitaker, Kealy, and Parnaby (2012).

18. For an overview of the modern CSIS and how it got to where it is, see Littlewood (2021).

19. See, for example, an archived version of Canadian Security Intelligence Service (1999).

20. This is based on CSIS public reports, which used RAP in 2005–2006 and then IAB in 2007–2008. An assessment quoted by a newspaper also refers to a "2007 document from the CSIS intelligence assessment branch."

21. This is a point made by an individual who reviewed a draft of this chapter.

22. An individual who reviewed a draft of this chapter noted that CSIS is trying to move to lower the classification of many products and produce more unclassified assessments to increase their distribution in government as well as make them accessible to more computer networks.

23. On this issue, see Carvin and Forcese (2019).

Chapter 3: Managing Intelligence Policy Dynamics

1. There is no method to objectively quantify policy or intelligence literacy. As such, our assessment of its evolution here is based on our interviews.

2. Of course, as will be discussed below, intelligence literacy in policy circles in Canada is also lower than in the US and the UK.

3. For more on the Bureau of Intelligence and Research, see King (2017).

4. See the ICA's *Annual Report 2018–19* for more detail (Innovation, Science, and Economic Development Canada 2019).

5. Privy Council Office, *Intelligence Priorities Binder Overview for the NSIA*, April 2015, quoted in NSICOP *Annual Report 2018* (National Security and Intelligence Committee of Parliamentarians 2019, 36).

6. The description of the intelligence priorities process that follows is based on our interviews as well as on NSICOP's *Annual Report 2018* (National Security and Intelligence Committee of Parliamentarians 2019, 33–55).

7. A memorandum to cabinet is the document that a minister submits to cabinet when they seek a decision on a specific proposal. See Government of Canada (2018).

8. The NSICOP *Annual Report 2018* also contains a detailed discussion of the accountability and performance measurement dimensions of the process, which are not the focus here (National Security and Intelligence Committee of Parliamentarians 2019).

9. As some interviewees noted, this is far from limited to the intelligence community: Elsewhere in government, and often outside government, it is also a frequent problem. Some suggested that there is a case to be made that the intelligence community ranks below average on this score, but this would be virtually impossible to empirically verify. As one noted, "silos are the biggest disease in government."

10. The Government established in 2006 the *Commission of Inquiry into the Investigation of the Bombing of Air India Flight 182* to look into the worst terrorist attack in Canadian history, which killed 329 in 1985. Its final report, delivered in 2010, provided a

comprehensive assessment of challenges facing Canada's security and law enforcement agencies. See Major (2010).

11. We thank one of the government officials who reviewed this chapter for this point.

12. This report, known as the Manley Report as it was chaired by the former Liberal politician John Manley, was commissioned by Prime Minister Harper to analyze efforts in Afghanistan and make recommendations for the way head (Manley et al. 2008).

13. See for example Saideman (2016), especially chapter 6, and the insider perspective of Golberg and Kaduck (2011).

14. On politicization, see Rovner (2011).

15. As one interviewee said, "It would be naïve to say that politics don't play a role, but it is also appropriate that politics plays a role. We live in a democracy; elected leaders should be the ones making decisions about stances, geopolitical approaches, relationships, and priorities that we have. So just because something is national security, it doesn't mean that the elected political leaders shouldn't be the ones making decisions about how we approach those issues."

16. When one of us (Juneau) tweeted in January 2020 that there is no case of the hard politicization of intelligence analysis in Canada (in reference to Prime Minister Justin Trudeau's press conference in which he quoted Canadian intelligence as assessing that Ukrainian International Airlines Flight 752 had likely been shot down by Iranian air defenses—which turned out to be correct), we received significant criticism, with many arguing that there have been frequent instances of the politicization of intelligence in Canada, particularly in relation to Indigenous issues. Upon further discussion online, it was clear that we were each referring to different categories of cases; for their part, critics meant that security operations—specifically, RCMP, provincial police forces, and other police forces targeting and harassing Indigenous people—were systematically politicized. As operations, especially those relating to provincial policing, were not the focus of our research, we cannot offer any evidence to support or refute these allegations, although we note that recent inquiries have found that the RCMP's culture is biased and "toxic" (Bastarache 2020). For critical takes on surveillance and Canada's Indigenous communities, see Crosby and Monaghan (2018) and Monaghan and Walby (2017). Other critical perspectives can be found in Hewitt (2002); Kealey (2017); and Sethna and Hewitt (2018).

17. On this deal and the controversy surrounding it, see Juneau (2019a).

18. There have been some limited concerns recently about the politicization of the public service more broadly. Nevertheless, the absence of any case of hard politicization of intelligence analysis is consistent with the well-established values of nonpartisanship and professionalism of the public service in Canada. See Aucoin (2012) and Jarvis (2016).

19. The name and precise responsibilities of this office have evolved over the years; it was known for a long time as the Director General for Security and Intelligence and then as the Counter-Terrorism, Crime and Intelligence Bureau. It was renamed the Intelligence Bureau in 2020.

20. Exceptions include countries where Canada has a presence on the ground and the US does not, such as Cuba and, until 2012, Iran.

21. *Report 4—Physical Security at Canada's Missions Abroad—Global Affairs Canada* assessed that GAC "had not taken all measures needed to keep pace with evolving security threats at its missions abroad" and that deficiencies were "significant" (Office of the Auditor General of Canada 2018). It also "found that most of the Department's capital projects to upgrade security were at least three years behind schedule." For a follow-up, see *Safety and Security for Global Affairs Canada Employees and Canadians Abroad*, a report of the Standing Senate Committee on Foreign Affairs and International Trade (2018).

22. For more information, see GAC's response to the auditor general's report (Global Affairs Canada 2019a).

23. GAC has three ministers—for foreign affairs, international trade, and development—who each have their own deputy minister.

24. Swords's testimony to the Standing Senate Committee on National Security and Defence (2007).

25. *Rumint*, or *rumor intelligence*, is the dismissive term used to denote information that is merely rumor or gossip.

26. Some of our interviewees revealed details about some of these cases, including names of officers and countries involved. Here and elsewhere in this section, however, we are withholding more detailed information.

27. One interviewee noted that "50 percent of GSRP officers are female, which really opens up old guys to talk to them."

28. For more on how this on-the-ground presence in Tehran was appreciated in Washington, see Juneau (2019b).

Chapter 4: Approaches to Analysis

1. As one of the anonymous reviewers of this manuscript noted—and as those who have worked in both academia and national security often understand—there are interesting parallels between the challenges faced by both academics and intelligence analysts in producing relevant analysis. There is a voluminous literature on this on the academic side. See for example Desch (2019) and Lepgold and Nincic (2001).

2. As one interviewee argued, for some in the intelligence community, "performance is volume."

3. As part of efforts to identify options to reduce expenses (the Deficit Reduction Action Plan), one scenario discussed in the Privy Council, and confirmed by interviews, was to eliminate the IAS. This would have allowed PCO as a whole to reach its deficit-reduction targets.

4. An interviewee offered an interesting parallel here: intelligence analysis of this kind is much like journalism, in that it has to work with tight deadlines, dig for scoops, make sure that its insights are relevant, work with sources, and so on.

5. One interviewee noted that this was unpopular with many analysts. Many, especially those with more seniority, more attachment to "traditional" analysis, and less concern with the notion of supporting clients, condescendingly considered short pieces

as "glorified journalism." It "took one year to overcome this resistance, and even today complaining still goes on."

6. This point was raised by some interviewees, especially those at the level of analysts, as well as by one of the anonymous reviewers of this manuscript.

7. One official who reviewed a draft of this chapter added: "There is no link between the seniority of the client and who does the briefing. It depends mostly on the level of detail required, the time allocated, and the briefing skills of the analysts."

8. This model is similar to how the intelligence community prepares the *Presidential Daily Brief* in the US, also with a designated briefer.

9. As one official who reviewed a draft of this chapter claimed here, only half in jest, "as history proves, not much."

10. For background, see Miller (2010) and Wilder (2011).

11. For more on this debate, see Kerbel and Olcott (2010).

12. Of course, such analysis might then have to be classified as CEO, for "Canadian-Eyes Only."

13. OSINT includes a wide range of sources of information: media (including social media), public data (published by governments), and professional and academic publications. OSINT, importantly, is not gathered through clandestine means, but it still needs to be collected, processed, and analyzed.

14. Importantly, Twitter recently—and finally—became available on the unclassified desktops of some CFINTCOM analysts. For a good discussion of how open-source investigations have changed investigative journalism—with important parallels to the work of intelligence—see Ahmad (2019).

15. For an overview of the program by its former director general, see Tiernan (2017). The program has taken on a more operational focus since 2019, not only bringing in external expertise, but also supporting CSIS engagement with external stakeholders who may benefit from briefings. For example, during the COVID-19 pandemic, Academic Outreach and Stakeholder Engagement has been actively involved in discussing security concerns with laboratories involved in research to ensure they are aware of cyberthreats.

16. As one official who reviewed a draft of this chapter noted, there is also a certain pressure for Canadian analysts to "speak the same language" as allied colleagues—who in some cases do use conditional language, such as to make comparisons among key judgements.

17. These are not without their share of criticism. See Carvin (2021a).

18. There is little public information on the National Fisheries Intelligence Service. That said, its work has been recognized: In 2019, the International Association of Law Enforcement Intelligence Analysts provided this service with an award for its leadership in intelligence analysis (Fisheries and Oceans Canada 2018).

19. This is a common problem that has also been documented in the US context. See Kerbel and Olcott 2010.

20. The Canadian Centre for Cyber Security, part of CSE, is the government's authority on cybersecurity. Created in 2018, it leads the government's responses to

cybersecurity events. It is also charged with informing Canadian citizens and businesses on cybersecurity matters. See Canadian Centre for Cyber Security (2019).

21. At the time, the other important director general position was for intelligence collection.

22. The DIR also called for the creation of new capabilities for the defense intelligence function, notably in geospatial and imagery intelligence. One interviewee also explained that the DIR called for the establishment of a defense intelligence human intelligence capability, which did not exist before and which—in this individual's view—has been successful since, notably having deployed with the military in operations.

23. One interviewee made the interesting comment that some of the proposed reforms in the DIR were not implemented, or only partly implemented, because the military soon became actively involved in heavy combat operations in Kandahar, Afghanistan, in 2005. This forced DND and the CAF to focus on the combat mission and distracted them from institutional reform efforts. This is a notion we propose to study in a future book.

24. Little has been published on Canadian defense intelligence. For two exceptions, see Rudner (2002) and Charters (2012).

Chapter 5: Recommendations and the Way Ahead

1. We heard this criticism from a small number of interviewees, and from one of the anonymous reviewers for this manuscript. On the broader debate on the role of the Privy Council, see the contrasting perspectives of Brodie (2018) and Savoie (1999).

2. To this end, the head of the IAS, who has the rank of assistant secretary to the cabinet and is currently an EX-4 (typically the equivalent of a junior assistant deputy minister) should be upgraded to an EX-5 (senior assistant deputy minister). For background on the DNI, see Office of the Director of National Intelligence (n.d.). See also Gentry (2015).

3. For a timeline of Incident Response Group meetings, see Canadian Press (2020).

4. Of note, the pandemic has resulted in a marked increase in intelligence analysis being briefed to cabinet and cabinet committees.

5. The Security and Intelligence Policy Program coordinates the secondment of young policy and intelligence analysts throughout the national security community.

6. These competitions were for EX-1 positions, the first level as an executive; the IAS has three director positions for regional and thematic analysis.

7. On this debate, see Epstein (2019).

8. We discuss professionalization further in the conclusion.

9. For an overview of this dynamic in the US context and a list of recommendations, see Katz (2019).

10. Joshua Rovner's work shows how increased transparency raises risks of politicization (2011).

11. See Bellingcat (2020).

12. The CSIS Academic Outreach program was recently broadened to include stakeholder engagement. While it will continue many of the academic outreach activities it

has successfully run in recent years, the *CSIS Public Report 2019* indicates that it will be more actively engaged in providing advice to external stakeholders, notably academic institutions on how to protect their students, their research, and academic integrity from adversaries seeking to undermine the openness and collaborative nature of higher education in Canada (Canadian Security Intelligence Service 2020, 30).

13. On Mobilizing Insights in National Defence and Security, see Juneau and Lagassé (2020).

14. We thank one of the anonymous reviewers for suggesting that we attempt to offer preliminary answers to this question.

Conclusion: The Future of the Canadian Intelligence and National Security Community

1. As this interviewee put it bluntly, "the intelligence community and national security folks think they are unique, but this is horsesh*t."

2. Bill C-59, which received royal assent in 2019, led to the most significant reforms to the architecture of Canadian national security and intelligence since the creation of CSIS in the 1980s. Unlike earlier legislation that brought changes to the Canadian national security and intelligence community (Bill C-36 in 2001 and Bill C-51 in 2015), C-59 went through a lengthy consultation process with stakeholders and was not rushed through parliament.

Appendix: A Guide to the Canadian Government and to the National Security and Intelligence Community

1. The authors are grateful to Philippe Lagassé for his assistance in writing this appendix.

2. Here "confidence of the House" refers to the ability to pass legislation with a majority of votes. If a vote of no confidence is passed, the government falls and an election is held.

3. The precise structure of the NSIA's office has evolved over time. See chapter 1 for more detail.

4. The RCMP's federal policing responsibilities are distinct from its contract policing activities done on behalf of provinces and territories. While the former is responsible for violent extremism, money laundering, and cybercrime, the latter is done on the basis of an agreement with certain provinces to provide police services, particularly in remote areas. The scope of our book only covers the federal aspect.

5. The terms *oversight* and *review* have specific meanings in Canada, distinct from how they are used in other countries. *Oversight* means the active monitoring of ongoing operations whereas *review* is ex post facto, ensuring that all operations and procedures complied with the law and were ethically sound.

BIBLIOGRAPHY

Adams, Barbara D., Michael H. Thomson, Natalia Derbentseva, and David R. Mandel. 2012. *Capability Challenges in the Human Domain for Intelligence Analysis: Report on Community-Wide Discussions with Canadian Intelligence Professions.* Contractor Report. CR 2011-182. Toronto: Defence Research and Development Canada. https://cradpdf.drdc-rddc.gc.ca/PDFS/unc118/p536570_A1b.pdf.

Ahmad, Muhammad I. 2019. "Bellingcat and How Open Source Reinvented Investigative Journalism." *New York Review of Books,* June 10. https://www.nybooks.com/daily/2019/06/10/bellingcat-and-how-open-source-reinvented-investigative-journalism/.

Allison, Graham T., and Morton H. Halperin. 1972. "Bureaucratic Politics: A Paradigm and Some Policy Implications." *World Politics: A Quarterly Journal of International Relations,* 24, supplement "Theory and Policy in International Relations": 40–79.

Aucoin, Peter. 2012. "New Political Governance in Westminster Systems: Impartial Public Administration and Management Performance at Risk." *Governance: An International Journal of Policy, Administrations, and Institution* 25, no. 2: 177–99.

Barnes, Alan. 2016. "Making Intelligence Analysis More Intelligent: Using Numeric Probabilities." *Intelligence and National Security* 31, no. 3: 327–44.

———. 2020. "Getting It Right: Canadian Intelligence Assessments on Iraq, 2002–2003." *Intelligence and National Security* 35, no. 7: 925–53.

Bastarache, Michael. 2020. *Broken Dreams, Broken Lives: The Devastating Effects of Sexual Harassment on Women in the RCMP.* https://www.rcmp-grc.gc.ca/wam/media/4773/original/8032a32ad5dd014db5b135ce3753934d.pdf.

Bellingcat. 2020. Latest Investigations. https://www.bellingcat.com/.

Berman, David, and Christina Pellegrini. 2016. "Canada Given Lukewarm Grade on Anti-Money Laundering Efforts." *Globe and Mail.* https://www.theglobeandmail.com/report-on-business/canada-given-lukewarm-grade-on-anti-money-laundering-efforts/article31892936.

Betts, Richard K. 1988. "Policy Makers and Intelligence Analysts: Love, Hate, or Indifference?" *Intelligence and National Security* 3, no. 1: 184–89.

Betts, Richard K., and Thomas Mahnken, eds. 2003. *Paradoxes of Strategic Intelligence: Essays in Honour of Michael I. Handel.* London: Frank Cass.

Bozeman, Adda B. 1992. *Strategic Intelligence and Statecraft: Selected Essays*. Washington, DC: Brassey's.

Brodie, Ian. 2018. *At the Centre of Government: The Prime Minister and Limits of Political Power*. McGill-Queen's Press.

Canadian Centre for Cyber Security. 2019. "About the Cyber Centre." https://cyber.gc.ca/en/about-cyber-centre.

Canadian Press. 2020. "A Timeline of Some Incident Response Group Meetings." *National Post*, February 17. https://nationalpost.com/pmn/news-pmn/canada-news-pmn/a-timeline-of-some-incident-response-group-meetings.

Canadian Security Intelligence Service. 1999. "Trends in Terrorism." *Perspectives*. Report no. 2000/01.

———. 2018. "Remarks by Director David Vigneault at the Economic Club of Canada." https://www.canada.ca/en/security-intelligence-service/news/2018/12/remarks-by-director-david-vigneault-at-the-economic-club-of-canada.html.

———. 2020. *CSIS Public Report 2019*. Ottawa: Minister of Minister of Public Safety and Emergency Preparedness, Public Works and Government Services Canada. https://www.canada.ca/content/dam/csis-scrs/documents/publications/PubRep-2019-E.pdf.

Carvin, Stephanie. 2021a. "The Integrated Terrorism Assessment Centre." In *Top Secret Canada: Understanding the Canadian Intelligence and National Security Community*, edited by Stephanie Carvin, Thomas Juneau, and Craig Forcese. Toronto: University of Toronto Press.

———. 2021b. *Stand On Guard: Reassessing Threats to Canada's National Security*. Toronto: University of Toronto Press.

Carvin, Stephanie, and Craig Forcese, hosts. 2019. "Ep 97 An INTREPID Podsight—Tricia Geddes ADP CSIS." *INTREPID* (podcast), July 23, 2019. https://www.intrepidpodcast.com/podcast/2019/7/23/ep-97-an-intrepid-podsight-tricia-geddes-adp-csis.

Central Intelligence Agency. 2015. *Director's Diversity in Leadership Study: Overcoming Barriers to Advancement*. April. https://www.cia.gov/static/d8681a6dc20446042a8c-3020459ca1d4/Directors-Diversity-in-Leadership-Study-Overcoming-Barriers-to-Advancement.pdf.

Charters, David. 2012. "Canadian Military Intelligence in Afghanistan." *International Journal of Intelligence and Counterintelligence* 25 no. 3: 470–507.

Crosby, Andrew, and Jeffrey Monaghan. 2018. *Policing Indigenous Movements: Dissent and the Security State*. Black Point and Winnipeg: Fernwood Publishing.

Collins, David. 2002. "Spies Like Them: The Canadian Security Intelligence Service and Its Place in World Intelligence." *Sydney Law Review* 24, no. 4: 505–28.

Davis, Jack. 2015. "Intelligence Analysts and Policymakers: Benefits and Dangers of Tension in the Relationship." In *Essentials of Strategic Intelligence*, edited by Loch K. Johnson. Santa Barbara, CA: Praeger.

Department of National Defence. 2017a. DAOD 8008-0, Defence Intelligence. Government of Canada. https://www.canada.ca/en/department-national-defence/

corporate/policies-standards/defence-administrative-orders-directives/8000-
series/8008/8008–0-defence-intelligence.html.

———. 2017b. DAOD 8002–2, Canadian Forces National Counter-Intelligence Unit.
Government of Canada. https://www.canada.ca/en/department-national-defence/
corporate/policies-standards/defence-administrative-orders-directives/8000-
series/8002/8002–2-canadian-forces-national-counter-intelligence-unit.html.

———. 2017c. *Strong, Secure, Engaged: Canada's Defence Policy.* Government of Canada. https://www.canada.ca/en/department-national-defence/corporate/policies-
standards/canada-defence-policy.html.

———. 2018. "Organizational Structure of the Department of National Defence and
the Canadian Armed Forces." Government of Canada. http://www.forces.gc.ca/en/
about-org-structure/cfintcom-mission.page.

———. 2019a. "Canadian Forces School of Military Intelligence." Government of
Canada. https://www.canada.ca/en/department-national-defence/services/bene-
fits-military/education-training/establishments/canadian-forces-school-military-
intelligence.html.

———. 2019b. "Policy Officer Recruitment Programme." Government of Canada.
https://www.canada.ca/en/department-national-defence/corporate/job-opportu-
nities/civilian-jobs/civilian-job-opportunities/students-and-new-grads/policy-
officer-recruitment-programme.html.

Derbentseva, Natalia, Lianne McLellan, and David R. Mandel. 2010. *Issues in Intelligence Production: Summary of Interviews with Canadian Managers of Intelligence
Analysts.* Technical Report DRDC Toronto TR 2010-144. Defence R&D Canada.
https://cradpdf.drdc-rddc.gc.ca/PDFS/unc111/p534903_A1b.pdf.

Desch, Michael. 2019. *Cult of the Irrelevant: The Waning Influence of Social Science on
National Security.* Princeton, NJ: Princeton University Press.

Epstein, David. 2019. *Range: How Generalists Triumph in a Specialized World.* London:
Macmillan.

Farson, Stuart, and Nancy Teeple. 2015. "Increasing Canada's Foreign Intelligence Capability: Is It a Dead Issue? *Intelligence and National Security* 30, no. 1: 47–76.

Financial Transactions and Reports Analysis Centre of Canada. 2018. *Annual Report
2017–18.*

Fisher, Luke. 1996. "Bizarre Right from Day 1: The Man Who Tried to Kill Jean Chrétien Is Found Guilty—but Not Responsible." *McLeans Magazine,* July 8. https://
archive.macleans.ca/article/1996/7/8/bizarre-right-fro-m-day-1.

Fisheries and Oceans Canada. 2018. "National Fisheries Intelligence Services Receives
International Award for Excellence." Government of Canada. https://www.canada.
ca/en/fisheries-oceans/news/2018/04/national-fisheries-intelligence-service-
receives-international-award-for-excellence.html.

Fingar, Thomas. 2011. *Reducing Uncertainty: Intelligence Analysis and National Security.*
Palo Alto, CA: Stanford University Press.

———. 2017. "Office of the Director of National Intelligence: From Pariah and Piñata to
Managing Partner." In *The National Security Enterprise: Navigating the Labyrinth,*

edited by Roger Z. George and Harvey Rishikof, 185–203. Washington, DC: Georgetown University Press.

Folker, Robert D., Jr. 2000. "Intelligence Analysis in Theater Joint Intelligence Centers: An Experiment in Applying Structured Methods." Occasional Paper Number Seven. Center for Strategic Intelligence Research. Washington, DC: Joint Military Intelligence College.

Forcese, Craig. 2018. "Bill C-59 and the Judicialization of Intelligence Collection." *Ottawa Faculty of Law Working Paper No. 2018–13*, 24. https://papers.ssrn.com/sol3/papers.cfm?abstract_id=3157921.

Forcese, Craig, and Jennifer Poirier. 2021. "The Department of Justice Canada (Justice Canada)." In *Top Secret Canada: Understanding the Canadian Intelligence and National Security Community*, edited by Stephanie Carvin, Thomas Juneau, and Craig Forcese. Toronto: University of Toronto Press.

Forcese, Craig, and Kent Roach. 2015. *False Security: The Radicalization of Canadian Anti-Terrorism*. Toronto: Irwin Law.

———. 2017. "The Roses and the Thorns of Canada's New National Security Bill." *Maclean's*, June 20, 2017. https://www.macleans.ca/politics/ottawa/the-roses-and-thorns-of-canadas-new-national-security-bill.

Forcese, Craig, and Leah West. 2021. *National Security Law*. Toronto: Irwin Press.

Friedland, Martin L. 1997. *Controlling Misconduct in the Military: A Study Prepared for the Commission of Inquiry into the Deployment of Canadian Forces in Somalia*. Ottawa: Minister of Public Works and Government Services Canada.

Fyffe, Greg. 2021. "The Privy Council and the Canadian Intelligence Community." In *Top Secret Canada: Understanding the Canadian Intelligence and National Security Community*, edited by Stephanie Carvin, Thomas Juneau, and Craig Forcese. Toronto: University of Toronto Press.

Gannon, John C. 2008. "Managing Analysis in the Information Age." In *Analyzing Intelligence: Origins, Obstacles, and Innovation*, edited by Roger Z. George and James B. Bruce, 213–25. Washington, DC: Georgetown University Press.

Gentry, John A. 1995. "Intelligence Analyst/Manager Relations at the CIA." *Intelligence and National Security* 10, no. 4: 133–46.

———. 2015. "Has the ODNI Improved U.S. Intelligence Analysis?" *International Journal of Intelligence and CounterIntelligence* 28, no. 4: 637–61.

———. 2016. "Managers of Analysts: The Other Half of Intelligence Analysis." *Intelligence and National Security* 31, no. 2: 154–77.

George, Roger Z., and James B. Bruce, eds. 2008. *Analyzing Intelligence: Origins, Obstacles, and Innovations*. Washington, DC: Georgetown University Press.

Ghez, Jeremy, and Gregory F. Treverton. 2017. "Making Strategic Analysis Matter." In *Strategic Analysis in Support of International Policy Making: Case Studies in Achieving Analytical Relevance*, edited by Thomas Juneau, 1–21. Lanham, MD: Rowman & Littlefield.

Global Affairs Canada. 2019a. *Global Affairs Canada Management Response and Action Plan*. Ottawa: Auditor General of Canada, Government of Canada. https://www.

ourcommons.ca/content/Committee/421/PACP/WebDoc/WD8148750/Action_
Plans/105-DepartmentOfForeign%20AffairsTradeAndDevelopment-e.pdf.

———. 2019b. *2018–19 Departmental Results Report*. Government of Canada. https://
www.international.gc.ca/gac-amc/assets/pdfs/publications/plans/drr-rrm/drr-
rrm_1819-en.pdf.

Golberg, Elissa, and Michael Kaduck. 2011. "Where Is Headquarters?: Diplomacy, Development, and Defence." In *Diplomacy in the Digital Age: Essays in Honour of Ambassador Gotlieb*, edited by Janice Gross Stein, 124–40. Toronto: McLelland & Stewart.

Government of Canada. 2017a. "Economics and Social Services." https://www.canada.
ca/en/treasury-board-secretariat/services/collective-agreements/occupational-
groups/economics-social-science-services.html#grp-ec.

———. 2017b. "Advanced Policy Analyst Program." https://apap.gc.ca/about-the-
apap/127.

———. 2018. "A Drafter's Guide to Cabinet Documents." https://www.canada.ca/en/
privy-council/services/publications/memoranda-cabinet/drafters-guide-docu-
ments.html.

———. 2019. "Recruitment of Policy Leaders." https://www.canada.ca/en/public-ser-
vice-commission/jobs/services/recruitment/graduates/recruitment-policy-leaders.
html.

———. 2020a. "Termium Plus: The Government of Canada's Terminology and Linguis-
tic Data Bank." https://www.btb.termiumplus.gc.ca/tpv2alpha/alpha-eng.html?lang
=eng&i=1&srchtxt=secondment&index=alt&codom2nd_wet=1#resultrecs.

———. 2020b. "Supporting Information on Sub-Programs." https://www.canada.ca/en/
privy-council/corporate/transparency/reporting-spending/departmental-results-
reports/2016–2017/supporting-information-sub-programs.html.

Hewitt, Steve. 2002. *Spying 101: The RCMP's Secret Activities at Canadian Universities,
1917–1997*. Toronto: University of Toronto Press.

Hulnick, Arthur S. 2015. "Intelligence Cycle." In *Intelligence: The Secret World of Spies*,
edited by Loch K. Johnson and James W. Wirtz, 81–92. Oxford: Oxford University
Press.

Innovation, Science, and Economic Development Canada. 2019. *Investment Canada
Act: Annual Report 2018–19*. Ottawa: Innovation, Science, and Economic Development Canada.

Intelligence and Security Committee of Parliament. 2018. *Diversity and Inclusion in
the UK Intelligence Community*. 1st sess., 57th Parliament of the United Kingdom.
https://assets.publishing.service.gov.uk/government/uploads/system/uploads/at-
tachment_data/file/740654/20180718_Report_Diversity_and_Inclusion.pdf.

Jarvis, Mark. 2016. *Creating a High-Performing Canadian Civil Service against a Back-
drop of Disruptive Change*. Toronto: University of Toronto, Mowat Centre.

Jensen, Kurt F. 2009. *Cautious Beginnings: Canadian Foreign Intelligence 1939–1951*.
Vancouver: University of British Columbia Press.

Jervis, Robert. 2010. *Why Intelligence Fails: Lessons from the Iranian Revolution and
Iraq War*. Ithaca, NY: Cornell University Press.

Johnson, Loch, and James Wirtz, eds., 2004. *Strategic Intelligence: Windows into a Secret World: An Anthology*. Oxford: Oxford University Press.

Juneau, Thomas. 2017. "Conclusion." In *Strategic Analysis in Support of International Policy Making: Case Studies in Achieving Analytical Relevance*, edited by Thomas Juneau, 243–58. Lanham, MD: Rowan & Littlefield.

———. 2019a. "A Surprising Spat: The Causes and Consequences of the Saudi-Canadian Dispute." *International Journal* 74, no. 2: 313–23.

———. 2019b. "A Story of Failed Re-engagement: Canada and Iran, 2015–2018." *Canadian Foreign Policy Journal* 25, no. 1: 35–53.

———. 2021. "The Department of National Defence and the Canadian Armed Forces." In *Top Secret Canada: Understanding the Canadian Intelligence and National Security Community*, edited by Stephanie Carvin, Thomas Juneau, and Craig Forcese. Toronto: University of Toronto Press.

Juneau, Thomas, and Philippe Lagassé. 2020. "Bridging the Academic-Policy Gap in Canadian Defence: What More Can Be Done?" *Canadian Public Administration Journal* 62, no. 2: 206–28.

Katz, Brian. 2019. "Policy and You: A Guide for Intelligence Analysts." *War on the Rocks*. https://warontherocks.com/2019/02/policy-and-you-a-guide-for-intelligence-analysts/.

Kealey, S. Gregory. 2017. *Spying on Canadians: The Royal Mounted Police Security Service and the Origins of the Long Cold War*. Toronto: University of Toronto Press.

Kerbel, Josh, and Anthony Olcott. 2010. "Synthesizing with Clients, Not Analyzing for Customers." *Studies in Intelligence* 54, no. 4: 11–27.

King, Tom. 2017. "Intelligence Informs Foreign Policy Making at the U.S. State Department: The Bureau of Intelligence and Research (INR)." In *Strategic Analysis in Support of International Policy Making: Case Studies in Achieving Analytical Relevance*, edited by Thomas Juneau, 95–110. Lanham, MD: Rowman & Littlefield.

Kovacs, Amos. 1997. "Using Intelligence." *Intelligence and National Security* 12, no. 4: 145–64.

Lapointe, Mike. 2020. "In Fast-Moving Political Reality, Trudeau Uses Incident Response Group to Seek 'Quick Resolutions' to Complex Problems." *Hill Times*, March 2, 2020. https://www.hilltimes.com/2020/03/02/in-fast-moving-complex-political-reality-trudeau-uses-incident-response-group-to-cut-through-social-media/237947.

Lepgold, Joseph, and Miroslav Nincic. 2001. *Beyond the Ivory Tower: International Relations Theory and the Issue of Policy Relevance*. New York: Columbia University Press.

Leuprecht, Christian, Kelly Sundberg, Todd Hataley, and Alexandra Green. 2021. "The Canada Border Services Agency (CBSA)." In *Top Secret Canada: Understanding the Canadian Intelligence and National Security Community*, edited by Stephanie Carvin, Thomas Juneau, and Craig Forcese. Toronto: University of Toronto Press.

Lilly, Meredith. 2021. "The Prime Minister's Office." In *Top Secret Canada: Understanding the Canadian Intelligence and National Security Community*, edited by

Stephanie Carvin, Thomas Juneau, and Craig Forcese. Toronto: University of Toronto Press.

Littlewood, Jez. 2021. "Canadian Security Intelligence Service." In *Top Secret Canada: Understanding the Canadian Intelligence and National Security Community*, edited by Stephanie Carvin, Thomas Juneau, and Craig Forcese. Toronto: University of Toronto Press.

Livermore, Daniel. 2009. "Does Canada Need a Foreign Intelligence Agency." *Centre for International Policy Studies*, Policy Brief No. 3.

Lowenthal, Mark. 2013. "A Disputation on Intelligence Reform and Analysis: My 18 Theses." *International Journal of Intelligence and CounterInterlligence* 26, no. 1: 31–37.

———. 2017. *Intelligence: From the Secrets to Policy.* Thousand Oaks, CA: CQ Press.

Major, John. 2010. *The Government of Canada Response to the Commission of Inquiry into the Investigation of the Bombing of Air India Flight 182.* Ottawa: Privy Council Office, Government of Canada. https://www.publicsafety.gc.ca/cnt/rsrcs/pblctns/rspns-cmmssn/index-en.aspx.

Mandel, David R. 2009. "Canadian Perspectives: Applied Behavioral Science in Support of Intelligence Analysis." PowerPoint presentation. Toronto: Defence Research and Development Canada, Government of Canada. https://www.cl.cam.ac.uk/~rja14/shb09/mandel.pdf.

———. 2015. "Accuracy of Intelligence Forecasts from the Intelligence Consumer's Perspective." *Policy Insights from the Behavioral and Brain Sciences* 2, no. 1: 111–20.

Mandel, David R., and Alan Barnes. 2018. "Geopolitical Forecasting Skill in Strategic Intelligence." *Journal of Behavioral Decision Making* 31, no. 1: 127–37.

Manley, John, Derek H. Burney, Jake Epp, Paul Tellier, and Pamela Wallin. 2008. *Independent Panel on Canada's Future Role in Afghanistan.* Ottawa: Independent Panel on Canada's Future Role in Afghanistan, Government of Canada. http://publications.gc.ca/collections/collection_2008/dfait-maeci/FR5-20-1-2008E.pdf.

Marrin, Stephen. 2007. "Intelligence Analysis: Structured Methods or Intuition?" *American Intelligence Journal* 25, no. 1: 7–16.

———. 2011. *Improving Intelligence Analysis: Bridging the Gap between Scholarship and Practice.* London: Routledge.

———. 2012a. "Evaluating the Quality of Intelligence Analysis: By What (Mis)Measure?" *Intelligence and National Security* 27, no. 6: 896–912.

———. 2012b. "Is Intelligence Analysis an Art or a Science?" *International Journal of Intelligence and CounterIntelligence* 25, no. 3: 529–45.

Miller, Paul D. 2010. "Lessons for Intelligence Support to Policymaking during Crises." *Studies in Intelligence* 54, no. 2: 1–8.

Momani, Bessma, and Jillian Stirk. 2017. *Diversity Dividend: Canada's Global Advantage.* Waterloo, Ontario, and Montréal, Quebec: Centre for International Governance Innovation and Pierre Elliott Trudeau Foundation. https://www.cigionline.org/sites/default/files/documents/DiversitySpecial%20Report%20WEB_0.pdf.

Monaghan, Jeffrey, and Kevin Walby. 2017. "Making Up 'Terror Identities': Security

Intelligence, Canada's Integrated Threat Assessment Centre and Social Movement Suppression." *Policing and Society* 22, no. 2: 133–51.

Moore, David T. 2005. "Species of Competencies for Intelligence Analysis." *American Intelligence Journal* 23: 29–43.

Moore, David T., Lisa Krizan, and Elizabeth J. Moore. 2005. "Evaluating Intelligence: A Competency-Based Model." *International Journal of Intelligence and CounterIntelligence* 18, no. 2: 204–20.

National Security and Intelligence Committee of Parliamentarians. 2019. *Annual Report 2018*. Ottawa: NSICOP. https://nsicop-cpsnr.ca/reports/rp-2019-04-09/2019-04-09_annual_report_2018_public_en.pdf.

———. 2020a. *Annual Report 2019*. Ottawa: NSICOP. https://www.nsicop-cpsnr.ca/reports/rp-2020-03-12-ar/annual_report_2019_public_en.pdf.

———. 2020b. *Special Report on the Collection, Use, Retention and Dissemination of Information on Canadians in the Context of the Department of National Defence and Canadian Armed Forces Defence Intelligence Activities*. Ottawa: NSICOP. https://www.nsicop-cpsnr.ca/reports/rp-2020-03-12-sr/special_report_20200312_public_en.pdf.

Nesbitt, Michael. "Global Affairs Canada (GAC)." 2021. In *Top Secret Canada: Understanding the Canadian Intelligence and National Security Community*, edited by Stephanie Carvin, Thomas Juneau, and Craig Forcese. Toronto: University of Toronto Press.

Office of the Auditor General of Canada. 2018. *Report 4—Physical Security at Canada's Missions Abroad—Global Affairs Canada*. https://www.oag-bvg.gc.ca/internet/English/parl_oag_201811_04_e_43202.html.

Office of the Director of National Intelligence. N.d. "Organization." https://www.dni.gov/index.php/who-we-are/organizations.

Pherson, Randolph H., and Richards J. Heuer Jr. 2011. *Structured Analytic Techniques for Intelligence Analysis*. Thousand Oaks, CA: CQ Press.

Pickford, Andrew, and Jeffrey Collins. 2016. "Canada Can Only Learn So Much from Australian Defence Policy." *Inside Policy*. Macdonald-Laurier Institute. https://www.macdonaldlaurier.ca/canada-can-only-learn-so-much-from-australian-defence-policy-andrew-pickford-and-jeffrey-collins-for-inside-policy/.

Public Safety Canada. 2019. "Minister Goodale Launches Advisory Group on National Security Transparency." Government of Canada. https://www.canada.ca/en/public-safety-canada/news/2019/07/minister-goodale-launches-advisory-group-on-national-security-transparency.html.

Pyrik, John. 2021. "Financial Transactions and Reports Analysis Centre of Canada (FINTRAC)." In *Top Secret Canada: Understanding the Canadian Intelligence and National Security Community*, edited by Stephanie Carvin, Thomas Juneau, and Craig Forcese. Toronto: University of Toronto Press.

Rimsa, Kostas. 2011. "Spy Catchers." In *Inside Canadian Intelligence: Exposing the New Realities of Espionage and International Terrorism*, 2nd ed., edited by Dwight Hamilton, 37–50. Toronto: Dundurn Press.

Roach, Kent. 2011. *The 9/11 Effect: Comparative Counter-Terrorism*. Cambridge, UK: Cambridge University Press.

Roach, Kent. 2021. "Royal Canadian Mounted Police (RCMP)." In *Top Secret Canada: Understanding the Canadian Intelligence and National Security Community*, edited by Stephanie Carvin, Thomas Juneau, and Craig Forcese. Toronto: University of Toronto Press.

Roi, Michael, and Paul Dickson. 2017. "Balancing Responsiveness, Relevance and Expertise: Lessons from History of Strategic Analysis in the Canadian Department of National Defence." In *Strategic Analysis in Support of International Policy Making: Case Studies in Achieving Analytical Relevance*, edited by Thomas Juneau, 225–42. Lanham, MD: Roman & Littlefield.

Rosenwasser, Jon J., and Michael Warner. 2017. "History of the Interagency Process for Foreign Relations in the United States: Murphy's Law?" In *The National Security Enterprise: Navigating the Labyrinth*, edited by Roger Z. George and Harvey Rishikof, 13–31. Washington, DC: Georgetown University Press.

Rovner, Joshua. 2011. *Fixing the Facts: National Security and the Politics of Intelligence*. Ithaca, NY: Cornell University Press.

Rudner, Martin. 2002. "The Future of Canada's Defence Intelligence." *International Journal of Intelligence and Counterintelligence* 15 no. 4: 540–64.

Saideman, Steve. 2016. *Adapting in the Dust: Lessons Learned from Canada's War in Afghanistan*. Toronto: University of Toronto Press.

Sallot, Jeff, and Andrew Mitrovica. 2000. "Mounties Blamed CSIS for Sanitized Sidewinder." *Globe and Mail*. https://www.theglobeandmail.com/news/national/mounties-blamed-csis-for-sanitizing-sidewinder/article18422995/.

Savoie, Donald J. 1999. *Governing from the Centre: The Concentration of Power in Canadian Politics*. Toronto: University of Toronto Press.

Sayle, Timothy Andrews. 2017. "Taking the Off-Ramp: Canadian Diplomacy, Intelligence, and Decision-Making before the Iraq War." In *Australia, Canada, and Iraq: Perspectives on an Invasion*, edited by Ramesh Thakur and Jack Cunningham, 210–27. Toronto: Dundurn Press.

Security Intelligence Review Committee. 2017. *Accelerating Accountability: Annual Report 2016–2017*. http://www.sirc-csars.gc.ca/pdfs/ar_2016–2017-eng.pdf.

Sethna, Christabelle, and Steve Hewitt. 2018. *Just Watch Us: RCMP Surveillance of the Women's Liberation Movement in Cold War Canada*. Montreal: McGill-Queen's University Press.

Shane, Scott. 2015. "C.I.A. Officers and F.B.I. Agents, Meet Your New Partner: The Analyst." *New York Times*, March 26. https://www.nytimes.com/2015/03/27/us/cia-officers-and-fbi-agents-meet-your-new-partner-the-analyst.html.

Silberman, Laurence H., and Charles S. Robb. 2005. *The Commission on the Intelligence Capabilities of the United States Regarding Weapons of Mass Destruction*. US Government. Washington, DC: Commission on the Intelligence Capabilities Regarding Weapons of Mass Destruction.

Smith, Conor. 2014. "Canadian Innovation and the DARPA Model." NATO Association of Canada. http://natoassociation.ca/canadian-innovation-and-the-darpa-model/.

Standing Senate Committee on Foreign Affairs and International Trade. 2018. *Report on Safety and Security for Global Affairs Canada Employees and Canadians Abroad.* 1st sess. 43rd Parliament of Canada. https://sencanada.ca/content/sen/committee/421/AEFA/reports/AEFA_Security_e.pdf.

Standing Senate Committee on National Security and Defence. 2007. *The Fifteenth Report of the Committee: Supplementary Release of Funds.* 1st sess. 39th Parliament of Canada. Committee Report 15. https://sencanada.ca/en/Content/Sen/committee/391/defe/16ev-e.

St. John, Richard Geoffrey. 2017. "Should Canada Have a Foreign Espionage Service." *Canadian Military Journal* 17, no. 4: 56–66.

Tiernan, Jean-Louis. 2017. "The Practice of Open Intelligence: The Experience of the Canadian Security Intelligence Service." In *Strategic Analysis in Support of International Policy Making: Case Studies in Achieving Analytical Relevance*, edited by Thomas Juneau, 147–62. Lanham, MD: Rowman & Littlefield.

Tierney, Michael. 2015. "Past, Present and Future: The Evolution of Canadian Foreign Intelligence in a Globalized World." *Canadian Military Journal* 15, no. 2: 44–54.

Treasury Board of Canada Secretariat. 2010. "Archived—Department of Foreign Affairs and International Trade—Report. Government of Canada. https://www.tbs-sct.gc.ca/dpr-rmr/2009–2010/inst/ext/ext02-eng.asp.

———. 2017a. "Occupational Groups for the Public Service." Government of Canada. https://www.canada.ca/en/treasury-board-secretariat/services/collective-agreements/occupational-groups.html.

———. 2017b. *Building a Diverse and Inclusive Public Service: Final Report of the Joint Union/Management Task Force on Diversity and Inclusion.* Government of Canada. https://www.canada.ca/en/treasury-board-secretariat/corporate/reports/building-diverse-inclusive-public-service-final-report-joint-union-management-task-force-diversity-inclusion.html.

Treverton, F. Gregory. 2008. "Intelligence Analysis: Between 'Politicization' and Irrelevance." In *Analyzing Intelligence: Origins, Obstacles, and Innovations*, edited by Roger Z. George and James B. Bruce, 91–104. Washington, DC: Georgetown University Press.

West, Leah. 2021. "National Security Review and Oversight." In *Top Secret Canada: Understanding the Canadian Intelligence and National Security Community*, edited by Stephanie Carvin, Thomas Juneau, and Craig Forcese. Toronto: University of Toronto Press.

Wilder, Dennis C. 2011. "An Educated Consumer Is Our Best Customer." *Studies in Intelligence* 55, no. 2: 23–31.

Wilner, Alex. 2021. "Public Safety Canada." In *Top Secret Canada: Understanding the Canadian Intelligence and National Security Community*, edited by Stephanie Carvin, Thomas Juneau, and Craig Forcese. Toronto: University of Toronto Press.

Whitaker, Reg, Gregory S. Kealy, and Andrea Parnaby. 2012. *Secret Service: Political Policing in Canada from the Fenians to Fortress America.* Toronto: University of Toronto Press.

INDEX

assessments provision, 103–4. *See also* Five Eyes

United States (US): diversity in intelligence and national security community, 54; exchanges and secondments, 69; and ILO office, 101–2; impact of Trumpism, 174–75; literacy in policy, 85, 86; and open source, 126–27, 162–63; opportunity analysis, 122; overclassification, 130; policy making and intelligence, 172; rivalries and coordination in intelligence, 26–27; staff in analysis units, 46; training and education, 57; trickle down of intelligence analysis, 22–23. *See also* Five Eyes

United States (US) and Canada: blue force analysis by Canada, 125, 160; coordination of agencies, 16; foreign intelligence, 31–32, 33, 146–47, 148, 174, 175; intelligence analysis differences, 6; liaison position in Canadian embassy, 148; supply of intelligence, 33–34

Vigneault, David, 79, 83

Westminster system of government, 35, 181–82

whole-of-government policy making, 94–96

WMD Commission (Silbermann-Robb Commission), 3

The authorized representative in the EU for product safety and compliance is:
Mare Nostrum Group
B.V Doelen 72
4831 GR Breda
The Netherlands

www.ingramcontent.com/pod-product-compliance
Lightning Source LLC
Chambersburg PA
CBHW030314270326
41926CB00010B/1367